JEPPESEN
A Boeing Company

GUIDED FLIGHT DISCOVERY

INSTRUMENT COMMERCIAL SYLLABUS

Contains:
- Instrument Rating Course
- Commercial Pilot Certification Course
- Multi-Engine Rating Course

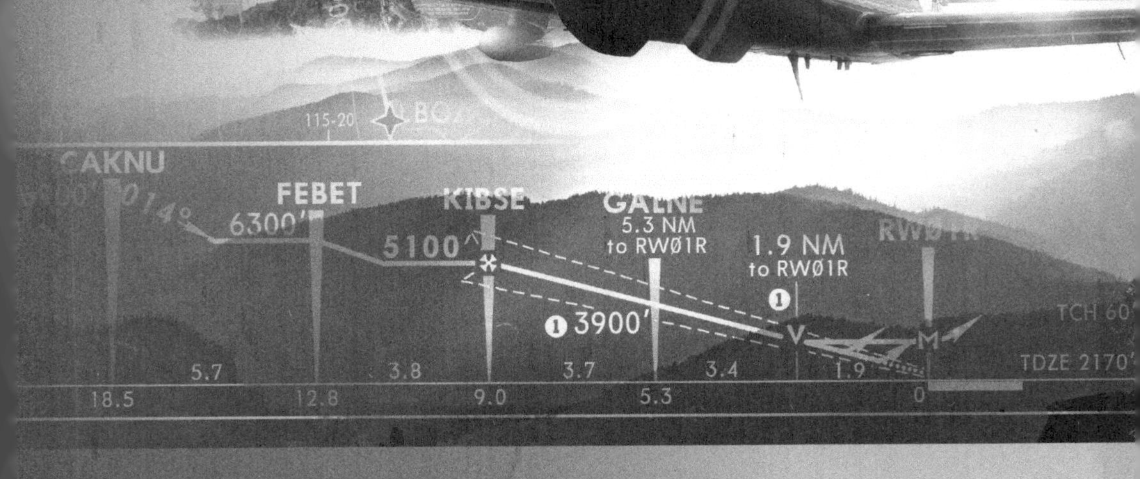

The charts, tables, and graphs used in this publication are for illustration purposes only and cannot be used for navigation or to determine actual aircraft performance.

Cover Photo
Piper Mirage 350 in flight courtesy of Piper Aircraft, Inc.

978-0-88487-656-4

Jeppesen
55 Inverness Drive East
Englewood, CO 80112-5498
Web site: www.jeppesen.com
Email: Captain@jeppesen.com

Published 1998, 1999, 2000, 2001, 2002, 2003, 2004, 2006, 2012, 2015, 2016, 2021
Printed in the United States of America

10001785-005

Preface

COURSES

The *Guided Flight Discovery Instrument/Commercial Syllabus* is an outline, or framework, for three separate courses of training: the Instrument Rating Course, the Commercial Pilot Certification Course, and the Multi-Engine Rating Course. These courses are designed to meet Title 14 CFR Part 141 aeronautical knowledge (ground) training and flight training requirements. However, the courses can be adapted to meet Title 14 CFR Part 61 requirements.

NOTE: *This syllabus will refer to Title 14 of the Code of Federal Regulations (CFR) as the Federal Aviation Regulations (FARs).*

Each course is divided into stages and includes a Ground Training Syllabus and a Flight Training Syllabus. A stage *check* is included at the end of each stage of *flight* training, and a stage *exam* is included at the end of each stage of *ground* training. In addition, End-of-Course Exams and End-of-Course Flight Checks are included in the syllabus prior to the conclusion of the respective ground and flight segments in each course.

INSTRUMENT RATING COURSE

The Instrument Rating Course provides the ground and flight lessons to obtain an instrument rating. The course:

- Meets the requirements of Appendix C to FAR Part 141 — Instrument Rating Course.
- Is comprised of Stages I, II, and III of the Instrument Ground Training Syllabus and Instrument Flight Training Syllabus.

COMMERCIAL PILOT CERTIFICATION COURSE

The Commercial Pilot Certification Course provides the ground and flight lessons to obtain a commercial pilot single-engine land certificate. The course:

- Meets the requirements of Appendix D to FAR Part 141 — Commercial Pilot Certification Course.
- Is comprised of Stages I, II of the Commercial Ground Training Syllabus and Stages I, II, and III of the Commercial Flight Training Syllabus.

NOTE: *No ground lessons are assigned in Stage III of the Commercial Pilot Certification Course so the Commercial Ground Training Syllabus does not include this stage.*

MULTI-ENGINE RATING COURSE

The Multi-Engine Rating Course provides the ground and flight lessons to add a multi-engine rating to the commercial pilot certificate. The course:

- Meets the requirements of Appendix I to FAR Part 141 —Additional Aircraft Category and/or Class Rating Course.
- Is comprised of Stage I of the Multi-Engine Ground Training Syllabus and Multi-Engine Flight Training Syllabus.

FAR REQUIREMENTS IN APPENDIX B

Tables in Appendix B depict how the objectives and tasks listed in the ground training and flight training lessons of each course correspond to the aeronautical knowledge training and flight training areas of operation required by FAR Part 141, FAR Part 61, and the FAA Airman Certification Standards (ACS).

FAA inspectors and school administrators should refer to these tables to verify that the courses include the required knowledge and flight training areas. Instructors should consult these tables and the pertinent sections of the regulations when teaching the courses to ensure that no aeronautical knowledge areas, flight training areas of operation or tasks are omitted during pilot training and that requirements are documented in appropriate records and endorsements. The following tables are included in Appendix B:

INSTRUMENT RATING COURSE

INSTRUMENT GROUND TRAINING — AERONAUTICAL KNOWLEDGE AREAS

This table depicts the ground training lessons that contain the aeronautical knowledge areas required by:

- Appendix C to Part 141 — Instrument Rating Course
  3. Aeronautical Knowledge Training
     (b) Ground training / aeronautical knowledge areas
- Part 61 Subpart B — Aircraft Ratings and Pilot Authorizations
  61.65 Instrument Rating Requirements
     (b) Aeronautical knowledge areas.

INSTRUMENT FLIGHT TRAINING — AREAS OF OPERATION

This table depicts the ground and flight training lessons that contain the areas of operation and tasks required by:

- Appendix C to Part 141 — Instrument Rating Course
  4. Flight Training
     (d) Areas of operation
- Part 61 Subpart B — Aircraft Rating and Pilot Authorization
  61.65 Instrument Rating Requirements
     (c) Flight proficiency
- Instrument Rating — Airplane Airman Certification Standards (ACS)

COMMERCIAL PILOT CERTIFICATION COURSE

COMMERCIAL GROUND TRAINING — AERONAUTICAL KNOWLEDGE AREAS

This table depicts the ground training lessons that contain the aeronautical knowledge areas required by:

- Appendix D to Part 141 — Commercial Pilot Certification Course
  3. Aeronautical Knowledge Training
     (b) Ground training / aeronautical knowledge areas
- Part 61 Subpart F — Commercial Pilots
  61.125 Aeronautical Knowledge
     (b) Aeronautical knowledge areas.

COMMERCIAL FLIGHT TRAINING — AREAS OF OPERATION

This table depicts the ground and flight training lessons that contain the areas of operation and tasks required by:

- Appendix D to Part 141 — Commercial Pilot Certification Course
  4. Flight Training
     (d) Areas of operation
        (1) For an airplane single-engine course
- Part 61 Subpart F — Commercial Pilots
  61.127 Flight Proficiency
     (d) Areas of operation
        (1) For an airplane single-engine course
- Commercial Pilot — Airplane Airman Certification Standards (ACS)

MULTI-ENGINE RATING COURSE

MULTI-ENGINE GROUND TRAINING — AERONAUTICAL KNOWLEDGE AREAS

This table depicts the ground training lessons that contain the aeronautical knowledge areas required by:

- Appendix I to Part 141 — Additional Aircraft Category and/or Class Rating Course
  3. Aeronautical Knowledge Training
     (c) Commercial pilot ground training / aeronautical knowledge areas
- Part 61 Subpart B — Aircraft Ratings and Pilot Authorizations
  61.63 Additional Aircraft Ratings
     (c) Additional class rating
        (1) Aeronautical knowledge areas appropriate to FAR 61.125 (b)

MULTI-ENGINE FLIGHT TRAINING — AREAS OF OPERATION

This table depicts the ground and flight training lessons that contain the areas of operation and tasks required by:

- Appendix I to Part 141 — Additional Aircraft Category and/or Class Rating Course
  4. Flight Training
     (2) Areas of operation appropriate to Part 141 Appendix D, 4. Flight Training (d)(2).
- Part 61 Subpart B — Aircraft Ratings and Pilot Authorizations
  61.63 Additional Aircraft Ratings
     (c) Additional class rating
        (1) Areas of operation appropriate to FAR 61.127 (b) (2)
- Commercial Pilot — Airplane Airman Certification Standards (ACS) Additional Rating Task Table — Addition of an Airplane Multi-Engine Land Rating to an Existing Commercial Pilot Certificate

COURSE SELECTION

Students may begin the appropriate courses provided the school determines they meet the prerequisite knowledge, experience, and proficiency requirements for that rating or certificate. The following course summaries indicate the enrollment and completion requirements for each course. Students should check the box of each course in which they will be enrolled.

____ is enrolled in the:
(Name)

❑ INSTRUMENT RATING COURSE

The student must hold a private pilot certificate and complete all of the lessons in Stages I, II, and III of the Instrument Rating Ground Training Syllabus and Instrument Rating Flight Training Syllabus.

❑ COMMERCIAL PILOT CERTIFICATION COURSE

The student must hold a private pilot certificate with an instrument rating and complete all of the lessons in Stages I and II of the Commercial Pilot Ground Training Syllabus and in Stages I, II, and III of the Commercial Pilot Flight Training Syllabus.

NOTE: *No ground lessons are assigned in Stage III of the Commercial Course so the Ground Training Syllabus does not include this stage.*

❑ INSTRUMENT COURSE AND COMMERCIAL COURSE — CONCURRENT ENROLLMENT

Concurrent enrollment requires the student to hold a private pilot certificate and be concurrently enrolled in the Instrument Rating Course and the Commercial Pilot Certification Course. Part 141 Appendix D, Section 2—Eligibility for Enrollment (b) (2) allows enrollment in the commercial pilot certification course if the student is concurrently enrolled in an instrument rating course. These enrollment requirements also state that the student must pass the Instrument Rating Practical Test prior to completing the Commercial Pilot Certification Course. For concurrent enrollment, the student must complete all of the lessons in:

- Stages I, II, and III of the Instrument Rating Ground Training Syllabus and Instrument Rating Flight Training Syllabus.
- Stages I and II of the Commercial Pilot Ground Training Syllabus and Stages I, II, and III of the Commercial Pilot Flight Training Syllabus.

❑ MULTI-ENGINE RATING COURSE

To add a multi-engine rating to the commercial pilot certificate, the student must hold a commercial pilot single-engine land certificate and complete all of the lessons in Stage I of the Multi-Engine Rating Ground Training Syllabus and Multi-Engine Flight Training Syllabus.

❑ MULTI-ENGINE COURSE AND COMMERCIAL COURSE — CONCURRENT ENROLLMENT

Concurrent enrollment requires the student to hold a private pilot certificate with an instrument rating and be concurrently enrolled in the Commercial Pilot Certification Course and the Multi-Engine Rating Course. The Commercial Pilot Certification Course is designed so that the student may earn the multi-engine rating without increasing the total flight time. The student must pass the Commercial Pilot–Airplane Single-Engine Land Practical Test prior to taking the Commercial Pilot Airplane–Multi-Engine Land Practical Test.

ADDITIONAL COURSE OPTIONS

This syllabus provides additional training options for the Instrument Rating Course and Commercial Pilot Certification Course. Operators should check the appropriate box for each option they select for their course of training.

INSTRUMENT RATING COURSE — FFS, FTD, AND ATD

The use of an aviation training device (ATD) is recommended for specified ground lessons and for use during flight lessons in the Instrument Rating Course. This syllabus also contains provisions for use of a full flight simulator (FFS) or flight training device (FTD) for instrument flight training. Operators who wish to utilize these options should check the appropriate box(es) when they apply for Training Course Outline (TCO) approval. The student copy of the syllabus also should be marked accordingly.

The Instrument Rating Course uses:

For ground training:

❑ Aviation training device (ATD).

For flight training:

❑ Basic aviation training device (BATD).

❑ Advanced aviation training device (AATD).

❑ Flight training device (FTD).

❑ Full flight simulator (FFS).

COMMERCIAL PILOT CERTIFICATION COURSE — FFS AND FTD

This syllabus contains provisions for use of a full flight simulator (FFS) or flight training device (FTD) for commercial pilot flight training. Operators who wish to utilize these options should check the appropriate box(es) when they apply for Training Course Outline (TCO) approval. The student copy of the syllabus also should be marked accordingly.

The Commercial Pilot Certification Course uses:

For flight training:

❑ Flight training device (FTD).

❑ Full flight simulator (FFS).

COMMERCIAL PILOT CERTIFICATION COURSE — COMPLEX AND TAA

The Commercial Pilot Certification Course requires 10 hours of training in one of the following airplanes:

- Turbine-powered
- A complex airplane—an airplane that has:
  - ◊ Retractable landing gear;
  - ◊ Flaps;
  - ◊ Controllable pitch propeller or full authority digital engine control (FADEC).
- Technically advanced airplane (TAA)—an airplane that has:
  - ◊ A primary flight display (PFD) with an airspeed indicator, turn coordinator, attitude indicator, heading indicator, altimeter, and vertical speed indicator;
  - ◊ A multifunction display (MFD) with a moving map using GPS navigation to display the aircraft position;
  - ◊ A two-axis autopilot integrated with the navigation and heading guidance system.

The Commercial Pilot Certification Course included in this syllabus provides flight lessons that cover a transition to a complex airplane or to a TAA. If operators want to incorporate the TAA transition lessons in place of, or combined with, the complex airplane transition lessons, they should check the appropriate box below. In cases where the student has already accomplished 10 hours of training in a TAA and does not require a TAA transition, these lessons may be conducted as review and to introduce commercial maneuvers in the TAA.

❑ **This syllabus utilizes a TAA for one or more of the Stage II flight lessons 46, 47, 48, 49, 50, 66, and 67 and Stage III flight lessons 78, 82, and 83 of the Commercial Pilot Certification Course.**

Table of Contents

Introduction

The *Instrument/Commercial Syllabus* uses the building-block method of teaching in which each instructional item is presented on the basis of previously learned knowledge and skill. The syllabus guides students and instructors through a lesson sequence in which new material builds on what a student has already mastered. The syllabus contains three courses: the Instrument Rating Course, the Commercial Pilot Certification Course, and the Multi-Engine Rating Course.

The basic syllabus is designed for the instrument rating (airplane) and the commercial pilot certificate (airplane single-engine). However, the Multi-Engine Rating Course includes additional ground and flight training to add a multi-engine rating to the commercial certificate. Applicants may complete only the single-engine courses, or they may continue through the multi-engine training.

Separate ground and flight training syllabi are contained within the Instrument Rating Course, Commercial Pilot Certification Course, and Multi-Engine Rating Course. Therefore, these courses may be conducted as integrated ground and flight training programs or be divided into separate components. When using the integrated sequence shown in the time allocation tables, aeronautical knowledge that is pertinent to a flight lesson is taught just before that flight.

GROUND TRAINING

Ground school is an integral part of pilot certification courses and the Instrument Rating Ground Training Syllabus, Commercial Pilot Ground Training Syllabus, and Multi-Engine Ground Training Syllabus meet FAR Part 141 requirements for ground training. When coordinating the ground school with flight training, each ground lesson is conducted at the point indicated in the Allocation Tables. In addition, tables in Appendix B specify the specific ground lessons in which each ground training task required by Part 141, Part 61, and the applicable FAA Airplane Airman Certification Standards (ACS) is introduced, reviewed, and evaluated.

In a classroom environment, ground lessons should normally be presented in numerical order. However, to provide some flexibility for adapting to individual student needs and to the training situation, the order of the lessons may be altered with approval of the chief flight instructor. Any deviation should not disturb the course continuity or objectives. Each lesson may be presented in one classroom session, or it may be divided into two or more sessions, as necessary.

To avoid confusion when conducting both the Instrument Rating Course and Commercial Pilot Certification Course and to facilitate concurrent enrollment in these courses (if selected) the ground lessons are numbered sequentially from Ground Lesson 1 to Ground Lesson 26 in the Instrument Rating Ground Training Syllabus and Ground Lesson 27 to Ground Lesson 46 in the Commercial Pilot Ground Training Syllabus.

GROUND TRAINING COMPONENTS

The Guided Flight Discovery Pilot Training System provides the necessary components to train for a private pilot certificate. Students and instructors should review the following list as a guide to assemble and effectively use the course materials.

Instrument/Commercial Syllabus—the outline of the Instrument Rating Course, Commercial Pilot Certification Course, and Multi-Engine Rating Course. The syllabus provides a basic framework for training in a logical sequence and assigns appropriate study material prior to each lesson.

Instrument/Commercial Textbook/e-Book—the primary source for initial study and review for the Instrument Rating Course and Commercial Pilot Certification Course. Textbook chapters are references for each ground lesson. The text contains complete and concise explanations of the advanced concepts and ideas that every pilot needs to know to operate effectively in the instrument and commercial flight environments. The subjects are logically organized to build upon previously introduced topics. Subjects are often expanded upon through the use of Discovery Insets, which are strategically placed throughout the chapters. The Summary Checklists, Key Terms, and Questions are designed to help you review and prepare for both the knowledge and practical tests. Chapter 14 — Commercial Maneuvers uses step-by-step procedure diagrams to help you visualize and understand each maneuver. Airman Certification Standards (ACS) excerpts for each maneuver also are included.

Multi-Engine Textbook/e-Book—the primary source for initial study and review for adding a multi-engine rating to your commercial certificate. The text contains complete and concise explanations of the advanced concepts and ideas that every pilot needs to know to operate as the pilot in command of a multi-engine airplane. Similar to the *Instrument/Commercial* textbook, Discovery Insets, Summary Checklists, Key Terms, and Questions are included, as well as step-by-step diagrams of multi-engine maneuvers and procedures. Textbook chapters are references for each multi-engine training ground lesson.

Jeppesen e-Books are electronic versions of traditional textbooks and reference materials that are available on iOS or Android devices and PC or Mac computers. Jeppesen e-Books provide valuable features, including the ability to quickly jump to specific information, bookmark pages, and take notes. Direct linking to chapters in each book is provided through the table of contents.

Instrument Rating Online and Commercial Pilot Online—provide academic content in ground lessons with exams and interactive maneuvers lessons in a complete ground school. Online lessons are listed as references for ground lessons in this syllabus. Lessons use a combination of audio, video, and graphics to clearly explain each topic. Maneuvers lessons provide step-by-step guidance with in-cockpit video showing what the pilot sees when performing each maneuver. A Learning Management System (LMS) tracks completions and test results specific to each question to assist in identifying student strengths and weaknesses.

Jeppesen FAR/AIM—includes the current Federal Aviation Regulations (FARs) and the Aeronautical Information Manual (AIM) in one publication available in printed form or as an e-Book. The FAR/AIM includes FAR Parts 1, 3, 11, 43, 48, 61, 67, 68, 71, 73, 91, 97, 103, 105, 107, 110, 119, 135, 136, 137, 141, 142, NTSB 830, and TSRs 1552 and 1562. The AIM is a complete reproduction of the FAA publication with full-color graphics and the Pilot/Controller Glossary. The AIM contains basic flight information and ATC procedures to operate effectively in the U.S. National Airspace System.

Instrument Rating Exams and Commercial Pilot Exams—provide essential testing components. Required by FAR Part 141, students take a stage exam after each stage of ground training and an End-of-Course Exam at the completion of each ground training course.

Instrument Rating Airman Knowledge Test Guide and Commercial Pilot Airman Knowledge Test Guide—help students understand the learning objectives for the test questions so that they can take the FAA Instrument Rating Airman Knowledge est and Commercial Pilot Airman Knowledge Test with confidence. The test guides contain sample knowledge test questions, with correct answers, explanations, and study references. Explanations of why the other choices are wrong are included where appropriate. Questions are organized by topic to correspond to the chapters and sections of the *Instrument/Commercial* textbook. Full-color figures identical to the those used for reference on the FAA test also are included. The test guides are intended to supplement your instructor-led flight and ground training.

LESSON EXAMS

Each ground lesson has a brief exam at the end. As applicable, students may complete the exam that accompanies the online lesson or complete the questions in the appropriate textbook chapter. As specified in the ground lesson completion standards, the exams must be scored and the student must discuss any incorrect responses with the instructor to ensure student understanding prior to beginning the next ground lesson. When a lesson is complete, the instructor assigns the next textbook chapter and section(s) or online lesson(s) for out-of-class study.

STAGE EXAMS

At the end of each stage, the student is required to successfully complete the stage exam outlined in the syllabus before beginning the next ground training stage. The stage exam evaluates the student's understanding of the knowledge areas within a stage. Successful completion of each stage exam and a review of each incorrect response is required before the student progresses to the next stage.

END-OF-COURSE EXAMS

When all of the ground lesson assignments are complete for the course, the student should take the End-of-Course Exam assigned in Stage III of the Instrument Rating Course, Stage III of the Commercial Pilot Certification Course and at the end of Stage I of the Multi-Engine Rating Course. Following the exam, the instructor should assign the student appropriate subject areas for review. After a thorough review, the student should complete the applicable FAA airman knowledge test without delay.

USING AN ATD FOR GROUND TRAINING

The syllabus provides for use of an ATD for ground training. An ATD is extremely effective for introducing procedures without the distraction of having to fly the airplane. If properly integrated into the ground training program, the ATD will enhance systems knowledge and procedural understanding before the student trains in the airplane.

In addition to skill enhancement, the introduction of maneuvers and procedures by instrument reference in the ATD has other advantages for both student and instructor. These include fewer distractions, more versatility in lesson presentation, repositioning, freeze functions, emergency training, and the ability to control the environment of the training session and allow the student to concentrate on the areas the instructor wants to emphasize. By following the recommended sequence of the syllabus, the student will gain maximum benefit from the integration of academic training, introduction of new maneuvers and procedures in the ATD, and subsequent practice in the airplane. The following ground lessons are particularly suited to the use of an ATD.

Ground Lesson 3 — Attitude Instrument Flying	(1 Hour)
Ground Lesson 4 — Instrument Navigation	(1 Hour)
Ground Lesson 12 — Holding Procedures	(1 Hour)
Ground Lesson 16 — VOR and NDB Approaches	(1 Hour)
Ground Lesson 17 — ILS Approaches	(1 Hour)
Ground Lesson 18 — RNAV Approaches	(1 Hour)

If the box for ATD utilization is checked in the Preface, then the ATD becomes part of the ground training segments for the approved course, and its use is required. If the box for ATD utilization is left blank, the ATD is not part of the approved course, and its use is not required. Not checking the ATD box does not preclude a ground instructor from using an ATD. An ATD may be used in ground training just like any other classroom instructional aid.

FLIGHT TRAINING

The Instrument Rating Course and Commercial Pilot Certification Course each have three stages of flight training. The Multi-Engine Rating Course has one stage of flight training. The Commercial Pilot Certification Course included in this syllabus provides flight lessons that cover a transition to a complex airplane or to a TAA. If operators want to incorporate the TAA transition lessons in place of, or combined with, the complex airplane transition lessons, they should check the appropriate box in the Preface. In cases where the student has already accomplished 10 hours of training in a TAA and does not require a TAA transition, these lessons may be conducted as review and to introduce commercial maneuvers in the TAA.

Each stage of flight training builds on previous learning and should be completed in sequence. However, to provide flexibility for adapting to individual student needs and the training environment, the syllabus lesson sequence may be altered with approval of the chief flight instructor. Any deviation should not disturb the course continuity or objectives. The following discussion presents a description of the primary areas of study in each stage.

To avoid confusion when conducting both the Instrument Rating Course and Commercial Pilot Certification Course and to facilitate concurrent enrollment in these courses (if selected) the flight lessons are numbered sequentially from Flight Lesson 1 to Flight Lesson 29 in the Instrument Rating Flight Training Syllabus and Flight Lesson 30 to Flight Lesson 87 in the Commercial Pilot Flight Training Syllabus.

INSTRUMENT RATING COURSE

STAGE I

Stage I of the syllabus is designed to provide the student with a strong foundation in attitude instrument flying and instrument navigation. At the completion of this stage, the student is thoroughly prepared for the introduction of holding patterns and instrument approach procedures.

STAGE II

During this stage, the student learns to perform holding patterns and instrument approaches. This training prepares the student for the introduction of IFR cross-country procedures in Stage III.

STAGE III

This stage of training teaches the student IFR cross-country procedures and provides a review of all previously learned maneuvers. Through the use of three instrument cross-country flights and review, the student is able to attain the proficiency level of an instrument-rated pilot.

The ground and flight training portions of the Instrument Rating Course are completed in Stage III. The student should also successfully pass the FAA Instrument Rating Airman Knowledge Test and take the FAA Instrument Rating Practical Test at the completion of this stage.

COMMERCIAL PILOT CERTIFICATION COURSE

STAGE I

Stage I builds upon previously learned ground and flight training. The student reviews and practices day and night VFR cross-country procedures to prepare for commercial pilot operations.

STAGE II

Stage II provides a thorough introduction and pilot-in-command checkout in the complex airplane. The remainder of the stage is devoted to the introduction and review of precision flight maneuvers.

STAGE III

Although no new maneuvers or procedures are introduced in Stage III, practice of commercial maneuvers in the complex airplane is included. This is an important stage of training. It provides a review of the skills learned throughout the syllabus and prepares the student for the FAA practical test. If the student has not previously completed the FAA Instrument Rating Practical Test, both the Instrument and

Commercial Practical Test Briefings that coincide with the End-of-Course Flight Check are to be utilized in this stage.

TAA OPTION STAGE II

Stage II provides a thorough introduction and pilot-in-command checkout in the technically advanced airplane (TAA). The remainder of the stage is devoted to the introduction and review of precision flight maneuvers.

TAA OPTION STAGE III

Although no new maneuvers or procedures are introduced in Stage III, practice of commercial maneuvers in the TAA is included. This is an important stage of training. It provides a review of the skills learned throughout the syllabus and prepares the student for the FAA practical test. If the student has not previously completed the FAA Instrument Rating Practical Test, both the Instrument and Commercial Practical Test Briefings that coincide with the End-of-Course Flight Check are to be utilized in this stage.

MULTI-ENGINE RATING COURSE

STAGE I

Stage I of the Multi-Engine Rating Course provides a foundation for all relevant multi-engine maneuvers and procedures, including normal and engine-out operations. The final portion of this stage concentrates on multi-engine procedures in the IFR environment with both normal instrument approaches and engine-out instrument approach procedures.

PREFLIGHT DISCUSSION

Prior to each dual and solo flight, the instructor should provide the student with a thorough briefing of the tasks to be covered during the lesson. The instructor should define unfamiliar terms, explain the maneuvers and objectives of each lesson, and discuss single-pilot resource management (SRM) concepts related to each lesson. The Preflight Discussion should be tailored to the specific flight, the local environment, and especially to the needs of the student.

AIRPLANE PRACTICE

Each flight should begin with a review of previously-learned maneuvers before any new maneuvers are introduced. To ensure that students efficiently utilize solo flight training lessons, the instructor should train the student in the maneuvers to be performed during the flight and discuss what is expected to be accomplished during that lesson.

If a flight simulation device is used, the instructor is not relieved of teaching during flight lessons. However, the student is expected to grasp new techniques more easily having already been introduced to them in the simulation device. If simulation devices are not utilized, both introduction and practice are to be accomplished in the airplane.

FFS, FTD, OR ATD

Some flight training time required for the Instrument Rating Course under Part 141 Appendix C and of the Commercial Pilot Course under Part 141 Appendix D may be conducted in an aviation training device (ATD) and/or a flight simulation training device (FSTD), which is defined as a full flight simulator (FFS) or flight training device (FTD).

An FFS is distinguished from an FTD by the simulator's motion cueing system. An FTD is distinguished from most ATDs by the FTD's full-size replica of the instruments, equipment, panels, and controls of an aircraft, or set of aircraft, in an open flight deck area or in an enclosed flight deck. Advanced aviation training devices (AATDs) have similar capabilities as FTDs. Basic ATDs (BATDs) can lack the physical controls contained in a simulator or FTD, or the device does not sufficiently replicate an aircraft flight deck to be an FTD. However, BATDs provide benefits such as versatility in lesson presentation, repositioning features, and freeze functions.

When applying for Training Course Outline (TCO), operators who wish to utilize an FSS, FTD, or ATD should:

- Check the appropriate box(es) in the Preface.
- Select the flight lessons in which they intend to use the flight simulator/training device and list the flight time in the appropriate row and column on the Allocation Tables.

NOTE: *The student copy of the syllabus also should be marked accordingly.*

INSTRUMENT FLIGHT TRAINING TIME

Part 141 Appendix C, 4. Flight Training (b) covers the use of full flight simulators, flight training devices, or aviation training devices. According to this regulation:

- An FFS that meets the requirements of FAR 141.41(a) may be used for up to 50 percent of the required instrument flight training time.
- An FTD that meets the requirements of FAR 141.41(a) or an AATD that meets the requirements of FAR 141.41(b) may be used for up to 40 percent of the required instrument flight training time.
- A BATD that meets the requirements of FAR 141.41(b) may be used for up to 25 percent of the required instrument flight training time.
- A combination of FFSs FTDs, and AATDs may be used for up to 50% of the of the required instrument flight training time. However, the total time in FTDs, AATDs may not exceed 40 percent of the flight time and total time in BATDs may not exceed 25 percent.

COMMERCIAL FLIGHT TRAINING TIME

Part 141 Appendix D, 4. Flight Training (c) covers the use of use of full flight simulators and flight training devices. According to this regulation:

- An FFS that meets the requirements of FAR 141.41(a) may be used for up to 30 percent of the required commercial flight training time.
- An FTD that meets the requirements of FAR 141.41(a) may be used for up to 20 percent of the required commercial flight training time.

- A combination of FFSs and FTDs may be used for up to 30% of the of the required commercial flight training time. However, the total time in FTDs may not exceed 20 percent of the flight time.

POSTFLIGHT DEBRIEFING

The Postflight Debriefing is as important as the Preflight Discussion. The student should perform a self-critique of maneuvers/procedures and SRM skills. This *learner-centered grading* is especially helpful in developing the student's decision-making ability. If the student is having trouble mastering a skill, both the student and instructor should develop a plan for improving performance. An effective Postflight Briefing increases retention and helps the student prepare for the next lesson. As a guide, a minimum of 1/2 hour per flight is recommended for the Preflight Discussion and Postflight Briefing combined.

STUDENT STAGE CHECKS

Stage checks measure the student's accomplishments during each stage of training in accordance with Part 141. The conduct of each stage check is the responsibility of the chief instructor. However, the chief instructor may delegate authority for conducting stage checks and the End-of-Course Flight Check to the assistant chief instructor or a designated check instructor. This procedure provides close supervision of training and provides another opinion on the student's progress. The stage check also helps the chief instructor check the effectiveness of the instructors.

An examination of the building-block theory of learning will show that it is extremely important for progress and proficiency to be satisfactory before the student enters a new stage of training. Therefore, the next stage should not begin until the student successfully completes the stage check. Failure to follow this progression might defeat the purpose of the stage check and degrade the overall effectiveness of the course.

PILOT BRIEFINGS

The following pilot briefings are assigned in the Flight Training Syllabi.

Instrument Rating Flight Training Briefings

- Instrument Approaches
- IFR Cross-Country
- Instrument Rating Practical Test

Commercial Pilot Flight Training Briefings

- Cross-Country Procedures (VFR)
- Complex/TAA Transition
- Commercial Flight Maneuvers
- Commercial Pilot Practical Test

Multi-Engine Rating Flight Training Briefings

- Multi-Engine Operations and Systems
- Engine-Out Operations
- Multi-Engine Instrument Flight
- Multi-Engine Rating Practical Test

Pilot briefings are contained in Appendix A of this syllabus. Each briefing consists of a series of questions to prepare the student for the knowledge and tasks required in subsequent solo lessons and the practical test. The student should review the appropriate briefing questions in advance and research the answers to gain optimum benefit from the briefing.

The briefings should be conducted as private tutoring sessions to test each student's comprehension. Hold the briefings in a comfortable classroom or office environment, and schedule ample time. Discuss every question thoroughly to ensure the student understands the key points. Correct placement of the briefings is indicated in the Allocation Tables

Implementing the Courses

The *Instrument/Commercial Syllabus* is presented in both an overview and a lesson-by-lesson format. The lesson sequence and content have been designed to provide the student with maximum academic and flight training prior to the introduction of new maneuvers or procedures. Therefore, the sequence of ground and flight training shown in the syllabus outline should not be altered significantly if the coordinated program is utilized.

If absolutely necessary, the placement of ground lesson assignments may be changed to allow the student to progress more rapidly in the academic study than outlined in the course. If this method is used, the student should not be allowed to progress into the ground lesson assignments of the next stage until the flight lessons in the current stage of training are completed. This is important, because the student's recall of academic knowledge decreases with an increase in time between subject introduction during ground training and its application in flight training.

INSTRUMENT RATING COURSE

The Instrument Rating Course is presented first in the *Instrument/Commercial Syllabus*. It consists of a minimum of 30 hours of ground training and 35 hours of instrument flight training in Stages I, II, and III of the syllabus. During Stage III the student should pass the FAA Instrument Rating Airman Knowledge Test. At the completion of Stage III, the FAA Instrument Rating Practical Test should be taken.

The Instrument Rating Course is presented in both an overview and a lesson-by-lesson format. The combined flight and ground training syllabi include the entire outline from Stage I through the completion of Stage III. The lesson sequence and content have been designed to provide the student with maximum academic and flight training prior to the introduction of new maneuvers and procedures. However, the sequence shown in the syllabus outline may be altered to meet special circumstances of the student or training environment.

COMMERCIAL PILOT CERTIFICATION COURSE

The Commercial Pilot Certification Course is presented in the next segment of the *Instrument/Commercial Syllabus*. This course consists of a minimum of 35 hours of ground training and 120 hours of flight training in Stages I, II and III. During Stage II, the student should pass the FAA Commercial Pilot Airman Knowledge Test. At the completion of Stage III, the FAA Commercial Pilot Practical Test should be taken.

NOTE: *No ground lessons are assigned in Stage III of the Commercial Pilot Certification Course so the Ground Training Syllabus does not include this stage.*

Students adding a multi-engine rating to their commercial pilot certificate must complete the Multi-Engine Rating Course, which includes 15 hours of ground training and 15 hours of multi-engine flight training.

The Commercial Pilot Certification Course is presented in both an overview and a lesson- by-lesson format. The lesson sequence and content have been designed to provide the student with maximum academic and flight training prior to the introduction of new maneuvers and procedures. While the ground and flight training syllabi provide a general training outline, the lesson sequence shown may be tailored to meet the individual needs of the student. For example, lessons 36, 37, 38, 39, 40 and 41 are designed to be solo cross-country flight lessons. However, these lessons may also be utilized for additional dual instruction to meet the proficiency requirements for the End-of-Course Flight Check and FAA practical test.

INSTRUMENT COURSE AND COMMERCIAL COURSE — CONCURRENT ENROLLMENT

Concurrent enrollment requires the student to hold a private pilot certificate and be concurrently enrolled in the Instrument Rating Course and the Commercial Pilot Certification Course. Part 141 Appendix D, Section 2—Eligibility for Enrollment (b) (2) allows enrollment in the commercial pilot certification course if the student is concurrently enrolled in an instrument rating course.

Concurrent enrollment includes a total of at least 65 hours of ground training and 155 hours of flight training. This total consists of 30 hours of ground training and 35 hours of flight training in Stages I, II, and III of the Instrument Rating Course. Stages I, II, and III of the Commercial Pilot Certification Course consists of an additional 35 hours of ground training and 120 hours of flight training.

Students adding a multi-engine rating to their commercial pilot certificate must complete the Multi-Engine Rating Course, which includes 15 hours of ground training and 15 hours of multi-engine flight training.

COMMERCIAL COURSE MULTI-ENGINE OPTIONS

The Allocation Tables for Flight Stages I, III, and III of the Commercial Pilot Certification Course provide two options for completing the course with a single-engine rating and a multi-engine rating. By enrolling in the Commercial and Multi-Engine Courses concurrently and shortening some of the single-engine flight lessons in Stage II and III, the courses are designed so that the student may earn the multi-engine rating without increasing the total flight time. The shortened times are listed in parenthesis in the Time Allocation tables. For Flight Stages II and III, the student must select one of two flight times listed in many of the Allocation Table rows:

- To take the Commercial Pilot–Airplane Single-Engine Land Practical Test at the end of Stage III, the student must complete the first flight time listed. After passing the practical test at the end of Stage III, the student may continue training to add a multi-engine rating to the commercial certificate by completing the Multi-Engine Rating Course. The student then takes the Commercial Pilot Airplane–Multi-Engine Land Practical Test.

- If the student chooses to be concurrently enrolled in the Commercial Pilot Certification Course and the Multi-Engine Rating Course, the student completes the second flight time listed (shown in parentheses) for Flight Stages II and III and the student must also complete the flight time in Stage I of the Multi-Engine Rating Course to meet the total time required for commercial pilot certification. In this case, the student completes the Multi-Engine Rating Course before taking the Commercial Pilot–Airplane Single-Engine Land Practical Test and the Commercial Pilot Airplane–Multi-Engine Land Practical Test.

CREDIT FOR PREVIOUS TRAINING

According to FAR 141.77(c), when a student transfers from one FAA-approved school to another approved school, course credits obtained in the previous course of training may be credited for 50 percent of the curriculum requirements by the receiving school. However, the receiving school must determine the amount of credits to be allowed based upon a proficiency test, knowledge test, or both, conducted by the receiving school. A student who enrolls in a course of training may receive credit for 25 percent of the curriculum requirements for knowledge and experience gained in a Part 61 flight school, and the credit must be based upon a proficiency test, knowledge test, or both, conducted by the receiving school. The amount of credit for previous training allowed, whether received from an FAA-approved school or other source, is determined by the receiving school. In addition, the previous provider of the training must certify the kind and amount of training given, and the result of each stage check and end-of-course test, if applicable.

PART 61 TRAINING

The *Instrument/Commercial Syllabus* is designed to meet all of the requirements of Part 141, Appendices, C, D, and I. It may also be adapted to meet the requirements of Part 61. Part 61 incorporates greater aeronautical experience requirements than are found in Part 141. For example, as indicated in FAR 61.65 for an instrument rating, you must have at least 50 hours of cross-country time as pilot in command and 40 hours of actual or simulated instrument time in the areas of operation specified in the FARs. This includes at least 15 hours of instrument flight training from an authorized instructor in the aircraft category for which the instrument rating is sought. If your training is accomplished under Part 141, you must have 35 hours of instrument training from an authorized instructor in the areas specified in Part 141, Appendix C and need not comply with the 50-hour PIC cross-country requirement.

Under Part 61, a commercial pilot applicant for an airplane category and single-engine class rating must log at least 250 hours of flight time as a pilot. This includes 100 hours in powered aircraft, of which 50 hours must be in airplanes. In addition, it must include 100 hours of pilot-in-command time, which includes at least 50 hours in cross-country flight of which at least 10 hours must be in airplanes. Further, 20 hours of flight training and 10 hours of solo flight also are required. Refer to FAR 61.125, 61.127, and 61.129.

Under Part 61, an applicant for a multi-engine class rating to be added to a pilot certificate must meet the requirements of FAR 61.63 (c). Essentially, there are no established minimum amounts of ground training or flight training time necessary in order to add an additional aircraft class rating to a pilot certificate. As a result, class ratings are often referred to as competency-based. Part 61 requires instruction be received appropriate to the desired rating, and that a flight instructor recommendation be obtained. Of course, the appropriate practical test also must be successfully completed.

The ground training requirements under Part 61 specify that an applicant for a knowledge test is required to have a logbook endorsement from an authorized instructor who conducted the training or reviewed the person's home study course. The endorsement must indicate satisfactory completion of the ground instruction or home study course required for the certificate or rating sought. A home study course for the purposes of Part 61 is a course of study in those aeronautical knowledge areas specified in FAR 61.125, and organized by a pilot school, publisher, flight or ground instructor, or by the student. The Instrument/Commercial Course easily meets this requirement. As a practical consideration, students seeking pilot certification under Part 61 should receive some formal ground training, either in the classroom or from an authorized flight or ground instructor.

An applicant who applies for an additional class rating to be added on a pilot certificate need not take an additional knowledge test, provided the applicant holds an airplane, rotorcraft, powered-lift, or airship rating at that pilot certificate level.

Courses Overview

INTRODUCTION

The *Instrument/Commercial Syllabus* is designed to coordinate the academic study assignments and flight training required by pilots operating in an increasingly complex aviation environment. New subject matter is introduced during the ground lessons, which include the following:

1. Textbook/e-Book assignments with study questions.
2. The Instrument Rating and Commercial Pilot Online courses.
3. Instructor/student discussions
4. Stage exams and end-of-course exams

After completing the ground lesson, the student will apply these new principles in a simulation device or in the airplane during the flight lesson. The Allocation Tables indicate placement of the ground lessons when the coordinated sequence is used.

Optimum effectiveness is realized when ground lessons are completed just prior to the respective flight lessons, as outlined in the syllabus. However, it is also acceptable to present lessons in a formal ground school before the student is introduced to the airplane. If a considerable length of time has elapsed between the ground lesson and the associated flight, the instructor may wish to conduct a short review of essential material. Flight lessons should not be conducted until related ground lessons have been completed.

INSTRUMENT RATING COURSE

COURSE OBJECTIVE

The student will obtain the knowledge, skill, and aeronautical experience necessary to meet the requirements for an instrument rating (airplane).

COURSE COMPLETION STANDARD

The student must demonstrate through knowledge tests, flight tests, and appropriate records that he/she meets the knowledge, skill, and experience requirements necessary to obtain an instrument rating (airplane).

STUDENT INFORMATION

COURSE ENROLLMENT

To enroll in the flight portion of the Instrument Rating Course, you must hold at least a private pilot certificate with an airplane category rating and a single-engine land class rating.

REQUIREMENTS FOR GRADUATION

To obtain an instrument rating, you must be able to read, speak, write, and understand the English language and hold a private pilot certificate with at least a third-class medical certificate. In addition, you must meet the aeronautical experience requirements specified in Part 141, Appendix C to be eligible for graduation.

LESSON DESCRIPTION AND STAGES OF TRAINING

This syllabus fully describes each lesson, including the objectives, references, topics, and completion standards. The stage objectives and standards are described at the beginning of each stage within the syllabus.

TESTS AND CHECKS

The syllabus incorporates stage and end-of-course flight checks in accordance with Part 141, Appendix C. These checks are given by the chief instructor, an assistant chief instructor, or check instructor designated by the chief instructor. The student will also complete the stage exams and pilot briefings that are described within the syllabus. In addition, the student must satisfactorily complete the End-of-Course Exam and End-of-Course Flight Check after completing all the stages.

Curriculum Overview
Instrument Rating Course

Completion of this course is based solely upon compliance with the minimum requirements of FAR Part 141. The time tables are provided for guidance in achieving regulatory compliance.

	GROUND TRAINING				FLIGHT TRAINING			
	Ground Lessons	ATD	Briefings, Stage, and Final Exams	Ground Training Totals	Instrument Training	Cross-Country Training	FFS, FTD, ATD	Flight Training Totals
STAGE I	8.0	(2.0)	1.0	9.0	13.0		As Req.	13.0
STAGE II	10.0	(3.0)	1.5	11.5	11.0		As Req.	11.0
STAGE III	6.0		3.5	9.5	11.0	(10.0)	As Req.	11.0
TOTALS	24.0	(5.0)	6.0	30.0	35.0	(10.0)	As Req.	35.0

NOTE: **Ground Training:**

1. Ground lessons may include class discussion or online lessons.
2. Operators using the ATD option for ground training may credit ATD time for up to 5 hours toward the 30-hour requirement. Suggested ATD hours for ground training are shown in parentheses.

NOTE: **Flight Training:**

1. Cross-country hours (shown in parentheses) are included in the instrument training time for Stage III and in the total flight training time.
2. All flight training in the Instrument Rating Course is dual.
3. As shown in the following table, operators using the FFS, FTD, and/or ATD options may credit FFS, FTD, or ATD time for instrument flight training time according to Part 141 Appendix C, 4. Flight Training (b) Use of full flight simulators, flight training devices, or aviation training devices.

Type of Device	FAR Equipment Requirements	Instrument Flight Time Allowed by Part 141 Appendix C, 4. (b)	Flight Hours
Full Flight Simulator (FFS)	141(a)	50%	17.5
Flight Training Device (FTD)	141(a)	40%	14
Advanced Aviation Training Device (AATD)	141(b)	40%	14
Basic Aviation Training Device (BATD)	141(b)	25%	8.75
Combination of Devices	141(a) and (b)	50% (Total time in FTDs, AATDs, and BATDs may not exceed percentages specified above.)	17.5 14 (total in FTDs and AATDs) 8.75 (total in BATDs)

COMMERCIAL PILOT CERTIFICATION COURSE

COURSE OBJECTIVE

The student will obtain the knowledge, skill, and aeronautical experience necessary to meet the requirements for a commercial pilot certificate with an airplane category rating and a single-engine land class rating.

COURSE COMPLETION STANDARD

The student must demonstrate through knowledge tests, flight tests, and appropriate records that he/she meets the knowledge, skill, and experience requirements necessary to obtain a commercial pilot certificate with an airplane category rating and a single-engine land class rating.

STUDENT INFORMATION

COURSE ENROLLMENT

To enroll in the flight portion of the Commercial Pilot Certification Course, you must hold at least a private pilot certificate. In addition, you must hold an instrument rating or be concurrently enrolled in an instrument rating (airplane) course.

REQUIREMENTS FOR GRADUATION

To obtain a commercial pilot certificate, you must be at least 18 years of age and be able to read, speak, write, and understand the English language. In addition, you must have a valid FAA third-class medical certificate. However, to exercise the privileges of a commercial pilot you must possess a valid second-class medical certificate. In addition, you must meet the aeronautical experience requirements specified in Part 141, Appendix D, to be eligible for graduation.

LESSON DESCRIPTION AND STAGES OF TRAINING

This syllabus fully describes each lesson, including the objectives, references, topics, and completion standards. The stage objectives and standards are described at the beginning of each stage within the syllabus.

TESTS AND CHECKS

The syllabus incorporates stage and end-of-course flight checks in accordance with Part 141, Appendix D. These checks are given by the chief instructor, an assistant chief instructor, or check instructor designated by the chief instructor. The student will also complete the stage exams and pilot briefings that are described within the syllabus. In addition, the student must satisfactorily complete the End-of-Course Exam and End-of-Course Flight Check after completing all the stages.

MULTI-ENGINE RATING COURSE

COURSE OBJECTIVE

The student will obtain the knowledge, skill, and aeronautical experience necessary to meet the requirements for a adding a multi-engine class rating to a commercial pilot certificate.

COURSE COMPLETION STANDARD

The student must demonstrate through knowledge tests, flight tests, and appropriate records that he/she meets the knowledge, skill, and experience requirements necessary to add a multi-engine land class rating to a commercial pilot certificate.

STUDENT INFORMATION

COURSE ENROLLMENT

To enroll in the flight portion of the Multi-Engine Rating Course, you must hold at least a commercial pilot certificate with an airplane single-engine land rating or be concurrently enrolled in a commercial pilot certification course.

REQUIREMENTS FOR GRADUATION

To add a multi-engine class rating to a commercial pilot certificate, you must be at least 18 years of age and be able to read, speak, write, and understand the English language. In addition, you must have a valid FAA third-class medical certificate. However, to exercise the privileges of a commercial pilot with a multi-engine rating, you must possess a valid second-class medical certificate. In addition, you must meet the aeronautical experience requirements specified in Part 141, Appendix I, to be eligible for graduation.

LESSON DESCRIPTION AND STAGES OF TRAINING

This syllabus fully describes each lesson, including the objectives, references, topics, and completion standards. The stage objectives and standards are described at the beginning of each stage within the syllabus.

TESTS AND CHECKS

The syllabus incorporates stage and end-of-course flight checks in accordance with Part 141, Appendix I. These checks are given by the chief instructor, an assistant chief instructor, or check instructor designated by the chief instructor. The student will also complete the stage exams and pilot briefings that are described within the syllabus. In addition, the student must satisfactorily complete the End-of-Course Exam and End-of-Course Flight Check after completing all the stages.

CURRICULUM OVERVIEW
Commercial Pilot Certification Course

Completion of this course is based solely upon compliance with the minimum requirements of FAR Part 141. The time tables are provided for guidance in achieving regulatory compliance.

		GROUND TRAINING			
		Ground Lessons	Stage and End-of-Course Exams	Briefings/ Debriefings	Ground Training Totals
	STAGE I	9.0	1.0	As Required	10.0
	STAGE II	22.0	3.0	As Required	25.0
COMM'L SINGLE ENGINE →	TOTALS	31.0	4.0	As Required	35.0
MULTI-ENGINE →	STAGE I	9.0	2.0	4.0	15.0

NOTE: 1. Ground lessons may include class discussion or online lessons.

2. No ground lessons are assigned in Stage III of the Commercial Course so the Ground Training Syllabus does not include this stage.

		FLIGHT TRAINING												
		Dual								Solo				
		Day Local	Day X-C	Night	FFS or FTD	Dual Stage Totals	Complex or TAA	Multi-Engine	Instru-ment	Day Local	Day X-C	Night	Solo Stage Totals	Dual/ Solo Comb. Totals
	STAGE I		8.0 (8.0)	5.0 (5.0)	As Req.	13.0 (13.0)			As Req.		34.0*	6.0	40.0	53.0 (53.0)
	STAGE II	20.0 (14.0)			As Req.	20.0 (14.0)	10.0 (7.0)		As Req.	9.0			9.0	29.0 (23.0)
	STAGE III	20.0 (12.0)	2.0 (1.0)		As Req.	22.0 (13.0)	5.0 (3.0)		As Req.	16.0			16.0	38.0 (29.0)
SE →	TOTALS	40.0 (26.0)	10.0 (9.0)	5.0 (5.0)	As Req.	55.0 (40.0)	15.0 (10.0)		As Req.	25.0	34.0*	6.0	65.0	120.0 (105.0)
ME →	STAGE I	(9.0)	(3.0)	(3.0)		(15.0)		(15.0)	As Req.					(15.0)
SE + ME →	TOTALS	40.0 (35.0)	10.0 (12.0)	5.0 (8.0)	As Req.	55.0 (55.0)	15.0 (10.0)	(15.0)	As Req.	25.0	34.0*	6.0		120.0 (120.0)

NOTE:
1. * Indicates some solo cross-country hours may be used for additional dual instruction to meet the proficiency requirements for the End-of-Course Flight Check and FAA Commercial Pilot Practical Test.
2. Complex, TAA, and Multi-Engine flight time is included as a portion of Day Local, Day X-C (Cross-Country), or Night hours so is not added to these hours to determine Dual Stage Totals.
3. In blocks where two times are shown, the first time is for students taking the Commercial Pilot–Airplane Single-Engine Land Practical Test at the end of Stage III. If the student chooses to complete the second flight time listed (shown in parentheses) for Flight Stages II and III, the student must also complete the multi-engine flight training time in Stage I of the Multi-Engine Rating Course to meet the total time required for commercial pilot certification. For example, the dual time totals for Stages I, II, and III are 55.0 hours for students not completing the multi-engine training and 40 hours for those who will complete the remaining 15 hours in the multi-engine airplane during Flight Stage I of the Multi-Engine Rating Course. In each case, the student will receive a minimum of 55.0 hours dual.
4. The 15 hours of flight time in Stage I of the Multi-Engine Rating Course are all dual instruction in the multi-engine airplane.
5. Check the applicable box in the Preface to use the Stage II and Stage III TAA Options–conduct the specified lessons in the Allocation Tables in a TAA in lieu of a complex airplane to meet the hour requirements shown here.
6. As shown in the following table, operators using the FFS or FTD options may credit FFS or FTD time for commercial flight training time according to Part 141 Appendix D, 4. Flight Training (c) Use of full flight simulators and flight training devices.

Type of Device	FAR Equipment Requirements	Percentage of Commercial Flight Training Time Allowed	Flight Hours
Full Flight Simulator (FFS)	141(a)	30%	16.5
Flight Training Device (FTD)	141(a)	20%	11
Combination of Devices	141(a)	30% (20% in FTDs)	16.5 (11 in FTDs)

Allocation Tables

Lesson Time Allocation

Ground Training: Ground Lessons	Ground Training: ATD	Ground Training: Pilot Briefings	Ground Training: Stage/Final Exams	Ground Training: Exam Debriefings		Dual Flight Training: Day Local	Dual Flight Training: Day Cross-Country	Dual Flight Training: Night Local	Dual Flight Training: Night Cross-Country	Dual Flight Training: Instrument	Dual Flight Training: FFS	Dual Flight Training: FTD or AATD	Dual Flight Training: BATD
					Instrument Rating Course — Stage I								
1.0					GL 1 – Instrument Rating Requirements/Human Factors								
1.0					GL 2 – Flight Instrument Systems								
1.0	As Req.				GL 3 – Attitude Instrument Flying								
					FL 1 – Instrument Flight – Basic Maneuvers	1.0				1.0			
					FL 2 – Basic Maneuvers and IFR Systems	1.0				1.0			
					FL 3 – Review Full Panel	1.0				1.0			
					FL 4 – Unusual Attitude Recovery / Autopilot Use	1.0				1.0			
					FL 5 – Systems/Equipment Malfunctions / Partial Panel	1.0				1.0			
					FL 6 – Unusual Attitude Recovery – Partial Panel	1.0				1.0			
					FL 7 – Review Instrument Flight – Full and Partial Panel	1.0				1.0			
1.0	As Req.				GL 4 – Instrument Navigation								
					FL 8 – VOR Navigation	1.0				1.0			
1.0					GL 5 – Airports, Airspace, and Flight Inform								
					FL 9 – GPS Navigation	1.0				1.0			
					FL 10 - GPS Navigation Review	1.0				1.0			
1.0			1.0	As Req.	GL 6 – ATC Services								
1.0					GL 7 – ATC Clearances								
1.0					GL 8 – Instrument FARs								
					FL 11 – Localizer Tracking	1.0				1.0			
					FL 12 – Navigation Review	1.0				1.0			
					GL 9 – Stage I Exam								
					FL 13 – Stage I Check	1.0				1.0			
8.0	As Req.		1.0	As Req.	Stage Totals	13.0				13.0			

NOTE: 1. Ground lessons may include class discussion or online lessons.

2. The ATD may be used as required in the ground lessons indicated. Operators utilizing the ATD option in the Instrument/Commercial or Instrument Rating Course may credit up to 5 hours of ATD time toward ground training requirements.

3. The individual times shown on the Allocation Tables are for instructor/student guidance only; they are not mandatory for each ground lesson, flight lesson, or stage of training. At the completion of this course, the student must meet the minimum requirements of Part 141 for ground and flight training in order to graduate. Preflight and postflight briefings are as required.

4. If using the FFS, FTD, and/or ATD options:
   - Indicate the flight time for the selected lesson row in the appropriate column.
   - Ensure that the total flight training time for a specific device does not exceed that indicated in Part 141 Appendix C 4. (b). (Refer to the Curriculum Overview for the Instrument Course in this syllabus.)

Ground Lessons	ATD	Pilot Briefings	Stage/Final Exams	Exam Debriefings	Lesson Time Allocation	Day Local	Day Cross-Country	Night Local	Night Cross-Country	Instrument	FFS	FTD or AATD	BATD
Ground Training						Dual Flight Training							
					Instrument Rating Course — Stage II								
1.0					GL 10 – Departure Charts and Procedures								
1.5					GL 11 – Enroute Charts and Procedures								
1.0	As Req.				GL 12 – Holding Procedures								
					FL 14 – GPS/VOR Holding	1.0				1.0			
1.0					GL 13 – Arrival Charts and Procedures								
					FL 15 – Localizer Holding	1.0				1.0			
1.5					GL 14 – Approach Charts								
1.0					GL 15 – Approach Procedures								
1.0	As Req.				GL 16 – VOR and NDB Approaches								
		.5			Briefing – Instrument Approaches								
					FL 16 and 17 – RNAV (GPS) Approach	2.0				2.0			
1.0	As Req.				GL 17 – ILS Approaches								
1.0					FL 18 – ILS and Localizer Approaches	1.0				1.0			
					GL 18 – VOR and NDB Approaches								
					FL 19 – VOR and VOR/DME Approaches	1.0				1.0			
					FL 20 – Partial-Panel Approaches	1.0				1.0			
					FL 21 – Review Partial-Panel Approaches	1.0				1.0			
					FL 22 – Review Holding and Approaches	1.5				1.5			
			1.0	As Req.	GL 19 – Stage II Exam								
					FL 23 – Stage II Check	1.5				1.5			
10.0	As Req.	.5	1.0	As Req.	Stage Totals	11.0				11.0			

NOTE:
1. Ground lessons may include class discussion or online lessons.
2. The ATD may be used as required in the ground lessons indicated. Operators utilizing the ATD option in the Instrument/Commercial or Instrument Rating Course may credit up to 5 hours of ATD time toward ground training requirements.
3. The individual times shown on the Allocation Tables are for instructor/student guidance only; they are not mandatory for each ground lesson, flight lesson, or stage of training. At the completion of this course, the student must meet the minimum requirements of Part 141 for ground and flight training in order to graduate. Preflight and postflight briefings are as required.
4. If using the FFS, FTD, and/or ATD options:
   - Indicate the flight time for the selected lesson row in the appropriate column.
   - Ensure that the total flight training time for a specific device does not exceed that indicated in Part 141 Appendix C 4. (b). (Refer to the Curriculum Overview for the Instrument Course in this syllabus.)

Lesson Time Allocation

Ground Training						Dual Flight Training							
Ground Lessons	ATD	Pilot Briefings	Stage/Final Exams	Exam Debriefings		Day Local	Day Cross-Country	Night Local	Night Cross-Country	Instrument	FFS	FTD or AATD	BATD
					Instrument Rating Course — Stage III								
1.0					GL 20 – Weather Factors and Hazards								
1.0					GL 21 – Interpreting Weather Information								
1.0					GL 22 – IFR Flight Planning								
		.5			Briefing – IFR Cross-Country								
					FL 24 – IFR Cross-Country Procedures		1.0			1.0			
					GL 23 – IFR Single-Pilot Resource Management								
1.0					GL 24 – IFR Emergencies								
1.0					FL 25 – IFR Cross-Country / Emergency Operations		2.0			2.0			
1.0					FL 26 – Long IFR Cross-Country		3.0			3.0			
		1.0			Briefing – Instrument Rating Practical Test								
					FL 27 – IFR Cross-Country Review		2.0			2.0			
			1.0	As Req.	GL 25 – Stage III Exam								
					FL 28 – Stage III Check	1.5				1.5			
			1.0	As Req.	GL 26 – Instrument Rating End-of-Course Exam								
					FL 29 – End-of-Course Flight Check	1.5				1.5			
6.0		1.5	2.0	As Req.	Stage Totals	3.0	8.0			11.0			
24.0	(5.0)	2.0	4.0	As Req.	Instrument Rating Course Totals	27.0	8.0			35.0			

NOTE: 1. Ground lessons may include class discussion or online lessons.

2. The ATD may be used as required in the ground lessons indicated. Operators utilizing the ATD option in the Instrument/Commercial or Instrument Rating Course may credit up to 5 hours of ATD time toward ground training requirements.

3. The individual times shown on the Allocation Tables are for instructor/student guidance only; they are not mandatory for each ground lesson, flight lesson, or stage of training. At the completion of this course, the student must meet the minimum requirements of Part 141 for ground and flight training in order to graduate. Preflight and postflight briefings are as required.

4. If using the FFS, FTD, and/or ATD options:
   - Indicate the flight time for the selected lesson row in the appropriate column.
   - Ensure that the total flight training time for a specific device does not exceed that indicated in Part 141 Appendix C 4. (b). (Refer to the Curriculum Overview for the Instrument Course in this syllabus.)

Lesson Time Allocation														
Ground Training					Flight Training									
					Dual							Solo		
Ground Lessons	Pilot Briefings	Stage/Final Exams	Exam Debriefings		Day Local	Day Cross-Country	Night	Complex	Instrument	FFS	FTD	Day Local	Day Cross-Country	Night
Commercial Pilot Certification Course — Stage I														
1.0				GL 27 – Commercial Pilot Requirements										
1.5				GL 28 – Airports, Airspace, and Flight Information										
1.5				GL 29 – Meteorology										
2.0				GL 30 – Cross-County Planning & Instrument Nav										
	As Req.			Briefing – Cross-Country Procedures (VFR)										
				FL 30 – Cross-Country		3.0			As Req.					
				FL 31 – Cross-Country									4.0	
1.0				GL 31 – Aviation Physiology and SRM Concepts										
				FL 32 – Night Local			1.0							
				FL 33 – Night Cross-Country			4.0		As Req.					
2.0				GL 32 – Commercial FARs										
				FL 34 – Night Local										1.5
				FL 35 – Night Local										1.5
				FL 36 – Night Cross-Country										3.0
		1.0	As Req.	GL 33 – Stage I Exam										
				FL 37 – Cross-Country									5.0	
				FL 38 – Cross-Country									5.0	
				FL 39 – Cross-Country									5.0	
				FL 40 – Cross-Country									5.0	
				FL 41 – Cross-Country									5.0	
				FL 42 – Cross-Country		3.0			As Req.					
				FL 43 – Long Cross-Country									5.0	
				FL 44 – Stage I Check		2.0								
9.0	As Req.	1.0	As Req.	Stage Totals		8.0	5.0		As Req.				34.0	6.0

NOTE: 1. Ground lessons may include class discussion or online lessons.

2. The individual times shown on the Allocation Tables are for instructor/student guidance only; they are not mandatory for each ground lesson, flight lesson, or stage of training. At the completion of this course, the student must meet the minimum requirements of Part 141 for ground and flight training in order to graduate. Preflight and postflight briefings are as required.

3. Flight lessons 37 through 41 are designed for solo or dual flight as necessary to meet the proficiency requirements for the End-of-Course Flight Check and FAA Commercial Pilot Practical Test.

4. If using the FFS and/or FTD options:
   - Indicate the flight time for the selected lesson row in the appropriate column.
   - Ensure that the total flight training time for a specific device does not exceed that indicated in Part 141 Appendix D 4.(c). (Refer to the Curriculum Overview for the Commercial Course in this syllabus.)

Lesson Time Allocation

Ground Training					Flight Training									
					Dual							Solo		
Ground Lessons	Pilot Briefings	Stage/Final Exams	Exam Debriefings		Day Local	Day X-Country	Night	Complex	Instrument	FFS	FTD	Day Local	Day X-Country	Night
				Commercial Pilot Certification Course — Stage II										
				FL 45 – Basic Flight Maneuvers								1.0		
2.0				GL 34 – High Performance Powerplants										
2.0				GL 35 – Environmental & Ice Control Systems										
2.0				GL 36 – Retractable Landing Gear										
	As Req.			Briefing – Complex Airplane/TAA Transition										
				FL 46 – Complex Airplane or TAA	1.0 (1.0)			1.0 (1.0)						
2.0				GL 37 – Advanced Aerodynamics & Accelerated Stalls										
2.0				GL 38 – Predicting Performance										
2.0				GL 39 – Controlling Weight & Balance										
				FL 47 – Complex Airplane or TAA	1.5 (1.0)			1.5 (1.0)	As Req.					
2.0				GL 40 – Emergency Operations										
2.0				GL 41 – Soft-Field & Short-Field Takeoffs & Landings										
				FL 48 - Complex Airplane or TAA Transition	1.5 (1.0)			1.5 (1.0)	As Req.					
				FL 49 – Complex Airplane or TAA Transition	1.5 (1.0)			1.5 (1.0)	As Req.					
				FL 50 – Complex Airplane or TAA Transition	1.5 (1.0)			1.5 (1.0)						
				FL 51 – Stall/Spin Awareness	1.5 (1.0)									
	As Req.			Briefing – Commercial Flight Maneuvers										
2.0				GL 42 – Steep Turns & Chandelles										
				FL 52 – Steep Turns & Chandelles	1.5 (1.0)									
2.0				GL 43 – 8s on Pylons, Steep Spirals, & Accuracy Landings										
				FL 53 – 8s on Pylons, Steep Spirals, & Accuracy Landings	1.5 (1.0)									
				FL 54 – Commercial Maneuvers Review	1.5 (1.0)							1.0		
2.0				GL 44 – Commercial Pilot SRM										
				FL 55 – Commercial Maneuvers								1.0		
				FL 56 – Commercial Maneuvers								1.0		
				FL 57 – Commercial Maneuvers										
				FL 58 – Emergency Operations Review	1.5 (1.0)				As Req.					
				FL 59 – Commercial Maneuvers								1.0		
				FL 60 – Commercial Maneuvers								1.0		
				FL 61 – Commercial Maneuvers								1.0		
				FL 62 – Commercial Maneuvers								1.0		
				FL 63 – Commercial Maneuvers								1.0		
				FL 64 – Commercial Maneuvers	1.5 (1.0)									
				FL 65 – Commercial Maneuvers	1.0 (1.0)									
				FL 66 – Complex Airplane or TAA	2.0 (1.0)			2.0 (1.0)	As Req.					
		1.0	As Req.	GL 45 – Stage II Exam										
		2.0	As Req.	GL 46 – Commercial Pilot End-of-Course Exam										
				FL 67 – Stage II Check (Complex Airplane or TAA)	1.0 (1.0)			1.0 (1.0)	As Req.					
22.0	As Req.	3.0	As Req.	**Stage Totals**	20.0 (14.0)			10.0 (7.0)	As Req.			9.0		

NOTE: 1. Ground lessons may include class discussion or online lessons.

2. The individual times shown on the Allocation Tables are for instructor/student guidance only; they are not mandatory for each ground lesson, flight lesson, or stage of training. At the completion of this course, the student must meet the minimum requirements of Part 141 for ground and flight training in order to graduate. Preflight and postflight briefings are as required.

3. In blocks with two times, the first time is for students taking the Commercial Pilot–Airplane Single-Engine Land Practical Test at the end of Stage III. If the student chooses to complete the second flight time (in parentheses) for Flight Stages II and III, the student must also complete the multi-engine flight training time in Stage I of the Multi-Engine Rating Course to meet the total time for commercial pilot certification.

4. Check the box in the Preface to use the Stage II TAA Option—conduct flight lessons 46, 47, 48, 49, 50, 66, and 67 in a TAA.

5. If using the FFS and/or FTD options:
   - Indicate the flight time for the selected lesson row in the appropriate column.
   - Ensure that the total flight training time for a specific device does not exceed that indicated in Part 141 Appendix D 4. (c). (Refer to the Curriculum Overview for the Commercial Course in this syllabus.)

Lesson Time Allocation

Ground Training: Ground Lessons	Ground Training: Pilot Briefings	Ground Training: Stage/Final Exams	Ground Training: Exam Debriefings		Flight Training Dual: Day Local	Flight Training Dual: Day Cross-Country	Flight Training Dual: Night	Flight Training Dual: Complex	Flight Training Dual: Instrument	Flight Training Dual: FFS	Flight Training Dual: FTD	Flight Training Solo: Day Local	Flight Training Solo: Day Cross-Country	Flight Training Solo: Night
				Commercial Pilot Certification Course — Stage III										
				FL 68 – Instrument/Commercial Review	2.0 (1.0)				As Req.					
				FL 69 – Instrument/Commercial Review	2.0 (1.0)				As Req.					
				FL 70 – Commercial Maneuvers								2.0		
				FL 71 – Commercial Maneuvers								2.0		
				FL 72 – Commercial Maneuvers	2.0 (1.0)									
				FL 73 – Commercial Maneuvers								2.0		
				FL 74 – Commercial Maneuvers								2.0		
				FL 75 – Commercial Maneuvers								2.0		
				FL 76 – Instrument/Commercial Review	2.0 (1.0)				As Req.					
				FL 77 – Instrument/Commercial Review	2.0 (1.0)				As Req.					
				FL 78 – Complex Airplane or TAA Review	2.0 (1.0)			2.0 (1.0)						
				FL 79 – Solo Review								2.0		
				FL 80 – Solo Review								2.0		
				FL 81 – Solo Review								2.0		
				FL 82 – Complex Airplane or TAA Cross-Country		2.0 (1.0)		2.0 (1.0)	As Req.					
				FL 83 – Complex Airplane or TAA	1.0 (1.0)			1.0 (1.0)						
	As Req.			Briefing – Commercial Pilot Practical Test										
				FL 84 – Final Stage Review		2.0 (1.0)								
				FL 85 – Final Stage Review	2.0 (1.0)									
				FL 86 – Stage III Check	1.5 (1.5)									
				FL 87 – End-of-Course Flight Check	1.5 (1.5)									
	As Req.			**Stage Totals**	20.0 (12.0)	2.0 (1.0)		5.0 (3.0)	As Req.			16.0		
31.0	As Req.	4.0	As Req.	**Commercial Pilot Course Totals**	40.0 (26.0)	10.0 (9.0)	5.0	15.0 (10.0)	As Req.			25.0	34.0	6.0

NOTE:
1. Stage III does not contain ground lessons. The total ground training time listed is from Stages I and II.
2. The individual times shown on the Allocation Tables are for instructor/student guidance only; they are not mandatory for each ground lesson, flight lesson, or stage of training. At the completion of this course, the student must meet the minimum requirements of Part 141 for ground and flight training in order to graduate. Preflight and postflight briefings are as required.
3. In blocks with two times, the first time is for students taking the Commercial Pilot–Airplane Single-Engine Land Practical Test at the end of Stage III. If the student chooses to complete the second flight time (in parentheses) for Flight Stages II and III, the student must also complete the multi-engine flight training time in Stage I of the Multi-Engine Rating Course to meet the total time for commercial pilot certification.
4. Check the box in the Preface to use the Stage III TAA Option—conduct flight lessons 78, 82, and 83 in a TAA.
5. If using the FFS and/or FTD options:
   - Indicate the flight time for the selected lesson row in the appropriate column.
   - Ensure that the total flight training time for a specific device does not exceed that indicated in Part 141 Appendix D 4.(c). (Refer to the Curriculum Overview for the Commercial Course in this syllabus.)

Lesson Time Allocation

Ground Training					Flight Training							
					Dual					Solo		
Ground Lessons	Pilot Briefings	Stage/Final Exams	Exam Debriefings		Day Local	Day Cross-Country	Night	Complex	Instrument	Day Local	Day Cross-Country	Night
				Multi-Engine Rating Course — Stage I								
2.0				GL 1 – The ME Rating, SRM, and Normal Operations								
	.5			Briefing – Multi-Engine Operations and Systems								
				FL 1 – Introduction Multi-Engine Airplane and Maneuvers	1.0			1.0	.2			
2.0				GL 2 – ME Systems, Weight & Balance, and Performance								
	.5			Briefing – Multi-Engine Performance Considerations								
				FL 2 – Maneuvers – VR/IR	1.0			1.0	.3			
				FL 3 – Short-Field Takeoffs and Landings	1.0			1.0	.2			
1.5				GL 3 – ME/Engine-Out Aerodynamics and Maneuvers								
1.5				GL 4 – Engine-Out Operations								
	.5			Briefing – Engine-Out Operations								
				FL 4 – Engine-Out Operations	1.0			1.0	.2			
				FL 5 – Engine-Out Operations	1.0			1.0	.2			
2.0				GL 5 – Instrument Flight and Applying SRM								
	.5			Briefing – Multi-Engine Instrument Flight								
				FL 6 – Engine-Out Operations by Instrument Reference	1.0			1.0	.2			
				FL 7 – Instrument Procedures	1.0			1.0	.7			
				FL 8 – Multi-Engine Instrument (Day Cross-Country)		3.0		3.0	1.0			
				FL 9 – Multi-Engine Instrument (Night Cross-Country)			3.0	3.0	1.0			
		1.0	1.0	GL 6 – Stage I Exam								
				Briefing—Multi-Engine Rating Practical Test								
				FL 10 – Stage I Check	1.0			1.0	.5			
		1.0	1.0	GL 7 – Multi-Engine End-of-Course Exam								
				FL 11 – End-of-Course Flight Check	1.0			1.0	.5			
9.0	2.0	2.0	2.0	Multi-Engine Stage Totals	9.0	3.0	3.0	15.0	5.0			

NOTE: 1. The individual times shown on the Allocation Tables are for instructor/student guidance only; they are not mandatory for each ground lesson, flight lesson, or stage of training. At the completion of this course, the student must meet the minimum requirements of Part 141 for ground and flight training in order to graduate. Preflight and postflight briefings are as required.

2. The dual instrument flight training time is shown to indicate the recommended portion of the flights that should be devoted to instrument training.

Instrument Rating Ground Training Syllabus

GROUND TRAINING COURSE OBJECTIVES

The student will obtain the aeronautical knowledge required by FAR Part 141 and Part 61 for an instrument rating and meet the prerequisites in Part 61 for the FAA Instrument Rating Airman Knowledge Test.

GROUND TRAINING COURSE COMPLETION STANDARDS

Through knowledge exams and records, the student must demonstrate the aeronautical knowledge required by FAR Part 141 and Part 61 for an instrument rating. The student must also demonstrate the knowledge necessary to pass the FAA Instrument Rating Airman Knowledge Test and show that the prerequisites specified in Part 61 have been met.

Stage I

STAGE OBJECTIVES

During this stage, the student learns about the principles of instrument flight, including the operation, use, and limitations of flight instruments and instrument navigation systems, and how the air traffic control system functions. Stage I also introduces single-pilot resource management (SRM) and human factors concepts related to flight in the IFR environment.

STAGE COMPLETION STANDARDS

The student must pass the Stage I Exam with a minimum score of 80 percent, and review each incorrect response with the instructor to ensure complete understanding before starting Stage II.

GROUND LESSON 1

REFERENCES

Instrument/Commercial Textbook/e-Book
Chapter 1 — Building Professional Experience
Section A — Instrument Rating Requirements

Instrument Online
GL01 — Discovering Instrument Flight
GL02 — Human Factors

NOTE: Prior to Ground Lesson 1, students should read Chapter 1, Section A — Instrument Rating Requirements, Section C — Aviation Physiology, and Section D — SRM Concepts.

OBJECTIVES

Lesson Objective	Part 141/61 Aeronautical Knowledge	ACS Task
Recognize the requirements for an instrument rating. Identify the recency of experience requirements to act as PIC under instrument flight rules.	Applicable Federal Aviation Regulations for IFR flight operations	Pilot Qualifications
Become familiar with single-pilot resource management (SRM) concepts that apply to flight in the IFR environment. Explain aviation physiology factors that apply to flight in the IFR environment.	Aeronautical decision making and judgment	Throughout the practical test, the evaluator must assess the applicant's ability to use ADM, SRM, and CRM, as applicable to the risk management tasks.

CONTENT

COURSE OVERVIEW

- ❑ Course Components
- ❑ Exams and Tests
- ❑ Policies and Procedures
- ❑ Student/Instructor Expectations
- ❑ Use of a Full Flight Simulator (FFS), Flight Training Device (FTD), and/or Aviation Training Device (ATD)

SECTION A — INSTRUMENT RATING REQUIREMENTS
GL01 — DISCOVERING INSTRUMENT FLIGHT

- ❑ Instrument Rating Privileges
- ❑ Instrument Training
- ❑ Instrument Currency
- ❑ FAA WINGS—Pilot Proficiency Program

SECTION C — AVIATION PHYSIOLOGY
GL02 — HUMAN FACTORS

- ❑ Vision in Flight
- ❑ Spatial Disorientation
- ❑ Visual Illusions
- ❑ Hypoxia
- ❑ Ear and Sinus Block
- ❑ Decompression Sickness
- ❑ Hyperventilation
- ❑ Fitness for Flight
- ❑ Stress
- ❑ Fatigue
- ❑ Alcohol and Drugs
- ❑ Hypothermia

SECTION D — SRM CONCEPTS

- ❑ Aeronautical Decision Making
- ❑ Risk Management
- ❑ Task Management
- ❑ Situational Awareness
- ❑ Controlled Flight Into Terrain Awareness
- ❑ Automation Management

COMPLETION STANDARDS

- Demonstrate understanding of policies and procedures that apply to the school's pilot training program during oral quizzing by the instructor.
- Demonstrate understanding of instrument training and recency of experience requirements during oral quizzing by the instructor.
- Demonstrate understanding of aviation physiology and SRM concepts that apply to the IFR flight environment during oral quizzing by the instructor.
- Complete with a minimum score of 80 percent: questions for Chapter 1A, 1C, and 1D; or online exams for GL02. With the instructor, review each incorrect response to ensure complete understanding before staring Ground Lesson 2.

STUDY ASSIGNMENT

Instrument/Commercial Textbook/e-Book

Chapter 2 — Principles of Instrument Flight
  Section A — Analog Flight Instruments
  Section B — Electronic Flight Displays

Instrument Online

GL03 — Analog Flight Instruments
GL04 — Digital Flight Instruments

GROUND LESSON 2

REFERENCES

Instrument/Commercial Textbook/e-Book

Chapter 2 — Principles of Instrument Flight
  Section A — Analog Flight Instruments
  Section B — Electronic Flight Displays

Instrument Online

GL03 — Analog Flight Instruments
GL04 — Digital Flight Instruments

OBJECTIVES

Lesson Objective	Part 141/61 Aeronautical Knowledge	ACS Task
Identify the instruments required for flight under IFR.	Applicable Federal Aviation Regulations for IFR flight operations	Instrument Flight Deck Check
Explain the function and operation of analog and digital flight instrument systems and components. Recognize the limitations and common errors of analog and digital flight instrument systems and components.	Safe and efficient operation of aircraft under instrument flight rules and conditions	Airplane Flight Instruments and Navigation Equipment Checking Instruments and Equipment

CONTENT

CHAPTER 2, SECTION A — ANALOG FLIGHT INSTRUMENTS
GL03 — ANALOG FLIGHT INSTRUMENTS

INSTRUMENTS FOR FLIGHT UNDER IFR
- ❏ FAA Instrument Requirements
- ❏ Inspection Requirements

GYROSCOPIC FLIGHT INSTRUMENTS
- ❏ System Operation
- ❏ System Errors
- ❏ Instrument Check

MAGNETIC COMPASS
- ❏ System Operation
- ❏ System Errors
- ❏ Instrument Check

PITOT-STATIC INSTRUMENTS
- ❏ System Operation
- ❏ System Errors
- ❏ Instrument Check
- ❏ V-Speeds and Color Codes

CHAPTER 2, SECTION B — ELECTRONIC FLIGHT DISPLAYS
GL04 — DIGITAL FLIGHT INSTRUMENTS

PRIMARY FLIGHT DISPLAY (PFD)
- ❏ Attitude and Heading Reference System (AHRS)
- ❏ Attitude Indicator
- ❏ Horizontal Situation Indicator (HSI)
- ❏ Air Data Computer (ADC)
- ❏ Airspeed Indicator
- ❏ Altimeter
- ❏ Vertical Speed Indicator (VSI)
- ❏ PFD Failure

MULTIFUNCTION DISPLAY (MFD)
- ❏ Features
- ❏ Map Display

AUTOMATION
- ❑ Operation
- ❑ Flight Director

COMPLETION STANDARDS

- Demonstrate understanding of IFR instrument requirements and instrument flight systems, operations, and errors during oral quizzing by the instructor.
- Complete with a minimum score of 80 percent: questions for Chapter 2A and 2B; or online exams for GL03 and GL04. With the instructor, review each incorrect response to ensure complete understanding before starting Ground Lesson 3.

STUDY ASSIGNMENT

Instrument/Commercial Textbook/e-Book
Chapter 2 — Principles of Instrument Flight
Section C — Attitude Instrument Flying

Instrument Online
GL05 — Attitude Instrument Flying

GROUND LESSON 3

REFERENCES

Instrument/Commercial Textbook/e-Book
Chapter 2 — Principles of Instrument Flight
Section C — Attitude Instrument Flying

Instrument Online
GL05 — Attitude Instrument Flying

OBJECTIVES

Lesson Objective	Part 141/61 Aeronautical Knowledge	ACS Task
Identify the fundamental procedures related to instrument cross-check, instrument interpretation, and aircraft control. Recognize the techniques that apply to attitude instrument flying, including common methods, performing basic maneuvers, managing instrument system failures, and partial-panel flying procedures. Explain how to recognize and recover from unusual flight attitudes.	Safe and efficient operation of aircraft under instrument flight rules and conditions	Instrument Flight Recovery from Unusual Flight Attitudes Approach with Loss of Primary Flight Instrument Indicators

CONTENT

FUNDAMENTAL SKILLS
- ❑ Instrument Cross-Check
- ❑ Instrument Interpretation
- ❑ Aircraft Control

ATTITUDE INSTRUMENT FLYING METHODS
- ❑ Control and Performance Method
- ❑ Primary and Supporting Method

BASIC FLIGHT MANEUVERS
- ❑ Straight-and-Level Flight
- ❑ Standard-Rate Turns
- ❑ Steep Turns
- ❑ Constant Airspeed Climbs
- ❑ Constant Rate Climbs
- ❑ Constant Airspeed Descents
- ❑ Constant Rate Descents
- ❑ Leveloff From Climbs and Descents
- ❑ Climbing and Descending Turns
- ❑ Common Errors

PARTIAL-PANEL FLYING
- ❑ Gyroscopic Instrument Failure
- ❑ Compass Turns
- ❑ Timed Turns
- ❑ Pitot-Static Instrument Failures

UNUSUAL ATTITUDE RECOVERY
- ❑ Nose-High Unusual Attitude
- ❑ Nose-Low Unusual Attitude

INTRODUCTION TO THE ATD (OPTION)
- ❑ Orientation and Flight Familiarization
- ❑ Overview of Physical and Virtual Controls
- ❑ Instrument Flight Deck Check
- ❑ Full-Panel Basic Flight Maneuvers
- ❑ Partial-Panel Flying

COMPLETION STANDARDS
- Demonstrate understanding of attitude instrument flying, coping with instrument failures, and unusual attitude recovery during oral quizzing by the instructor.
- Complete with a minimum score of 80 percent: questions for Chapter 2C; or online exam for GL05. With the instructor, review each incorrect response to ensure complete understanding before starting Ground Lesson 4.

STUDY ASSIGNMENT

Instrument/Commercial Textbook/e-Book
Chapter 2 — Principles of Instrument Flight
Section D — Instrument Navigation

Instrument Online
GL06 — Instrument Navigation

GROUND LESSON 4

REFERENCES

Instrument/Commercial Textbook/e-Book
Chapter 2 — Principles of Instrument Flight
Section D — Instrument Navigation

Instrument Online
GL06 — Instrument Navigation

OBJECTIVES

Lesson Objective	Part 141/61 Aeronautical Knowledge	ACS Task
Explain the operation and limitations of VOR, DME, and GPS equipment. Identify how to navigate using VOR, DME, and GPS equipment.	IFR navigation and approaches by use of navigation systems	Airplane Flight Instruments and Navigation Equipment Intercepting and Tracking Navigational Systems and Arcs

CONTENT

VOR NAVIGATION
- ❑ Horizontal Situation Indicator
- ❑ Intercepting a Course
- ❑ Tracking
- ❑ Determining Your Progress
- ❑ Station Passage
- ❑ VOR Operational Considerations
- ❑ VOR Checks
- ❑ Distance Measuring Equipment
- ❑ DME Arcs

AREA NAVIGATION (RNAV)
- ❑ Required Navigation Performance (RNP)
- ❑ Inertial Navigation System (INS)
- ❑ Flight Management Systems (FMS)

SATELLITE NAVIGATION — GPS
- ❑ Trilateration
- ❑ Wide Area Augmentation System (WAAS)
- ❑ Ground-Based Augmentation System (GBAS)
- ❑ Requirements for IFR GPS Navigation
- ❑ Navigating with GPS

ATD (OPTION)
- ❑ VOR Orientation
- ❑ HSI Orientation
- ❑ Intercepting and Tracking a VOR Radial

- ❑ Intercepting and Tracking DME Arcs
- ❑ GPS Programming
- ❑ Intercepting and Tracking GPS Courses
- ❑ Electronic Flight Display Orientation

COMPLETION STANDARDS

- Demonstrate understanding of navigating with VOR and GPS equipment and the operation and limitations of navigation systems during oral quizzing by the instructor.
- Complete with a minimum score of 80 percent: questions for Chapter 2D; or online exam for GL06. With the instructor, review each incorrect response to ensure complete understanding before starting Ground Lesson 5.

STUDY ASSIGNMENT

Instrument/Commercial Textbook/e-Book

Chapter 3 — The Flight Environment

Section A — Airports, Airspace, and Flight Information

Instrument Online

GL 7 — Airports, Airspace, and Flight Information

GROUND LESSON 5

REFERENCES

Instrument/Commercial Textbook/e-Book

Chapter 3 — The Flight Environment

Section A — Airports, Airspace, and Flight Information

Instrument Online

GL07 — Airports, Airspace, and Flight Information

OBJECTIVES

Lesson Objective	Part 141/61 Aeronautical Knowledge	ACS Task
Interpret airport markings, lighting, and signs. Explain the structure and requirements of the National Airspace System. Identify procedures to avoid runway incursions and to perform land and hold short operations (LAHSO).	Applicable Federal Aviation Regulations for IFR flight operations Appropriate information in the Aeronautical Information Manual	Compliance with Air Traffic Control Clearances
Identify the flight information sources that apply to IFR operations. Recognize how to use flight information to plan a flight.	Appropriate information in the Aeronautical Information Manual	Cross-Country Flight Planning

CONTENT

THE AIRPORT ENVIRONMENT

- ❑ Runway and Taxiway Markings and Signs
- ❑ Runway Incursion Avoidance
- ❑ Land and Hold Short Operations (LAHSO)
- ❑ Approach Light System
- ❑ Visual Glideslope Indicators
- ❑ Runway Lighting
- ❑ Airport Beacons and Obstruction Lights
- ❑ Aircraft Lighting
- ❑ Airport Security

AIRSPACE

- ❑ Uncontrolled Airspace (Class G)
- ❑ Controlled Airspace (Class A, B, C, D, and E)
- ❑ Special VFR
- ❑ Airspeed Limitations
- ❑ Special Use Airspace
- ❑ Other Airspace Areas
- ❑ Temporary Flight Restrictions (TFRs)
- ❑ Air Defense Identification Zone (ADIZ)
- ❑ Washington DC Special Flight Rules Area (SFRA)
- ❑ Intercept Procedures

FLIGHT INFORMATION

- ❑ Aeronautical Charts—VFR and IFR
- ❑ Chart Supplements
- ❑ Airport/Facility Directory
- ❑ Electronic Flight Bag (EFB)
- ❑ Notices to Airman (NOTAMs)
- ❑ Federal Aviation Regulations (FARs)
- ❑ *Aeronautical Information Manual* (AIM)
- ❑ Advisory Circulars

COMPLETION STANDARDS

- Demonstrate understanding of airport markings, lighting, and signs, and the procedures for runway incursion avoidance, LAHSO, and airport security during oral quizzing by the instructor.
- Demonstrate understanding of airspace requirements and flight information sources during oral quizzing by the instructor.
- Complete with a minimum score of 80 percent: questions for Chapter 3A; or online exam for GL07. With the instructor, review each incorrect response to ensure complete understanding before starting Ground Lesson 7.

STUDY ASSIGNMENT

Instrument/Commercial Textbook/e-Book

Chapter 3 — The Flight Environment
Section B — Air Traffic Control System

Instrument Online

GL 8 — Air Traffic Control System

GROUND LESSON 6

REFERENCES

Instrument/Commercial Textbook/e-Book

Chapter 3 — The Flight Environment
Section B — ATC Services

Instrument Online

GL08 — Air Traffic Control System

OBJECTIVES

Lesson Objective	Part 141/61 Aeronautical Knowledge	ACS Task
Recognize the types of services provided by the air traffic control system. Explain the use of enroute and terminal facilities in the IFR environment.	Appropriate information in the Aeronautical Information Manual Air traffic control system and procedures for instrument flight operations:	Compliance with Air Traffic Control Clearances Departure, Enroute, and Arrival Operations

CONTENT

ADS-B SYSTEM

- ❑ ADS-B Services
- ❑ ADS-B Data Links

AIR ROUTE TRAFFIC CONTROL CENTER
❑ ARTCC Traffic Separation
❑ Processing the IFR Flight Plan
❑ Air Route Surveillance Radar (ARSR)
❑ Traffic Separation
❑ Weather Avoidance
❑ Safety Alerts
❑ Emergency Assistance

TERMINAL FACILITIES
❑ Terminal Radar Approach Control (TRACON)
❑ Control Tower
❑ ATIS
❑ Clearance Delivery

ATC SERVICES FOR VFR AIRCRAFT
❑ Pilot Responsibilities
❑ Interpreting Traffic Advisories

COMPLETION STANDARDS

- Demonstrate understanding of enroute and terminal ATC services for IFR operations during oral quizzing by the instructor.
- Complete with a minimum score of 80 percent: questions for Chapter 3B; or online exam for GL08. With the instructor, review each incorrect response to ensure complete understanding before starting Ground Lesson 8.

STUDY ASSIGNMENT

Instrument/Commercial Textbook/e-Book
Chapter 3 — The Flight Environment
Section C — ATC Clearances

Instrument Online
GL09 — ATC Clearances

GROUND LESSON 7

REFERENCES

Instrument/Commercial Textbook/e-Book
Chapter 3 — The Flight Environment
Section C — ATC Clearances

Instrument Online
GL09 — ATC Clearances

OBJECTIVES

Lesson Objective	Part 141/61 Aeronautical Knowledge	ACS Task
Recognize the elements of an IFR clearance. Explain ATC clearance procedures in the IFR environment. Demonstrate how to write clearance shorthand.	Air traffic control system and procedures for instrument flight operations	Compliance with Air Traffic Control Clearances

CONTENT

PILOT RESPONSIBILITIES

- ❑ See and Avoid
- ❑ IFR Climb Considerations

IFR FLIGHT PLAN AND ATC CLEARANCE

- ❑ Elements of an IFR Clearance
- ❑ Abbreviated IFR Departure Clearance
- ❑ VFR on Top
- ❑ Approach Clearances
- ❑ VFR Restrictions to an IFR Clearance
- ❑ Composite Flight Plan
- ❑ Tower Enroute Control Clearance
- ❑ Departure Restrictions
- ❑ Clearance Readback
- ❑ Clearance Shorthand

COMPLETION STANDARDS

- Demonstrate understanding of IFR clearances, ATC procedures, pilot responsibilities, and clearance shorthand during oral quizzing by the instructor.
- Complete with a minimum score of 80 percent: questions for Chapter 3C; or online exam for GL09. With the instructor, review each incorrect response to ensure complete understanding before starting Ground Lesson 9.

STUDY ASSIGNMENT

FAR/AIM

Instrument FARs

GROUND LESSON 8

REFERENCES

FAR/AIM
Instrument FARs

OBJECTIVES

Lesson Objective	Part 141/61 Aeronautical Knowledge	ACS Task
Explain the Federal Aviation Regulations related to instrument flight. Explain the accident and incident reporting requirements in NTSB Part 830.	Applicable Federal Aviation Regulations for IFR flight operations	Compliance with Air Traffic Control Clearances

CONTENT

- ❑ FAR Part 1
- ❑ FAR Part 61
- ❑ FAR Part 91
- ❑ NTSB Part 830

COMPLETION STANDARDS

- Demonstrate understanding of the FARs in Parts 1, 61, and 91 related to instrument flight and the accident and incident reporting requirements of NTSB Part 830 during oral quizzing by the instructor before starting Ground Lesson 6.

STUDY ASSIGNMENT

Review the content of Ground Lessons 1 – 8 to prepare for the Stage I Exam.

GROUND LESSON 9
STAGE I EXAM

REFERENCES

Ground Lessons 1 – 8

OBJECTIVE
Demonstrate knowledge of the subjects covered in Ground Lessons 1 – 8 by passing the Stage I Exam.

CONTENT
STAGE I EXAM
- ❑ Instrument Rating Requirements
- ❑ Aviation Physiology
- ❑ SRM Concepts
- ❑ Analog Flight Instruments
- ❑ Electronic Flight Displays
- ❑ Attitude Instrument Flying
- ❑ Instrument Navigation
- ❑ Airports, Airspace, and Flight Information
- ❑ ATC Services
- ❑ ATC Clearances
- ❑ Instrument FARs

COMPLETION STANDARDS
To complete the lesson and stage, pass the Stage I Exam with a minimum score of 80 percent. With the instructor, review each incorrect response to ensure complete understanding before starting Stage II.

STUDY ASSIGNMENT
Instrument/Commercial Textbook/e-Book
Chapter 4 — Departure

Instrument Online
GL11 — Departure Charts and Procedures

STAGE II

STAGE OBJECTIVES

During this stage, the student learns how to interpret instrument charts and explores the procedures for performing IFR departure, enroute, arrival, and approach operations.

STAGE COMPLETION STANDARDS

The student must pass the Stage II Exam with a minimum score of 80 percent, and review each incorrect response with the instructor to ensure complete understanding before starting Stage III.

GROUND LESSON 10

REFERENCES

Instrument/Commercial Textbook/e-Book
Chapter 4 — Departure

Instrument Online
GL11 — Departure Charts and Procedures

OBJECTIVES

Lesson Objective	Part 141/61 Aeronautical Knowledge	ACS Task
Interpret the information on instrument departure charts. Explain how to perform IFR departure procedures.	Appropriate information in the Aeronautical Information Manual Air traffic control system and procedures for instrument flight operations Safe and efficient operation of aircraft under instrument flight rules and conditions Use of IFR enroute and instrument approach procedure charts	Departure, Enroute, and Arrival Operations

CONTENT

SECTION A — DEPARTURE CHARTS

GL11 — DEPARTURE CHARTS AND PROCEDURES

- ❏ Instrument Departure Procedures (DPs)
- ❏ Climb Gradients

- ❑ Standard Instrument Departure (SID)
- ❑ Vector SID Chart Features
- ❑ Pilot Navigation SID Chart Features
- ❑ RNAV SID Chart Features
- ❑ Obstacle Departure Procedure (ODP)
- ❑ Diverse Vector Area

SECTION B — DEPARTURE PROCEDURES

GL11 — DEPARTURE CHARTS AND PROCEDURES

- ❑ Takeoff Minimums
- ❑ Climb Gradients
- ❑ Visual Climb Over Airport (VCOA)
- ❑ Obstacle Clearance
- ❑ Briefing the Departure
- ❑ Performing a SID
- ❑ Climb Via Clearance
- ❑ Obstacle Departure Procedures
- ❑ Vectors
- ❑ VFR Departures

COMPLETION STANDARDS

- Demonstrate understanding of interpreting instrument departure charts and following departure procedures during oral quizzing by the instructor.
- Complete with a minimum score of 80 percent: questions for Chapter 4; or online exam for GL11. With the instructor, review each incorrect response to ensure complete understanding before starting Ground Lesson 11.

STUDY ASSIGNMENT

Instrument/Commercial Textbook/e-Book

Chapter 5 — Enroute

Section A — Enroute and Area Charts

Section B — Enroute Procedures

Instrument Online

GL12 — Enroute Charts

GL13 — Enroute Procedures

GROUND LESSON 11

REFERENCES

Instrument/Commercial Textbook/e-Book

Chapter 5 — Enroute

Section A — Enroute and Area Charts

Section B — Enroute Procedures

Instrument Online

GL12 — Enroute Charts

GL13 — Enroute Procedures

OBJECTIVES

Lesson Objective	Part 141/61 Aeronautical Knowledge	ACS Task
Interpret the information on IFR enroute and area charts. Explain how to perform the proper procedures for flying enroute in the IFR environment.	Appropriate information in the Aeronautical Information Manual Air traffic control system and procedures for instrument flight operations Safe and efficient operation of aircraft under instrument flight rules and conditions	Departure, Enroute, and Arrival Operations

CONTENT

SECTION A — ENROUTE AND AREA CHARTS

GL12 — ENROUTE CHARTS

- ❏ Enroute Charts
- ❏ Front Panel
- ❏ Navigation Aids
- ❏ Victor Airways
- ❏ RNAV Routes
- ❏ Communication
- ❏ Airports
- ❏ Airspace
- ❏ Area Charts

SECTION B — ENROUTE PROCEDURES

GL13 — ENROUTE PROCEDURES

- ❏ Enroute Radar Procedures
- ❏ Communication
- ❏ Reporting Procedures
- ❏ Enroute Navigation Using GPS
- ❏ IFR Cruising Altitudes
- ❏ Reduced Vertical Separation Minimums (RVSM)
- ❏ Descending from the Enroute Segment

COMPLETION STANDARDS

- Demonstrate understanding of IFR enroute charts and enroute procedures in the IFR environment during oral quizzing by the instructor.
- Complete with a minimum score of 80 percent: questions for Chapter 5A and 5B; or online exams for GL12 and GL13. With the instructor, review each incorrect response to ensure complete understanding before starting Ground Lesson 12.

STUDY ASSIGNMENT

Instrument/Commercial Textbook/e-Book

Chapter 5 — Enroute
  Section C — Holding Procedures

Instrument Online

GL14 — Holding Procedures

GROUND LESSON 12

REFERENCES

Instrument/Commercial Textbook/e-Book
Chapter 5 — Enroute
Section C — Holding Procedures

Instrument Online
GL14 — Holding Procedures

OBJECTIVE

Lesson Objective	Part 141/61 Aeronautical Knowledge	ACS Task
Describe how to perform holding patterns including entry, timing, and communication procedures.	Appropriate information in the Aeronautical Information Manual Air traffic control system and procedures for instrument flight operations Safe and efficient operation of aircraft under instrument flight rules and conditions	Compliance with Air Traffic Control Clearances Holding Procedures Departure, Enroute, and Arrival Operations

CONTENT

HOLDING PATTERN

❑ Timing
❑ Distance
❑ Crosswind Correction
❑ Maximum Holding Speed

HOLDING PATTERN ENTRIES

❑ Direct Entry
❑ Teardrop Entry
❑ Parallel Entry
❑ Visualizing Entry Procedures
❑ ATC Holding Instructions

ATD (OPTION)

❑ Holding Entries
❑ VOR and RNAV (GPS) Holding
❑ Wind Correction and Ground Track

COMPLETION STANDARDS

- Demonstrate understanding of holding pattern procedures, entries, and ATC holding instructions during oral quizzing by the instructor.
- Complete with a minimum score of 80 percent: questions for Chapter 5C; or online exam for GL14. With the instructor, review each incorrect response to ensure complete understanding before starting Ground Lesson 13.

STUDY ASSIGNMENT

Instrument/Commercial Textbook/e-Book

Chapter 6 — Arrival

Instrument Online

GL15 — Arrival Charts and Procedures

GROUND LESSON 13

REFERENCES

Instrument/Commercial Textbook/e-Book

Chapter 6 — Arrival

Instrument Online

GL15 — Arrival Charts and Procedures

OBJECTIVES

Lesson Objective	Part 141/61 Aeronautical Knowledge	ACS Task
Interpret the information on instrument arrival charts. Explain how to perform IFR arrival procedures.	Appropriate information in the Aeronautical Information Manual Air traffic control system and procedures for instrument flight operations Use of IFR enroute and instrument approach procedure charts Safe and efficient operation of aircraft under instrument flight rules and conditions	Departure, Enroute, and Arrival Operation

CONTENT

SECTION A — ARRIVAL CHARTS

GL15 — ARRIVAL CHARTS AND PROCEDURES

- ❑ Standard Terminal Arrival Route (STAR)
- ❑ Interpreting the STAR
- ❑ RNAV STAR

SECTION B — ARRIVAL PROCEDURES

GL15 — ARRIVAL CHARTS AND PROCEDURES

- ❑ Preparing for the Arrival
- ❑ Briefing the STAR Procedure
- ❑ Flying the Arrival
- ❑ Airspeed
- ❑ Descend Via Clearance
- ❑ Vertical Navigation Planning

COMPLETION STANDARDS

- Demonstrate understanding of interpreting instrument arrival charts and following arrival procedures during oral quizzing by the instructor.
- Complete with a minimum score of 80 percent: questions for Chapter 6; or online exams for GL15. With the instructor, review each incorrect response to ensure complete understanding before starting Ground Lesson 14.

STUDY ASSIGNMENT

Instrument/Commercial Textbook/e-Book

Chapter 7 — Approach

Section A — Approach Charts

Instrument Online

GL16 — Approach Considerations

GL17 — Approach Charts

GROUND LESSON 14

REFERENCES

Instrument/Commercial Textbook/e-Book

Chapter 7 — Approach

Section A — Approach Charts

Instrument Online

GL16 — Approach Considerations

GL17 — Approach Charts

OBJECTIVES

Lesson Objective	Part 141/61 Aeronautical Knowledge	ACS Task
Identify approach procedure types and the segments of an instrument approach procedure. Interpret and apply the information published on instrument approach charts.	Appropriate information in the Aeronautical Information Manual Air traffic control system and procedures for instrument flight operations Use of IFR enroute and instrument approach procedure charts Safe and efficient operation of aircraft under instrument flight rules and conditions	Nonprecision Approach Precision Approach Missed Approach Circling Approach Landing from an Instrument Approach

CONTENT

SECTION A — APPROACH CHARTS

GL16 — APPROACH CONSIDERATIONS

- ❑ Approach Procedure Types
- ❑ Transition from Enroute to Approach
- ❑ Initial Approach Segment
- ❑ Intermediate Approach Segment
- ❑ Final Approach Segment
- ❑ Missed Approach Segment
- ❑ Runway and Approach Lighting

SECTION A — APPROACH CHARTS

GL17 — APPROACH CHARTS

- ❑ Chart Layout
- ❑ Heading Section
- ❑ Communications Section
- ❑ Briefing Information
- ❑ Minimum Safe/Sector Altitude (MSA)
- ❑ Terminal Arrival Altitude (TAA)
- ❑ Plan View
- ❑ Profile View
- ❑ Descent/Timing Conversion Table
- ❑ Time and Speed Table and Rate of Climb/Descent Table
- ❑ Lighting Box
- ❑ Missed Approach Icons
- ❑ Landing Minimums
- ❑ Airport Sketch

AIRPORT CHART AND AIRPORT DIAGRAM

- ❑ Heading and Communications
- ❑ Airport Environment
- ❑ Runway Information
- ❑ Alternate Airports

COMPLETION STANDARDS

- Demonstrate understanding of instrument approach procedure types, segments and chart interpretation during oral quizzing by the instructor.
- Demonstrate understanding of airport chart/diagram interpretation during oral quizzing by the instructor.
- Complete with a minimum score of 80 percent: questions for Chapter 7A; or online exams for GL16 and GL17. With the instructor, review each incorrect response to ensure complete understanding before starting Ground Lesson 15.

Study Assignment Instrument/Commercial Textbook/e-Book

Chapter 7 — Approach

Section B — Approach Procedures

Instrument Online

GL18 — Approach Procedures

GROUND LESSON 15

REFERENCES

Instrument/Commercial Textbook/e-Book

Chapter 7 — Approach

Section B — Approach Procedures

Instrument Online

GL18 — Approach Procedures

OBJECTIVES

Lesson Objective	Part 141/61 Aeronautical Knowledge	ACS Task
Describe how to prepare for an approach by performing an approach overview and approach briefing. Explain how to perform an approach by following the proper procedures depicted on the approach chart.	Appropriate information in the Aeronautical Information Manual Air traffic control system and procedures for instrument flight operations Use of IFR enroute and instrument approach procedure charts Safe and efficient operation of aircraft under instrument flight rules and conditions	Nonprecision Approach Precision Approach Missed Approach Circling Approach Landing from an Instrument Approach

CONTENT

PREPARING FOR THE APPROACH

- ❑ Approach Overview
- ❑ Approach Briefing
- ❑ Approach Clearance

PERFORMING THE APPROACH

- ❏ Straight-In Landing Versus Circling Approach
- ❏ Straight-In Approach
- ❏ Use of ATC Radar for Approaches
- ❏ Course Reversals
- ❏ Circling Approaches
- ❏ Sidestep Maneuver
- ❏ Missed Approach Procedures
- ❏ Visual and Contact Approaches

COMPLETION STANDARDS

- Demonstrate understanding of how to prepare for and perform an instrument approach procedure during oral quizzing by the instructor.
- Complete with a minimum score of 80 percent: questions for Chapter 7B; or online exam for GL18. With the instructor, review each incorrect response to ensure complete understanding before starting Ground Lesson 16.

STUDY ASSIGNMENT

Instrument/Commercial Textbook/e-Book

Chapter 8 — Instrument Approaches
  Section A — RNAV Approaches

Instrument Online

GL19 — RNAV Approach Procedures

GROUND LESSON 16

REFERENCES

Instrument/Commercial Textbook/e-Book

Chapter 8 — Instrument Approaches
  Section A — RNAV Approaches

Instrument Online

GL19 — RNAV Approach Procedures

OBJECTIVES

Lesson Objective	Part 141/61 Aeronautical Knowledge	ACS Task
Recognize the equipment required to fly to LNAV, LNAV/VNAV, LPV, and LP minimums. Recognize the characteristics of RNAV (RNP) approaches. Given an instrument approach chart, explain the procedures for performing an RNAV (GPS) approach.	Air traffic control system and procedures for instrument flight operations Use of IFR enroute and instrument approach procedure charts Safe and efficient operation of aircraft under instrument flight rules and conditions	Intercepting and Tracking Navigational Systems and Arcs Nonprecision Approach Precision Approach Missed Approach Landing from an Instrument Approach

CONTENT

APPROACH DESIGN AND EQUIPMENT

- ❑ Terminal Arrival Area
- ❑ Waypoints
- ❑ GPS Approach Equipment
- ❑ Landing Minimums
- ❑ LNAV
- ❑ LNAV/VNAV
- ❑ LPV
- ❑ LP
- ❑ RNP Approach
- ❑ RAIM Failure During an Approach

FLYING AN RNAV (GPS) APPROACH

- ❑ Flying an RNAV (GPS) Approach to LPV Minimums
- ❑ Preparing for the Approach
- ❑ Performing the Approach
- ❑ Flying an RNAV (GPS) Approach to LNAV Minimums

ATD (OPTION)

- ❑ RNAV (GPS) Approach Procedures

COMPLETION STANDARDS

- Demonstrate understanding of RNAV (GPS) approach procedures using instrument approach charts during oral quizzing by the instructor.
- Complete with a minimum score of 80 percent: questions for Chapter 8C; or online exams for GL19. With the instructor, review each incorrect response to ensure complete understanding before starting Ground Lesson 19.

STUDY ASSIGNMENT

Instrument/Commercial Textbook/e-Book

Chapter 8 — Instrument Approaches

Section B — ILS Approaches

Instrument Online

GL20 — ILS Approach Procedures

GROUND LESSON 17

REFERENCES

Instrument/Commercial Textbook/e-Book

Chapter 8 — Instrument Approaches

Section B — ILS Approaches

Instrument Online

GL20 — ILS Approach Procedures

OBJECTIVES

Lesson Objective	Part 141/61 Aeronautical Knowledge	ACS Task
Given an instrument approach chart, explain the procedures for performing an ILS approach. Given an instrument approach chart, explain the procedures for performing a localizer approach.	Air traffic control system and procedures for instrument flight operations Use of IFR enroute and instrument approach procedure charts Safe and efficient operation of aircraft under instrument flight rules and conditions	Intercepting and Tracking Navigational Systems and Arcs Nonprecision Approach Missed Approach Precision Approach Landing from an Instrument Approach

CONTENT

ILS CATEGORIES AND COMPONENTS
❑ Localizer
❑ Glide Slope
❑ Range Information

FLYING AN ILS APPROACH
❑ Flying a Straight-In ILS Approach
❑ Preparing for the Approach
❑ Performing the Approach
❑ ILS Approach with a Course Reversal
❑ Simultaneous Approaches to Parallel Runways
❑ Simultaneous Offset Instrument Approach
❑ Simultaneous Converging Instrument Approach

LOCALIZER APPROACHES
❑ Localizer Approach
❑ Localizer Back Course Approach
❑ Localizer-Type Directional Aid (LDA)

ATD (OPTION)
❑ ILS Approach Procedures
❑ Localizer Approach Procedures

COMPLETION STANDARDS

- Demonstrate understanding of ILS and localizer approach procedures using instrument approach charts during oral quizzing by the instructor.
- Complete with a minimum score of 80 percent: questions for Chapter 8B; or online exam for GL20. With the instructor, review each incorrect response to ensure complete understanding before starting Ground Lesson 18.

STUDY ASSIGNMENT

Instrument/Commercial Textbook/e-Book
Chapter 8 — Instrument Approaches
Section C — VOR and NDB Approaches

Instrument Online
GL21 — VOR Approach Procedures
GL22 — NDB Approach Procedures

GROUND LESSON 18

NOTE: *Because the FAA is phasing out NDB facilities and approaches, the NDB approach content of this lesson is optional.*

REFERENCES

Instrument/Commercial Textbook/e-Book
Chapter 8 — Instrument Approaches
Section C — VOR and NDB Approaches

Instrument Online
GL21 — VOR Approach Procedures
GL22 — NDB Approach Procedures

OBJECTIVES

Lesson Objective	Part 141/61 Aeronautical Knowledge	ACS Task
Given an instrument approach chart, explain the procedures for performing a VOR approach. Given an instrument approach chart, explain the procedures for performing an NDB approach.	Air traffic control system and procedures for instrument flight operations Use of IFR enroute and instrument approach procedure charts Safe and efficient operation of aircraft under instrument flight rules and conditions	Intercepting and Tracking Navigational Systems and Arcs Nonprecision Approach Missed Approach Landing from an Instrument Approach

CONTENT

SECTION A — VOR AND NDB APPROACHES

GL21 — VOR APPROACH PROCEDURES

- ❑ Off-Airport and On-Airport Facilities
- ❑ Flying a VOR/DME Approach
- ❑ Approach Briefing
- ❑ Performing the Approach

SECTION A — VOR AND NDB APPROACHES

GL22 — NDB APPROACH PROCEDURES

- ❑ Flying an NDB Approach
- ❑ Preparing for the Approach
- ❑ Performing the Approach

ATD (OPTION)

- ❑ VOR Approach Procedures
- ❑ NDB Approach Procedures

COMPLETION STANDARDS

- Demonstrate understanding of VOR and NDB approach procedures using instrument approach charts during oral quizzing by the instructor.

- Complete with a minimum score of 80 percent: questions for Chapter 8A; or online exams for GL21 and GL22. With the instructor, review each incorrect response to ensure complete understanding before starting Ground Lesson 19.

STUDY ASSIGNMENT

Review the content of Ground Lessons 10 – 18 to prepare for the Stage II Exam.

GROUND LESSON 19

STAGE II EXAM

REFERENCES

Ground Lessons 10 – 18

OBJECTIVE

Demonstrate knowledge of the subjects covered in Ground Lessons 10 – 18 by passing the Stage II Exam.

CONTENT

STAGE II EXAM

❑ Departure Charts and Procedures
❑ Enroute Charts and Procedures
❑ Holding Procedures
❑ Arrival Charts and Procedures
❑ Approach Charts and Procedures
❑ RNAV Approaches
❑ ILS Approaches
❑ VOR and NDB Approaches

COMPLETION STANDARDS

To complete the lesson and stage, pass the Stage II Exam with a minimum score of 80 percent. With the instructor, review each incorrect response to ensure complete understanding before starting Stage III.

STUDY ASSIGNMENT

Instrument/Commercial Textbook/e-Book

Chapter 9 — Meteorology
Section A — Weather Factors
Section B — Weather Hazards and Ice Control Systems

Instrument Online

GL24 — Weather Factors and Hazards

Stage III

STAGE OBJECTIVES

During this stage, the student learns about weather factors and hazards and how to obtain and interpret weather reports and forecasts and graphic weather products. In addition, the student explores IFR flight planning and emergency procedures and develops a greater understanding of using single-pilot resource management (SRM) in the IFR environment.

STAGE COMPLETION STANDARDS

The student must pass the Stage III Exam and the Instrument Rating End-of-Course Exam with minimum scores of 80 percent, and review each incorrect response with the instructor to ensure complete understanding.

GROUND LESSON 20

REFERENCES

Instrument/Commercial Textbook/e-Book
Chapter 9 — Meteorology
Section A — Weather Factors
Section B — Weather Hazards and Ice Control Systems

Instrument Online
GL24 — Weather Factors and Hazards

OBJECTIVES

Lesson Objective	Part 141/61 Aeronautical Knowledge	ACS Task
Recognize the factors that affect weather patterns. Identify the causes of and the risks associated with weather hazards that apply to flight operations. Explain the different types of aircraft icing and the operation of ice control systems on the airplane.	Recognition of critical weather situations and wind shear avoidance	Weather Information Airplane Systems Related to IFR Operations

CONTENT

SECTION A — WEATHER FACTORS

GL24 — WEATHER FACTORS AND HAZARDS

- ❑ The Atmosphere
- ❑ Atmospheric Circulation
- ❑ Moisture, Precipitation, and Stability
- ❑ Types of Clouds
- ❑ Air Mass
- ❑ Fronts
- ❑ High Altitude Weather

SECTION B — WEATHER HAZARDS AND ICE CONTROL SYSTEMS

GL24 — WEATHER FACTORS AND HAZARDS

WEATHER HAZARDS

- ❑ Thunderstorms
- ❑ Hydroplaning
- ❑ Low Level Turbulence
- ❑ Wake Turbulence
- ❑ Clear Air Turbulence
- ❑ Mountain Wave Turbulence
- ❑ Reporting Turbulence
- ❑ Wind Shear
- ❑ Low Visibility
- ❑ Volcanic Ash
- ❑ Cold Weather Operations
- ❑ Icing

ICE CONTROL SYSTEMS

- ❑ Airfoil Ice Control
- ❑ Windshield Ice Control
- ❑ Propeller Ice Control
- ❑ Other Ice Control Systems

COMPLETION STANDARDS

- Demonstrate understanding of weather factors, weather hazards, including icing, and ice control systems during oral quizzing by the instructor.
- Complete with a minimum score of 80 percent: questions for Chapters 9A and 9B; or online exams for GL24. With the instructor, review each incorrect response to ensure complete understanding before starting Ground Lesson 21.

STUDY ASSIGNMENT

Instrument/Commercial Textbook/e-Book

Chapter 9 — Meteorology

Section C — Aviation Weather Reports and Forecasts

Section D — Graphic Weather Products

Section E — Sources of Weather Information

Instrument Online

GL25 — Analyzing Weather

GROUND LESSON 21

REFERENCES

Instrument/Commercial Textbook/e-Book
Chapter 9 — Meteorology
- Section C — Aviation Weather Reports and Forecasts
- Section D — Graphic Weather Products
- Section E — Sources of Weather Information

Instrument Online
GL25 — Analyzing Weather

OBJECTIVES

Lesson Objective	Part 141/61 Aeronautical Knowledge	ACS Task
Recognize how to obtain and interpret aviation weather reports and forecasts for flight planning. Recognize how to obtain and interpret graphic weather products for flight planning. Recognize how to obtain preflight and in-flight sources of weather information.	Procurement and use of aviation weather reports and forecasts, and the elements of forecasting weather trends on the basis of that information and personal observation of weather conditions	Weather Information Cross-Country Flight Planning

CONTENT

SECTION C — AVIATION WEATHER REPORTS AND FORECASTS

GL25 — ANALYZING WEATHER

OBSERVATIONS
- ❑ Aviation Routine Weather Report (METAR)
- ❑ Pilot Weather Reports (PIREPs)

FORECASTS
- ❑ Terminal Aerodrome Forecast (TAF)
- ❑ Winds and Temperatures Aloft Forecast
- ❑ AIRMETs and SIGMETs
- ❑ Severe Weather Reports and Forecasts

SECTION D — GRAPHIC WEATHER PRODUCTS

GL25 — ANALYZING WEATHER

OBSERVATIONS
- ❑ Radar Observations
- ❑ Satellite Imagery
- ❑ Graphic Depictions of METARs

ANALYSIS
- ❑ Surface Analysis Chart
- ❑ Ceiling and Visibility Analysis (CVA)

FORECASTS
- ❑ Aviation Forecasts
- ❑ Short-Range Surface Prognostic (Prog) Charts
- ❑ U.S. Low-Level Significant Weather (SIGWX) Chart
- ❑ Mid- and High Level SIGWX Charts
- ❑ Wind and Temperature Aloft Forecast
- ❑ Freezing-Level Graphics
- ❑ Current and Forecast Icing Products (CIP/FIP)
- ❑ G-AIRMET
- ❑ Graphical Forecast for Aviation (GFA) Tool

SECTION E — SOURCES OF WEATHER INFORMATION

GL25 — ANALYZING WEATHER
- ❑ Preflight Weather Sources
- ❑ Flight Service
- ❑ National Weather Service
- ❑ In-Flight Weather Sources
- ❑ Weather Radar Services
- ❑ Center Weather Advisory (CWA)
- ❑ Automated Weather Reporting Systems
- ❑ Data Link Weather
- ❑ Airborne Weather Radar

COMPLETION STANDARDS
- Demonstrate understanding of how to interpret aviation weather reports and forecasts and graphic weather products and how to obtain and use preflight and in-flight weather sources during oral quizzing by the instructor.
- Complete with a minimum score of 80 percent: questions for Chapter 9C, 9D, and 9E; or the online exam for GL25. With the instructor, review each incorrect response to ensure complete understanding before starting Ground Lesson 22.

STUDY ASSIGNMENT
Instrument/Commercial Textbook/e-Book
Chapter 10 — IFR Flight Considerations
Section A — IFR Flight Planning

Instrument Online
GL27 — IFR Flight Planning

GROUND LESSON 22

REFERENCES

Instrument/Commercial Textbook/e-Book
Chapter 10 — IFR Flight Considerations
Section A — IFR Flight Planning

Instrument Online
GL27 — IFR Flight Planning

OBJECTIVES

Lesson Objective	Part 141/61 Aeronautical Knowledge	ACS Task
Identify the steps to plan an IFR cross-country flight.	Applicable Federal Aviation Regulations for IFR flight operations IFR navigation and approaches by use of navigation systems Use of IFR enroute and instrument approach procedure charts Procurement and use of aviation weather reports and forecasts, and the elements of forecasting weather trends on the basis of that information and personal observation of weather conditions	Cross-Country Flight Planning

CONTENT

SECTION A — IFR FLIGHT PLANNING

GL27 — IFR FLIGHT PLANNING

- ❏ Prepare a Flight Overview
- ❏ Develop the Route
- ❏ Obtain a Weather Briefing
- ❏ Complete the Nav Log
- ❏ File the Flight Plan
- ❏ Perform Preflight Tasks
- ❏ Closing the IFR Flight Plan

COMPLETION STANDARDS

- Demonstrate understanding of IFR flight planning during oral quizzing by the instructor.

- Complete with a minimum score of 80 percent: questions for Chapters 10A; or the online exams for GL27. With the instructor, review each incorrect response to ensure complete understanding before starting Ground Lesson 26.

STUDY ASSIGNMENT

Instrument/Commercial Textbook/e-Book

Chapter 10 — IFR Flight Considerations

Section B — IFR Single-Pilot Resource Management

Instrument Online

GL26 — IFR Single-Pilot Resource Management

GROUND LESSON 23

REFERENCES

Instrument/Commercial Textbook/e-Book

Chapter 10 — IFR Flight Considerations

Section B — IFR Single-Pilot Resource Management

Instrument Online

GL26 — IFR Single-Pilot Resource Management

OBJECTIVES

Lesson Objective	Part 141/61 Aeronautical Knowledge	ACS Task
Describe the skills that apply to effective SRM and CRM in the IFR environment. Explain the factors that affect decision making during IFR operations.	Aeronautical decision making and judgment Crew resource management, to include crew communication and coordination	Throughout the practical test, the evaluator must assess the applicant's ability to use ADM, SRM, and CRM, as applicable to the risk management tasks.

CONTENT

SECTION B — IFR SINGLE-PILOT RESOURCE MANAGEMENT

GL26 — IFR SINGLE-PILOT RESOURCE MANAGEMENT

- ❑ Aeronautical Decision Making
- ❑ Risk Management
- ❑ Task Management
- ❑ Situational Awareness
- ❑ Controlled Flight Into Terrain
- ❑ Automation Management

COMPLETION STANDARDS

- Demonstrate understanding of the skills that apply to effective SRM and CRM and that factors that affect aeronautical decision making in the IFR environment during oral quizzing by the instructor. Describe the skills that apply to effective SRM and CRM in the IFR environment.
- Complete with a minimum score of 80 percent: questions for Chapter 10B; or online exams for GL26. With the instructor, review each incorrect response to ensure complete understanding before starting Ground Lesson 23.

STUDY ASSIGNMENT

Instrument/Commercial Textbook/e-Book

Chapter 10 — IFR Flight Considerations
Section C — IFR Emergencies

Instrument Online

GL28 — IFR Emergencies

GROUND LESSON 24

REFERENCES

Instrument/Commercial Textbook/e-Book

Chapter 10 — IFR Flight Considerations
Section C — IFR Emergencies

Instrument Online

GL28 — IFR Emergencies

OBJECTIVES

Lesson Objective	Part 141/61 Aeronautical Knowledge	ACS Task
Identify emergency situations and recognize the correct procedures to manage emergencies in the IFR environment.	Applicable Federal Aviation Regulations for IFR flight operations Safe and efficient operation of aircraft under instrument flight rules and conditions Aeronautical decision making and judgment Crew resource management, to include crew communication and coordination	Loss of Communications Approach with Loss of Primary Flight Instrument Indicators

CONTENT

- ❑ Declaring an Emergency
- ❑ Malfunction Reports
- ❑ Minimum Fuel

❑ Loss of Primary Flight Instrument Indicators
❑ Loss of Communications
❑ Radar Approaches

COMPLETION STANDARDS

- Demonstrate understanding of how to recognize and respond appropriately to emergency situations in the IFR environment during oral quizzing by the instructor.
- Complete with a minimum score of 80 percent: questions for Chapter 10C; or online exam for GL28. With the instructor, review each incorrect response to ensure complete understanding before starting Ground Lesson 25.

STUDY ASSIGNMENT

Review the content of Ground Lessons 20 – 24 to prepare for the Stage III Exam.

GROUND LESSON 25
STAGE III EXAM

REFERENCES

Ground Lessons 20 – 24

OBJECTIVE

Demonstrate knowledge of the subjects covered in Ground Lessons 20 – 24 by passing the Stage III Exam.

CONTENT

STAGE III EXAM

❑ Weather Factors and Hazards
❑ Aviation Weather Reports and Forecasts
❑ Graphic Weather Products
❑ Sources of Weather Information
❑ IFR Flight Planning
❑ IFR Single-Pilot Resource Management
❑ IFR Emergencies

COMPLETION STANDARDS

To complete the lesson and stage, pass the Stage III Exam with a minimum score of 80 percent. With the instructor, review each incorrect response to ensure complete understanding before taking the End-of-Course Exam.

STUDY ASSIGNMENT

Review the content of Ground Lessons 1 – 25 to prepare for the Instrument Rating End-of-Course Exam

---

GROUND LESSON 26
END-OF-COURSE EXAM

REFERENCES

Ground Lessons 1 – 25

OBJECTIVE

Demonstrate comprehension of the material covered in Ground Lessons 1 – 25 by passing the Instrument Rating End-of-Course Exam to prepare for the FAA Instrument Rating Airman Knowledge Test.

CONTENT

❏ Instrument Rating End-of-Course Exam

COMPLETION STANDARDS

To complete the lesson and the Instrument Rating Ground Training, pass the Instrument Rating End-of-Course Exam with a minimum score of 80 percent. With the instructor, review each incorrect response to ensure complete understanding before taking the FAA Instrument Rating Airman Knowledge Test .

STUDY ASSIGNMENT

Review the content of Ground Lessons 1 – 26 to prepare for the FAA Instrument Rating Airman Knowledge Test.

Instrument Rating Flight Training Syllabus

FLIGHT TRAINING COURSE OBJECTIVES

The student will obtain the aeronautical skill and experience required by FAR Part 141 and Part 61 for an instrument rating.

FLIGHT TRAINING COURSE COMPLETION STANDARDS

Through flight tests and school records, the student must demonstrate that the necessary aeronautical skill and experience required by FAR Part 141 and Part 61 for an instrument rating have been met.

***NOTE:** Throughout the flight training course, the student must apply and be evaluated on single-pilot resource management (SRM) skills, including aeronautical decision-making (ADM), and risk management. The student must be able to counteract hazardous attitudes, apply the ADM process to make effective decisions, identify hazards and mitigate risks. In addition, the student must demonstrate the ability to manage tasks and automation, maintain situational awareness, and take actions to prevent controlled flight into terrain (CFIT).*

Stage I

STAGE OBJECTIVES

During Stage I, the student learns precise airplane attitude control by instrument reference by performing a variety of maneuvers. In addition, the student gains proficiency in VOR, GPS, and localizer navigation.

STAGE COMPLETION STANDARDS

This stage is complete when the student demonstrates precise airplane attitude control by full- and partial-panel instrument reference. In addition, the student must demonstrate proficiency in VOR, GPS, and localizer navigation by accurately tracking courses and maintaining positional awareness at all times.

***NOTE:** Completion of certain tasks listed in each lesson must be based on the type of instruments and navigation equipment available in the airplane.*

FLIGHT LESSON 1

DUAL — LOCAL

***NOTE:** As indicated in the Allocation Tables, complete Ground Lessons 1, 2, and 3 prior to this flight.*

OBJECTIVES

- Become familiar with the instrument training airplane's systems and equipment.
- Use proper instrument cross-check and interpretation.
- Apply the appropriate pitch, bank, power, and trim corrections to perform basic flight maneuvers solely by reference to instruments.

PREFLIGHT DISCUSSION

❏ Positive Exchange of Flight Controls
❏ Single-Pilot Resource Management (SRM)
❏ Crew Resource Management (CRM)

INTRODUCE

PREFLIGHT PREPARATION

❏ Pilot Qualifications
❏ Weather Information

FLIGHT BY REFERENCE TO INSTRUMENTS

Instrument Flight (Full Panel)
❏ Straight-and-Level Flight
❏ Change of Airspeed
❏ Standard-Rate Turns
❏ Constant Airspeed Climbs and Descents
❏ Constant Rate Climbs and Descents
❏ Climbing and Descending Turns
❏ Operations in Turbulence

REVIEW

PREFLIGHT PREPARATION

❏ Operation of Systems
❏ Human Factors

PREFLIGHT PROCEDURES

❏ Self-Assessment
❏ Preflight Inspection
❏ Passenger Briefing
❏ Flight Deck Management
❏ Use of Checklists
❏ Engine Starting
❏ Taxiing
❏ Before Takeoff Check/Runup

AIRPORT OPERATIONS

❏ Radio Communications
❏ Airport, Runway, and Taxiway Signs, Markings, and Lighting
❏ Traffic Patterns
❏ Runway Incursion Avoidance
❏ Wake Turbulence Avoidance
❏ Wind Shear Avoidance

BASIC MANEUVERS
- ❑ Positive Exchange of Flight Controls
- ❑ Collision Avoidance
- ❑ Controlled Flight Into Terrain (CFIT) Awareness

TAKEOFFS, LANDINGS, AND GO-AROUNDS
(Includes operations in crosswinds)
- ❑ Normal Takeoff and Climb
- ❑ Normal Approach and Landing

POSTFLIGHT PROCEDURES
- ❑ After Landing, Parking, and Securing

COMPLETION STANDARDS

- During flight solely by reference to instruments: maintain positive aircraft control with altitude ±200 feet, headings ±15°, airspeed ±15 knots, bank angles ±10°, and descent/climb rate ±150 feet per minute.
- Perform preflight preparation, preflight procedures, airport operations, basic maneuvers, takeoffs and landings, and postflight procedures at the private pilot proficiency level.

POSTFLIGHT DEBRIEFING

- ❑ Critique maneuvers/procedures and SRM.
- ❑ Create a plan for skills that need improvement.
- ❑ Update the record folder and logbook.

FLIGHT LESSON 2

DUAL — LOCAL

OBJECTIVES

- Become familiar with the aircraft systems, equipment, and preflight checks necessary for IFR flight.
- Gain proficiency in performing instrument cross-check and interpretation.
- Gain proficiency in applying the appropriate pitch, bank, power, and trim corrections to perform basic flight maneuvers solely by reference to instruments.

PREFLIGHT DISCUSSION

- ❑ Anti-icing and Deicing Systems
- ❑ Airplane Flight Instruments
- ❑ Runway Incursion Avoidance in Low Visibility

INTRODUCE

PREFLIGHT PROCEDURES
- ❑ Airplane Systems Related to IFR Operations (Anti-icing and Deicing)
- ❑ Airplane Flight Instruments Operation
- ❑ Instrument Flight Deck Check

POSTFLIGHT PROCEDURES

❑ Checking Instruments and Equipment
  - ◊ Check for proper operation.
  - ◊ Document improper operation or failure.

REVIEW

PREFLIGHT PREPARATION

❑ Pilot Qualifications
❑ Weather Information

FLIGHT BY REFERENCE TO INSTRUMENTS

Instrument Flight (Full Panel)

❑ Straight-and-Level Flight
❑ Change of Airspeed
❑ Standard-Rate Turns
❑ Constant Airspeed Climbs and Descents
❑ Constant Rate Climbs and Descents
❑ Climbing and Descending Turns
❑ Operations in Turbulence

POSTFLIGHT PROCEDURES

❑ After Landing, Parking, and Securing

COMPLETION STANDARDS

- Demonstrate understanding of flight instrument and anti-icing/deicing equipment operation.
- Perform preflight and postflight checks on the airplane's instruments and equipment necessary for an IFR flight.
- During flight solely by reference to instruments: maintain positive aircraft control with altitude ±200 feet, headings ±15°, airspeed ±15 knots, bank angles ±10°, and descent/climb rate ±150 feet per minute.

POSTFLIGHT DEBRIEFING

❑ Critique maneuvers/procedures and SRM.
❑ Create a plan for skills that need improvement.
❑ Update the record folder and logbook.

FLIGHT LESSON 3

DUAL — LOCAL

OBJECTIVES

- Become familiar with performing slow flight, stalls, and steep turns solely by reference to instruments.
- Increase proficiency in attitude instrument flying.

PREFLIGHT DISCUSSION

❑ Stall and Spin Awareness
❑ Situations that can Degrade Instrument Cross-Check

INTRODUCE

FLIGHT BY REFERENCE TO INSTRUMENTS

Instrument Flight (Full Panel)

- ❑ Maneuvering During Slow Flight
- ❑ Power-Off Stalls
- ❑ Power-On Stalls
- ❑ Stall and Spin Awareness
- ❑ Steep Turns

REVIEW

PREFLIGHT PROCEDURES

- ❑ Airplane Systems Related to IFR Operations (Anti-icing and Deicing)
- ❑ Airplane Flight Instruments Operation
- ❑ Instrument Flight Deck Check

FLIGHT BY REFERENCE TO INSTRUMENTS

Instrument Flight (Full Panel)

- ❑ Straight-and-Level Flight
- ❑ Change of Airspeed
- ❑ Standard-Rate Turns
- ❑ Constant Airspeed Climbs and Descents
- ❑ Constant Rate Climbs and Descents
- ❑ Climbing and Descending Turns
- ❑ Operations in Turbulence

POSTFLIGHT PROCEDURES

- ❑ Checking Instruments and Equipment
  - ◊ Check for proper operation.
  - ◊ Document improper operation or failure.

COMPLETION STANDARDS

- Maintain airplane control while maneuvering during slow flight and performing stalls and steep turns solely by reference to instruments.
- Properly perform preflight and postflight checks and operate the airplane instruments and equipment necessary for an IFR flight.

POSTFLIGHT DEBRIEFING

- ❑ Critique maneuvers/procedures and SRM.
- ❑ Create a plan for skills that need improvement.
- ❑ Update the record folder and logbook.

FLIGHT LESSON 4

DUAL — LOCAL

OBJECTIVES

- Become familiar with the procedures to recover from unusual flight attitudes solely by reference to instruments.

- Become familiar with engaging the autopilot (if so equipped) to perform straight-and-level flight, climbs, descents, and turns.
- Increase proficiency in full-panel attitude instrument flying.

PREFLIGHT DISCUSSION

❏ Spatial Disorientation and Optical Illusions.
❏ Unusual Attitude Causal Factors
❏ Procedures for Recovery from Unusual Flight Attitudes
❏ Automation Management

INTRODUCE

FLIGHT BY REFERENCE TO INSTRUMENTS

❏ Autopilot Use, if Equipped

Recovery From Unusual Flight Attitudes

❏ Nose- High Attitude
❏ Nose-Low Attitude

REVIEW

PREFLIGHT PROCEDURES

❏ Airplane Systems Related to IFR Operations (Anti-icing and Deicing)
❏ Airplane Flight Instruments Operation
❏ Instrument Flight Deck Check

FLIGHT BY REFERENCE TO INSTRUMENTS

Instrument Flight (Full Panel)

❏ Straight-and-Level Flight
❏ Change of Airspeed
❏ Standard-Rate Turns
❏ Constant Airspeed Climbs and Descents
❏ Constant Rate Climbs and Descents
❏ Climbing and Descending Turns
❏ Operations in Turbulence
❏ Maneuvering During Slow Flight
❏ Power-Off Stalls
❏ Power-On Stalls
❏ Stall and Spin Awareness
❏ Steep Turns

POSTFLIGHT PROCEDURES

❏ Checking Instruments and Equipment
  ◊ Check for proper operation.
  ◊ Document improper operation or failure.

COMPLETION STANDARDS

- Demonstrate understanding of the aircraft instrument systems, equipment, and preflight and postflight checks necessary for IFR flight.
- Demonstrate proficiency in full-panel attitude instrument flying by maintaining altitude ±100 feet, headings ±10°, airspeed ±10 knots, bank angles ±5°, and descent/climb rate ±100 feet per minute.

- Use the autopilot to perform straight-and-level flight, climbs, descents, and turns.
- Recognize the approach of stalls and perform the correct recovery procedures.
- Recognize unusual flight attitudes and perform the correct recovery procedures.

POSTFLIGHT DEBRIEFING

❑ Critique maneuvers/procedures and SRM.
❑ Create a plan for skills that need improvement.
❑ Update the record folder and logbook.

FLIGHT LESSON 5

DUAL — LOCAL

OBJECTIVES

- Perform the proper procedures to manage system and equipment malfunctions.
- Practice partial-panel attitude instrument flying by performing basic maneuvers.

PREFLIGHT DISCUSSION

❑ Managing Primary Instrument Malfunctions
❑ Instrument Malfunction Reporting Requirements

INTRODUCE

SYSTEMS AND EQUIPMENT MALFUNCTIONS

❑ Abnormal Instrument Indications
❑ Electrical System Failure
❑ Vacuum Pump Failure
❑ Gyroscopic Instrument Failure
❑ Pitot-Static Instrument Failure
❑ Loss of Primary Flight Instrument Indications
❑ Use of Secondary Flight Displays when Primary Displays Fail

FLIGHT BY REFERENCE TO INSTRUMENTS

Instrument Flight (Partial Panel)

❑ Straight-and-Level Flight
❑ Change of Airspeed
❑ Standard-Rate Turns
❑ Constant Airspeed Climbs and Descents
❑ Constant Rate Climbs and Descents
❑ Climbing and Descending Turns
❑ Operations in Turbulence

REVIEW

PREFLIGHT PROCEDURES

❑ Airplane Systems Related to IFR Operations
❑ Airplane Flight Instruments Operation
❑ Instrument Flight Deck Check

FLIGHT BY REFERENCE TO INSTRUMENTS

❏ Autopilot Use, if Equipped

Recovery From Unusual Flight Attitudes

❏ Nose- High Attitude
❏ Nose-Low Attitude

POSTFLIGHT PROCEDURES

❏ Checking Instruments and Equipment

COMPLETION STANDARDS

- Recognize abnormal instrument indications and determine the causes.
- Modify the instrument cross-check to maintain airplane control while flying with a partial panel.
- Effectively use the secondary flight displays when primary displays fail.
- Demonstrate proficiency in using the autopilot to perform straight-and-level flight, climbs, descents, and turns.

POSTFLIGHT DEBRIEFING

❏ Critique maneuvers/procedures and SRM.
❏ Create a plan for skills that need improvement.
❏ Update the record folder and logbook.

FLIGHT LESSON 6

DUAL — LOCAL

OBJECTIVES

- Perform compass turns and timed turns to magnetic compass headings.
- Recover from unusual flight attitudes solely by reference to instruments using a partial panel.
- Increase proficiency in full- and partial-panel attitude instrument flying.
- Manage instrument systems and equipment malfunctions.

PREFLIGHT DISCUSSION

❏ Magnetic Compass Errors

INTRODUCE

FLIGHT BY REFERENCE TO INSTRUMENTS

Instrument Flight (Partial Panel)

❏ Compass Turns
❏ Timed Turns to Magnetic Compass Headings
❏ Autopilot Use, if Equipped

Recovery From Unusual Flight Attitudes

❏ Nose- High Unusual Attitude
❏ Nose-Low Unusual Attitude

REVIEW

SYSTEMS AND EQUIPMENT MALFUNCTIONS

- ❑ Abnormal Instrument Indications
- ❑ Electrical System Failure
- ❑ Vacuum Pump Failure
- ❑ Gyroscopic Instrument Failure
- ❑ Pitot-Static Instrument Failure
- ❑ Loss of Primary Flight Instrument Indications
- ❑ Use of Secondary Flight Displays when Primary Displays Fail

FLIGHT BY REFERENCE TO INSTRUMENTS

Instrument Flight (Partial Panel)

- ❑ Straight-and-Level Flight
- ❑ Change of Airspeed
- ❑ Standard-Rate Turns
- ❑ Constant Airspeed Climbs and Descents
- ❑ Constant Rate Climbs and Descents
- ❑ Climbing and Descending Turns

COMPLETION STANDARDS

- Perform compass turns and timed turns to magnetic compass headings.
- Recognize unusual flight attitudes using a partial panel and perform the correct recovery procedures.
- Increase proficiency in full- and partial-panel attitude instrument flying.
- Perform the correct procedures to manage instrument systems and equipment malfunctions.
- Using partial-panel instrument reference: maintain altitude ±200 feet, headings ±15°, airspeed ±15 knots, bank angles ±10° during turns, and descent/climb rate ±150 feet per minute.

POSTFLIGHT DEBRIEFING

- ❑ Critique maneuvers/procedures and SRM.
- ❑ Create a plan for skills that need improvement.
- ❑ Update the record folder and logbook.

FLIGHT LESSON 7

DUAL — LOCAL

OBJECTIVE

Increase proficiency in full- and partial-panel instrument maneuvers.

PREFLIGHT DISCUSSION

- ❑ SRM in the IFR Environment
  - ◊ Aeronautical Decision Making
  - ◊ Risk Management
  - ◊ Task Management
  - ◊ Situational Awareness

◊ CFIT Awareness
◊ Automation Management

REVIEW

FLIGHT BY REFERENCE TO INSTRUMENTS

Instrument Flight (Full Panel and Partial Panel)

❑ Straight-and-Level Flight
❑ Standard-Rate Turns
❑ Constant Rate Climbs and Descents
❑ Constant Airspeed Climbs and Descents
❑ Autopilot Use, if Equipped

Recovery From Unusual Flight Attitudes

❑ Nose- High Unusual Attitude
❑ Nose-Low Unusual Attitude

COMPLETION STANDARDS

- Perform correct recovery techniques from unusual flight attitudes using full- and partial-panel instrument reference.
- Demonstrate proficiency in full- and partial-panel attitude instrument flying by maintaining: altitude ±100 feet, headings ±10°, airspeed ±10 knots, bank angles ±5°, and descent/climb rate ±100 feet per minute.
- Demonstrate proficiency in using the autopilot to perform straight-and-level flight, climbs, descents, and turns.

POSTFLIGHT DEBRIEFING

❑ Critique maneuvers/procedures and SRM.
❑ Create a plan for skills that need improvement.
❑ Update the record folder and logbook.

STUDY ASSIGNMENT

Ground Lesson 4

Instrument Navigation

FLIGHT LESSON 8

DUAL — LOCAL

OBJECTIVES

- Properly perform a VOR equipment check and operate VOR equipment.
- Gain proficiency in VOR orientation, radial interception, and tracking.
- Learn how to intercept and track a DME arc.
- Increase proficiency in attitude instrument flying.

PREFLIGHT DISCUSSION

❑ Identifying the VOR
❑ VOR Service Volumes

❑ VOR Indicators (Traditional, HSI)
❑ VOR Equipment Check Procedures

INTRODUCE

PREFLIGHT PROCEDURES

Instrument Flight Deck Check

❑ VOR Equipment Check

Airplane Flight Instruments and Navigation Equipment

❑ VOR Equipment Operation

NAVIGATION SYSTEMS

Intercepting and Tracking Navigational Systems and Arcs (Full Panel and Partial Panel)

❑ VOR Orientation
❑ VOR Radial Interception and Tracking
❑ Intercepting and Tracking DME Arcs
❑ Autopilot Use for Navigation, if Equipped
❑ NDB Orientation and Homing
❑ NDB Bearing Interception and Tracking

NOTE: *Students might be asked to demonstrate ADF equipment operation if the airplane used for the practical test is so equipped. In this case, NDB navigation tasks should be accomplished.*

REVIEW

FLIGHT BY REFERENCE TO INSTRUMENTS

Instrument Flight (Full Panel and Partial Panel)

❑ Straight-and-Level Flight
❑ Standard-Rate Turns
❑ Constant Rate Climbs and Descents
❑ Constant Airspeed Climbs and Descents
❑ Autopilot Use, if Equipped

Recovery From Unusual Flight Attitudes

❑ Nose- High Unusual Attitude
❑ Nose-Low Unusual Attitude

COMPLETION STANDARDS

- Demonstrate understanding of VOR equipment checks, orientation, radial interception, and tracking.
- Demonstrate understanding of intercepting and tracking DME arcs.
- Using full- and partial-panel instrument reference: maintain altitude ±100 feet, headings ±10°, airspeed ±10 knots, bank angles ±5°, and descent/climb rate ±100 feet per minute.

POSTFLIGHT DEBRIEFING

❑ Critique maneuvers/procedures and SRM.
❑ Create a plan for skills that need improvement.
❑ Update the record folder and logbook.

STUDY ASSIGNMENT

Ground Lesson 5
Airports, Airspace, and Flight Information

FLIGHT LESSON 9

DUAL — LOCAL

OBJECTIVES

- Properly perform a GPS equipment check and program GPS equipment.
- Gain proficiency in satellite navigation—GPS orientation, course interception, and tracking.
- Intercept and track a DME arc using GPS navigation.
- Increase proficiency in VOR orientation, radial interception, and tracking.

PREFLIGHT DISCUSSION

❑ "North Up" and "Track Up" Orientation
❑ Basic GPS Programming
❑ GPS Database Currency

INTRODUCE

PREFLIGHT PROCEDURES

Instrument Flight Deck Check
❑ GPS Equipment Check
❑ GPS Database Currency

Airplane Flight Instruments and Navigation Equipment
❑ GPS Programming

NAVIGATION SYSTEMS

Intercepting and Tracking Navigational Systems and Arcs (Full Panel and Partial Panel)
❑ GPS Orientation
❑ GPS Course Interception and Tracking
❑ Intercepting and Tracking DME Arcs
❑ Autopilot Use for Navigation, if Equipped

REVIEW

PREFLIGHT PROCEDURES

Instrument Flight Deck Check
❑ VOR Equipment Check

Airplane Flight Instruments and Navigation Equipment
❑ VOR Equipment Operation

NAVIGATION SYSTEMS

Intercepting and Tracking Navigational Systems and Arcs

(Full Panel and Partial Panel)
- ❑ VOR Orientation
- ❑ VOR Radial Interception and Tracking
- ❑ Intercepting and Tracking DME Arcs
- ❑ Autopilot Use for Navigation, if Equipped
- ❑ NDB Orientation and Homing
- ❑ NDB Bearing Interception and Tracking

NOTE: *Students might be asked to demonstrate ADF equipment operation if the airplane used for the practical test is so equipped. In this case, NDB navigation tasks should be accomplished.*

COMPLETION STANDARDS

- Demonstrate understanding of GPS equipment checks, orientation, course interception, and tracking.
- Demonstrate understanding of intercepting and tracking DME arcs using GPS navigation
- Demonstrate increased proficiency in VOR radial interception and tracking
- Using full- and partial-panel instrument reference: maintain altitude ±100 feet, headings ±10°, airspeed ±10 knots, bank angles ±5°, and descent/climb rate ±100 feet per minute.

POSTFLIGHT DEBRIEFING

- ❑ Critique maneuvers/procedures and SRM.
- ❑ Create a plan for skills that need improvement.
- ❑ Update the record folder and logbook.

FLIGHT LESSON 10

DUAL — LOCAL

OBJECTIVES

- Increase proficiency in performing a GPS equipment check and programming GPS equipment.
- Increase proficiency in satellite navigation—GPS orientation, course interception, tracking, and DME arcs.

PREFLIGHT DISCUSSION

- ❑ Requirements for Using GPS Under IFR
- ❑ AFM Supplements to Determine GPS Certification
- ❑ RAIM
- ❑ WAAS

REVIEW

PREFLIGHT PROCEDURES

Instrument Flight Deck Check

- ❑ GPS Equipment Check
- ❑ GPS Database Currency

Airplane Flight Instruments and Navigation Equipment

- ❑ GPS Programming

NAVIGATION SYSTEMS

Intercepting and Tracking Navigational Systems and Arcs (Full Panel and Partial Panel)

- ❑ GPS Orientation
- ❑ GPS Course Interception and Tracking
- ❑ Intercepting and Tracking DME Arcs
- ❑ Autopilot Use for Navigation, if Equipped

COMPLETION STANDARDS

- Demonstrate proficiency in performing GPS equipment checks, orientation, course interception, and tracking.
- Demonstrate proficiency in intercepting and tracking DME arcs using GPS navigation
- Using full- and partial-panel instrument reference: maintain altitude ±100 feet, headings ±10°, airspeed ±10 knots, bank angles ±5°, and descent/climb rate ±100 feet per minute.

POSTFLIGHT DEBRIEFING

- ❑ Critique maneuvers/procedures and SRM.
- ❑ Create a plan for skills that need improvement.
- ❑ Update the record folder and logbook.

STUDY ASSIGNMENT

Ground Lessons 6, 7 and 8

ATC Services
ATC Clearances
Instrument Regulations

FLIGHT LESSON 11

DUAL — LOCAL

OBJECTIVES

- Interpret the CDI indications associated with the increased sensitivity while intercepting and tracking a localizer course.
- Increase proficiency in VOR and satellite navigation (GPS) orientation, course interception, tracking, and DME arcs.

PREFLIGHT DISCUSSION

❏ Localizer Coverage Limits, Sensitivity, Frequencies
❏ Identifying the Localizer
❏ Front Course and Back Course Navigation

INTRODUCE

NAVIGATION SYSTEMS

Intercepting and Tracking Navigational Systems and Arcs (Full Panel and Partial Panel)
❏ Localizer Course Interception and Tracking

REVIEW

PREFLIGHT PROCEDURES

Instrument Flight Deck Check
❏ GPS Equipment Check
❏ GPS Database Currency

Airplane Flight Instruments and Navigation Equipment
❏ GPS Programming

NAVIGATION SYSTEMS

Intercepting and Tracking Navigational Systems and Arcs (Full Panel and Partial Panel)
❏ GPS Course Interception and Tracking
❏ VOR Radial Interception and Tracking
❏ Autopilot Use for Navigation, if Equipped

COMPLETION STANDARDS

- Demonstrate understanding of localizer course interception and tracking.
- Demonstrate proficiency in performing VOR and GPS equipment checks, orientation, course interception, and tracking.

POSTFLIGHT DEBRIEFING

❏ Critique maneuvers/procedures and SRM.
❏ Create a plan for skills that need improvement.
❏ Update the record folder and logbook.

FLIGHT LESSON 12

DUAL — LOCAL

OBJECTIVES

To prepare for the Stage I Check:

- Review full- and partial-panel instrument maneuvers and procedures.
- Review full- and partial-panel VOR, GPS, and localizer navigation.
- Correct any deficient skill and knowledge areas.

PREFLIGHT DISCUSSION

❑ Attitude Instrument Flying Review
❑ VOR, GPS, and Localizer Navigation Review

REVIEW

PREFLIGHT PREPARATION

❑ Pilot Qualifications
❑ Weather Information

PREFLIGHT PROCEDURES

❑ Airplane Systems Related to IFR Operations (Anti-icing and Deicing)
❑ Airplane Flight Instruments Operation
❑ Instrument Flight Deck Check

Airplane Flight Instruments and Navigation Equipment

❑ GPS Programming
❑ VOR Equipment Operation

FLIGHT BY REFERENCE TO INSTRUMENTS

Instrument Flight (Full Panel and Partial Panel)

❑ Straight-and-Level Flight
❑ Standard-Rate Turns
❑ Constant Rate Climbs and Descents
❑ Constant Airspeed Climbs and Descents
❑ Timed Turns to Magnetic Compass Headings
❑ Magnetic Compass Turns
❑ Autopilot Use, if Equipped

Recovery From Unusual Flight Attitudes

❑ Nose-High Attitude
❑ Nose-Low Attitude

SYSTEMS AND EQUIPMENT MALFUNCTIONS

❑ Loss of Primary Flight Instrument Indications
❑ Use of Secondary Flight Displays when Primary Displays Fail

NAVIGATION SYSTEMS

Intercepting and Tracking Navigational Systems and Arcs (Full Panel and Partial Panel)

❑ GPS Course Interception and Tracking
❑ VOR Radial Interception and Tracking

- ❑ Localizer Course Interception and Tracking
- ❑ Intercepting and Tracking DME Arcs
- ❑ Autopilot Use for Navigation, if Equipped

POSTFLIGHT PROCEDURES

- ❑ Checking Instruments and Equipment

COMPLETION STANDARDS

- Demonstrate proficiency in full- and partial-panel attitude instrument flying by maintaining altitude ±100 feet, headings ±10°, airspeed ±10 knots, bank angles ±5°, and descent/climb rate ±100 feet per minute.
- Perform correct recovery techniques from unusual flight attitudes using full- and partial-panel instrument reference.
- Demonstrate proficiency in VOR, GPS, and localizer navigation using full- and partial-panel instrument reference.
- Demonstrate proficiency in using the autopilot (if equipped) to perform straight-and-level flight, climbs, descents, turns, and navigation.
- Apply proper correction to maintain a course, allowing no more than ¾-scale deflection of the CDI. Maintain DME arcs ±1 nautical mile.
- Demonstrate the ability to use SRM to make effective decisions, maintain situational awareness, prevent CFIT, and manage risk, tasks, and automation.

POSTFLIGHT DEBRIEFING

- ❑ Critique maneuvers/procedures and SRM.
- ❑ Create a plan for skills that need improvement.
- ❑ Update the record folder and logbook.

STUDY ASSIGNMENT

Ground Lesson 9

Stage I Exam

Stage I Check

Prepare for the Stage I Check in Flight Lesson 13.

FLIGHT LESSON 13

DUAL — LOCAL

STAGE I CHECK

OBJECTIVE

Demonstrate to the chief instructor, the assistant chief instructor, or the designated check instructor:

- Proficiency in full- and partial-panel instrument maneuvers and procedures.
- Proficiency in full- and partial-panel VOR, GPS, and localizer navigation.

PREFLIGHT DISCUSSION

Conduct for the Stage I Check, including:

- ❑ Maneuvers and Procedures
- ❑ Acceptable Performance Criteria
- ❑ Applicable Rules

EVALUATE

PREFLIGHT PREPARATION

- ❑ Pilot Qualifications
- ❑ Weather Information

PREFLIGHT PROCEDURES

- ❑ Airplane Systems Related to IFR Operations (Anti-icing and Deicing)
- ❑ Airplane Flight Instruments Operation
- ❑ Instrument Flight Deck Check

Airplane Flight Instruments and Navigation Equipment

- ❑ GPS Programming
- ❑ VOR Equipment Operation

FLIGHT BY REFERENCE TO INSTRUMENTS

Instrument Flight (Full Panel and Partial Panel)

- ❑ Straight-and-Level Flight
- ❑ Standard-Rate Turns
- ❑ Constant Rate Climbs and Descents
- ❑ Constant Airspeed Climbs and Descents
- ❑ Timed Turns to Magnetic Compass Headings
- ❑ Magnetic Compass Turns
- ❑ Autopilot Use, if Equipped

Recovery From Unusual Flight Attitudes

- ❑ Nose-High Attitude
- ❑ Nose-Low Attitude

SYSTEMS AND EQUIPMENT MALFUNCTIONS

- ❑ Loss of Primary Flight Instrument Indications
- ❑ Use of Secondary Flight Displays when Primary Displays Fail

NAVIGATION SYSTEMS

Intercepting and Tracking Navigational Systems and Arcs (Full Panel and Partial Panel)

❑ GPS Course Interception and Tracking
❑ VOR Radial Interception and Tracking
❑ Localizer Course Interception and Tracking
❑ Intercepting and Tracking DME Arcs
❑ Autopilot Use for Navigation, if Equipped

POSTFLIGHT PROCEDURES

❑ Checking Instruments and Equipment

COMPLETION STANDARDS

- Demonstrate proficiency in full- and partial-panel attitude instrument flying by maintaining altitude ±100 feet, headings ±10°, airspeed ±10 knots, bank angles ±5°, and descent/climb rate ±100 feet per minute.
- Perform correct recovery techniques from unusual flight attitudes using full- and partial-panel instrument reference.
- Demonstrate proficiency in VOR, GPS, and localizer navigation using full- and partial-panel instrument reference.
- Demonstrate proficiency in using the autopilot to perform straight-and-level flight, climbs, descents, turns, and navigation.
- Apply proper correction to maintain a course, allowing no more than ¾-scale deflection of the CDI. Maintain DME arcs ±1 nautical mile.
- Demonstrate the ability to use SRM to make effective decisions, maintain situational awareness, prevent CFIT, and manage risk, tasks, and automation.

POSTFLIGHT DEBRIEFING

❑ Evaluate maneuvers/procedures and SRM.
❑ Plan additional instruction for skills not meeting Stage I completion standards.
❑ Update the record folder and logbook.

STUDY ASSIGNMENT

Ground Lessons 10, 11, and 12

Departure Charts and Departure Procedures
Enroute Charts and Procedures
Holding Procedures

Stage II

STAGE OBJECTIVES

During Stage II, the student learns to perform holding patterns and instrument approaches, including circling and missed approach procedures. The student performs RNAV (GPS), ILS, localizer, and VOR approach procedures using full- and partial-panel instrument reference.

STAGE COMPLETION STANDARDS

This stage is complete when the student can demonstrate proficiency in performing holding patterns and all required instrument approach procedures.

NOTE: *Completion of the navigation, holding, and approach tasks listed in each lesson must be based on the available airplane equipment.*

FLIGHT LESSON 14

DUAL — LOCAL

OBJECTIVES

- Become familiar with VOR and GPS holding patterns: standard, non-standard, published, and unpublished.
- Become familiar with holding clearances.
- Become familiar with determining the appropriate holding entry: direct, teardrop, or parallel.
- Become familiar with how to correct for wind effects during the hold

PREFLIGHT DISCUSSION

❏ ATC Holding Instructions
❏ Recommended Holding Pattern Entries
❏ Wind Correction Procedures
❏ Airspeed Limitations

INTRODUCE

AIR TRAFFIC CONTROL CLEARANCES AND PROCEDURES

Compliance with Air Traffic Control Clearances

❏ Holding Clearance

Holding Procedures

❏ VOR Holding
❏ GPS Holding
❏ NDB Holding
❏ DME Holding

NOTE: *Students might be asked to demonstrate ADF and/or DME equipment operation if the airplane used for the practical test is so equipped. In this case, the NDB and DME holding tasks should be accomplished.*

REVIEW

NAVIGATION SYSTEMS

Intercepting and Tracking Navigational Systems and Arcs (Full Panel and Partial Panel)

❑ GPS Course Interception and Tracking
❑ VOR Radial Interception and Tracking

COMPLETION STANDARDS

- Demonstrate understanding of VOR and GPS holding patterns, including the appropriate entry, timing, and wind correction procedures.
- Demonstrate understanding of how to comply with a holding clearance.
- Demonstrate understanding of determining the appropriate holding entry.
- Maintain orientation at all times during holding procedures.

POSTFLIGHT DEBRIEFING

❑ Critique maneuvers/procedures and SRM.
❑ Create a plan for skills that need improvement.
❑ Update the record folder and logbook.

STUDY ASSIGNMENT

Ground Lesson 13

Arrival Charts and Procedures

FLIGHT LESSON 15

DUAL — LOCAL

OBJECTIVES

- Become familiar with intersection holding.
- Become familiar with localizer holding.
- Gain proficiency in performing VOR and GPS holding patterns.

PREFLIGHT DISCUSSION

❑ Task Management During Holding
❑ Situational Awareness During Holding

INTRODUCE

PREFLIGHT DISCUSSION

❑ Expect Further Clearance (EFC) Time
❑ Fuel Planning Considerations

AIR TRAFFIC CONTROL CLEARANCES AND PROCEDURES

Holding Procedures

❑ Intersection Holding
❑ Localizer Holding

REVIEW

AIR TRAFFIC CONTROL CLEARANCES AND PROCEDURES

Compliance with Air Traffic Control Clearances

❑ Holding Clearances

Holding Procedures

❑ VOR Holding
❑ GPS Holding
❑ NDB Holding
❑ DME Holding

NOTE: *Students might be asked to demonstrate ADF and/or DME equipment operation if the airplane used for the practical test is so equipped. In this case, the NDB and DME holding tasks should be accomplished.*

NAVIGATION SYSTEMS

Intercepting and Tracking Navigational Systems and Arcs (Full Panel and Partial Panel)

❑ GPS Course Interception and Tracking
❑ VOR Radial Interception and Tracking
❑ Localizer Course Interception and Tracking

COMPLETION STANDARDS

- Demonstrate understanding of localizer and intersection holding patterns, including the appropriate entry, timing, and wind correction procedures.
- Given a diagram of a holding pattern and the course from which you are approaching the holding fix, draw the recommended holding pattern entry.
- Demonstrate the ability to follow a holding clearance and to perform the correct holding procedures for VOR and GPS holding patterns, including the appropriate entry, timing, and wind correction procedures.
- Maintain altitude ±100 feet, heading ±10°, airspeed ±15 knots, bank angles ±5°, and CDI within 3/4-scale deflection.

POSTFLIGHT DEBRIEFING

❑ Critique maneuvers/procedures and SRM.
❑ Create a plan for skills that need improvement.
❑ Update the record folder and logbook.

STUDY ASSIGNMENT

Ground Lessons 14, 15, and 16

Approach Charts
Approach Procedures
RNAV Approaches

Instrument Approaches Briefing

FLIGHT LESSON 16

DUAL — LOCAL

OBJECTIVES

- Become familiar with performing nonprecision RNAV (GPS) approach procedures.
- Become familiar with performing missed approach procedures.
- Become familiar with landing from an instrument approach: straight-in landing or circling approach.
- Increase proficiency in performing all types of holding patterns.

NOTE: *According to the ACS, acceptable nonprecision approaches include RNAV (GPS) to LNAV, LNAV/VNAV or LPV line of minima as long as the LPV DA is greater than 300 feet HAT (height above touchdown).*

PREFLIGHT DISCUSSION

❑ RNAV (GPS) Approach Required Equipment, including RAIM and WAAS
❑ RNAV (GPS) Landing Minimums (LPV, LNAV/VNAV, LNAV, LP)
❑ Approach Procedures with Vertical Guidance (APV)
❑ Approach Briefing
❑ Continuous Descent Final Approach (CDFA)
❑ Visual Descent Point (VDP)

INTRODUCE

AIR TRAFFIC CONTROL CLEARANCES AND PROCEDURES

Compliance with Air Traffic Control Clearances
❑ Approach Clearances

INSTRUMENT APPROACH PROCEDURES

Nonprecision Approach
❑ RNAV (GPS) Approaches

Approach Procedures
❑ Procedure Turn/Course Reversal
❑ Terminal Arrival Area (TAA)
❑ Vectors to the Approach Course
❑ Approach Procedure to Straight-In or Circling Landing Minimums
❑ Circling Approach
❑ Missed Approach

Landing from an Instrument Approach
❑ Straight-In Landing
❑ Circling Approach
❑ Wake Turbulence Avoidance
❑ Wind Shear Avoidance
❑ Land and Hold Short Operations (LAHSO)

REVIEW

AIR TRAFFIC CONTROL CLEARANCES AND PROCEDURES

Compliance with Air Traffic Control Clearances

❏ Holding Clearances

Holding Procedures

❏ Intersection Holding
❏ Localizer Holding

COMPLETION STANDARDS

- Demonstrate understanding of nonprecision RNAV (GPS) approach procedures.
- Maintain altitude ±200 feet, selected heading ±15°, airspeed ±15 knots, prior to beginning the final approach segment.
- Perform the correct procedure to initiate a missed approach, establish a climb attitude, and configure the airplane.
- Properly transition at the decision altitude (DA), minimum descent altitude (MDA), or visual descent point (VDP) to a visual flight condition and maneuver safely for a normal landing.
- Avoid circling beyond visibility requirements and maintain the appropriate circling altitude until in a position from which a descent to a normal landing can be made.
- Demonstrate the ability to perform the correct holding pattern entries and procedures for all types of holding patterns.

POSTFLIGHT DEBRIEFING

❏ Critique maneuvers/procedures and SRM.
❏ Create a plan for skills that need improvement.
❏ Update the record folder and logbook.

FLIGHT LESSON 17

DUAL — LOCAL

OBJECTIVES

- Become familiar with performing RNAV (GPS) approach procedures to LPV minimums with a DA less than 300 feet HAT.
- Gain proficiency in performing nonprecision RNAV (GPS) approach procedures.
- Gain proficiency in performing missed approach procedures.
- Gain proficiency in landing from an instrument approach: straight-in landing or circle-to-land/circling approach.

NOTE: *According to the ACS:*

◊ *Localizer performance with vertical guidance (LPV) minimums with a decision altitude (DA) less than 300 feet height above touchdown (HAT) may be used to demonstrate precision approach proficiency.*

◊ *Acceptable nonprecision approaches include RNAV (GPS) to LNAV, LNAV/VNAV or LPV line of minima as long as the LPV DA is greater than 300 feet HAT (height above touchdown).*

PREFLIGHT DISCUSSION

- ❑ Straight-In Landing or Circle-to-Land/Circling Approach
- ❑ Straight-In Approach or Approach with Course Reversal
- ❑ Requirements to Descend Below the MDA or DA
- ❑ Land and Hold Short Operations (LAHSO)

INTRODUCE

INSTRUMENT APPROACH PROCEDURES

Precision Approach

- ❑ RNAV (GPS) Approaches (to LPV minimums with a DA less than 300 feet HAT)

REVIEW

AIR TRAFFIC CONTROL CLEARANCES AND PROCEDURES

Compliance with Air Traffic Control Clearances

- ❑ Approach Clearances

INSTRUMENT APPROACH PROCEDURES

Nonprecision Approach

- ❑ RNAV (GPS) Approaches

Approach Procedures

- ❑ Procedure Turn/Course Reversal
- ❑ Terminal Arrival Area (TAA)
- ❑ Vectors to the Approach Course
- ❑ Approach Procedure to Straight-In or Circling Landing Minimums
- ❑ Circling Approach
- ❑ Missed Approach

Landing from an Instrument Approach

- ❑ Straight-In Landing
- ❑ Circling Approach
- ❑ Wake Turbulence Avoidance
- ❑ Wind Shear Avoidance
- ❑ Land and Hold Short Operations (LAHSO)

COMPLETION STANDARDS

- Demonstrate understanding of RNAV (GPS) approach procedures to a DA less than 300 feet HAT.
- When performing nonprecision RNAV (GPS) approaches:
  - ◊ Prior to beginning the final approach segment: maintain altitude ±100 feet, selected heading ±10°, airspeed ±10 knots.
  - ◊ On final approach: maintain no more than a ¾-scale deflection of the CDI, and maintain airspeed ±10 knots.
  - ◊ Maintain altitude above the MDA, +100/-0 feet to the visual descent point (VDP) or missed approach point (MAP), as applicable; or maintain a stabilized final approach from the final approach fix (FAF) to the DA.

- Use the correct procedures to perform a missed approach, a straight-in landing, and circling to land.

POSTFLIGHT DEBRIEFING

- ❑ Critique maneuvers/procedures and SRM.
- ❑ Create a plan for skills that need improvement.
- ❑ Update the record folder and logbook.

STUDY ASSIGNMENT

Ground Lesson 17

ILS Approaches

FLIGHT LESSON 18

DUAL — LOCAL

OBJECTIVES

- Become familiar with ILS and localizer approach procedures.
- Increase proficiency in performing RNAV (GPS) approach procedures.
- Increase proficiency in performing missed approach procedures.
- Increase proficiency in landing from an instrument approach: straight-in landing or circle-to-land/circling approach.

PREFLIGHT DISCUSSION

- ❑ ILS Components
- ❑ ILS and Localizer Approach Required Equipment
- ❑ DME Arcs to the Approach Course
- ❑ Landing Minimums with Inoperative Equipment

INTRODUCE

INSTRUMENT APPROACH PROCEDURES

Precision Approach

- ❑ ILS Approaches

Nonprecision Approach

- ❑ Localizer Approaches

REVIEW

AIR TRAFFIC CONTROL CLEARANCES AND PROCEDURES

Compliance with Air Traffic Control Clearances

- ❑ Approach Clearances

INSTRUMENT APPROACH PROCEDURES

Precision Approach

- ❑ RNAV (GPS) Approaches (to LPV minimums with a DA less than 300 feet HAT)

Nonprecision Approach

- ❑ RNAV (GPS) Approaches

Approach Procedures
- ❑ Procedure Turn/Course Reversal
- ❑ Terminal Arrival Area (TAA)
- ❑ Vectors to the Approach Course
- ❑ Approach Procedure to Straight-In or Circling Landing Minimums
- ❑ Circling Approach
- ❑ Missed Approach

Landing from an Instrument Approach
- ❑ Straight-In Landing
- ❑ Circling Approach
- ❑ Wake Turbulence Avoidance
- ❑ Wind Shear Avoidance
- ❑ Land and Hold Short Operations (LAHSO)

COMPLETION STANDARDS

- During ILS approaches, demonstrate understanding of localizer tracking, intercepting and maintaining the glide slope, and using power and attitude changes to control airspeed and descent rates.
- Demonstrate understanding of localizer approach procedures.
- When performing RNAV (GPS) approaches:
  - ◊ Prior to beginning the final approach segment: maintain altitude ±100 feet, selected heading ±10°, airspeed ±10 knots.
  - ◊ On final approach: maintain no more than a ¾-scale deflection of the CDI, and maintain airspeed ±10 knots.
  - ◊ Maintain altitude above the MDA, +100/-0 feet to the visual descent point (VDP) or missed approach point (MAP), as applicable; or maintain a stabilized final approach from the final approach fix (FAF) to the DA.
- Use the correct procedures to perform a missed approach, a straight-in landing, and circling to land.

POSTFLIGHT DEBRIEFING

- ❑ Critique maneuvers/procedures and SRM.
- ❑ Create a plan for skills that need improvement.
- ❑ Update the record folder and logbook.

STUDY ASSIGNMENT

Ground Lesson 18
VOR and NDB Approaches

FLIGHT LESSON 19

DUAL — LOCAL

OBJECTIVES

- Become familiar with VOR and VOR/DME approach procedures.
- Increase proficiency in RNAV (GPS), ILS, and localizer approach procedures.

NOTE: *This syllabus does not require practice of NDB approaches because the ACS does not list NDB approaches as an example of an acceptable nonprecision approach. NDB approach procedures are being phased out and replaced by more accurate RNAV (GPS) procedures.*

PREFLIGHT DISCUSSION

❏ VOR and VOR/DME Approach Required Equipment
❏ On- and Off-Airport VORs
❏ Approach Briefing

INTRODUCE

INSTRUMENT APPROACH PROCEDURES

Nonprecision Approach
❏ VOR and VOR/DME Approaches

REVIEW

AIR TRAFFIC CONTROL CLEARANCES AND PROCEDURES

Compliance with Air Traffic Control Clearances
❏ Approach Clearances

INSTRUMENT APPROACH PROCEDURES

Precision Approach
❏ ILS Approaches
❏ RNAV (GPS) Approaches (to LPV minimums with a DA less than 300 feet HAT)

Nonprecision Approach
❏ Localizer Approaches
❏ RNAV (GPS) Approaches

Approach Procedures
❏ Procedure Turn/Course Reversal
❏ Terminal Arrival Area (TAA)
❏ Vectors to the Approach Course
❏ Approach Procedure to Straight-In or Circling Landing Minimums
❏ Circling Approach
❏ Missed Approach

Landing from an Instrument Approach
❏ Straight-In Landing
❏ Circling Approach
❏ Wake Turbulence Avoidance
❏ Wind Shear Avoidance
❏ Land and Hold Short Operations (LAHSO)

COMPLETION STANDARDS

- Demonstrate understanding of VOR and VOR/DME approach procedures.
- When performing RNAV (GPS), ILS, and localizer approaches:
  - ◊ Prior to beginning the final approach segment: maintain altitude ±100 feet, selected heading ±10°, airspeed ±10 knots.
  - ◊ On final approach: maintain no more than a ¾-scale deflection of the CDI, and maintain airspeed ±10 knots.
  - ◊ Maintain altitude above the MDA, +100/-0 feet to the visual descent point (VDP) or missed approach point (MAP), as applicable; or maintain a stabilized final approach from the final approach fix (FAF) to the DA.

POSTFLIGHT DEBRIEFING

- ❑ Critique maneuvers/procedures and SRM.
- ❑ Create a plan for skills that need improvement.
- ❑ Update the record folder and logbook.

FLIGHT LESSON 20

DUAL — LOCAL

OBJECTIVES

- Become familiar with flying approach procedures with a loss of the primary flight instrument indicators.
- Become familiar with no-gyro radar vectoring and approach procedures.
- Increase proficiency in full-panel nonprecision, precision, and APV instrument approach procedures.

PREFLIGHT DISCUSSION

- ❑ Approaches with Loss of Primary Flight Instrument Indicators
- ❑ No-Gyro Radar Vectoring and Approach Procedures
- ❑ Instrument and Equipment Malfunction Procedures
- ❑ Advising ATC and ATC Assistance

INTRODUCE

EMERGENCY OPERATIONS

Approaches with Loss of Primary Flight Instrument Indicators

- ❑ No-Gyro Radar Vectoring and Approach Procedures
- ❑ Partial-Panel Approach Procedures
- ❑ Partial-Panel Missed Approach Procedures

INSTRUMENT APPROACH PROCEDURES

Precision Approach (Partial Panel)

- ❑ ILS Approaches
- ❑ RNAV (GPS) Approaches (to LPV minimums with a DA less than 300 feet HAT)

Nonprecision Approach (Partial Panel)

- ❑ Localizer Approaches
- ❑ RNAV (GPS) Approaches
- ❑ VOR and VOR/DME Approaches

COMPLETION STANDARDS

- Demonstrate understanding of no-gyro radar vectoring and approaches.
- Demonstrate understanding of partial-panel approach and missed approach procedures.

POSTFLIGHT DEBRIEFING

- ❑ Critique maneuvers/procedures and SRM.
- ❑ Create a plan for skills that need improvement.
- ❑ Update the record folder and logbook.

STUDY ASSIGNMENT

Begin to review for the Stage II Check in Flight Lesson 23.

FLIGHT LESSON 21

DUAL — LOCAL

OBJECTIVES

- Gain proficiency in performing approach procedures with a loss of the primary flight instrument indicators, including no-gyro radar vectoring and approach procedures.
- Increase proficiency in full- and partial-panel RNAV (GPS), ILS, localizer, VOR, and VOR/DME instrument approach procedures.

PREFLIGHT DISCUSSION

- ❑ Task Management During Instrument and Equipment Malfunction
- ❑ Situational Awareness During Partial-Panel Approaches

REVIEW

EMERGENCY OPERATIONS

Approaches with Loss of Primary Flight Instrument Indicators

- ❑ No-Gyro Radar Vectoring and Approach Procedures
- ❑ Partial-Panel Approach Procedures
- ❑ Partial-Panel Missed Approach Procedures

INSTRUMENT APPROACH PROCEDURES

Precision Approach (Full Panel and Partial Panel)

- ❑ ILS Approaches
- ❑ RNAV (GPS) Approaches (to LPV minimums with a DA less than 300 feet HAT)

Nonprecision Approach (Full Panel and Partial Panel)

- ❑ Localizer Approaches
- ❑ RNAV (GPS) Approaches
- ❑ VOR and VOR/DME Approaches

COMPLETION STANDARDS

- Demonstrate proficiency in performing approach procedures with a loss of the primary flight instrument indicators.
- Demonstrate proficiency in performing approach procedures with a loss of the primary flight instrument indicators, including no-gyro radar vectoring and approach procedures.
- Demonstrate proficiency in full- and partial-panel RNAV (GPS), ILS, localizer, VOR, and VOR/DME instrument approach procedures.

POSTFLIGHT DEBRIEFING

❑ Critique maneuvers/procedures and SRM.
❑ Create a plan for skills that need improvement.
❑ Update the record folder and logbook.

STUDY ASSIGNMENT

Begin to review for the Stage II Check in Flight Lesson 23.

FLIGHT LESSON 22

DUAL — LOCAL

OBJECTIVES

To prepare for the Stage II Check:

- Review holding pattern entries and procedures.
- Review instrument approach procedures.
- Correct any deficient knowledge and skill areas.

PREFLIGHT DISCUSSION

❑ SRM During Holding and Approach Procedures

REVIEW

AIR TRAFFIC CONTROL CLEARANCES AND PROCEDURES

Compliance with Air Traffic Control Clearances

❑ Approach Clearances

Holding Procedures

❑ VOR Holding
❑ GPS Holding
❑ Localizer Holding
❑ Intersection Holding

EMERGENCY OPERATIONS

Approaches with Loss of Primary Flight Instrument Indicators

❑ No-Gyro Radar Vectoring and Approach Procedures
❑ Partial-Panel Approach Procedures
❑ Partial-Panel Missed Approach Procedures

INSTRUMENT APPROACH PROCEDURES

Precision Approach (Full Panel and Partial Panel)

❑ ILS Approaches
❑ RNAV (GPS) Approaches (to LPV minimums with a DA less than 300 feet HAT)

Nonprecision Approach (Full Panel and Partial Panel)

❑ Localizer Approaches
❑ RNAV (GPS) Approaches
❑ VOR and VOR/DME Approaches

Approach Procedures

❑ Procedure Turn/Course Reversal
❑ Terminal Arrival Area (TAA)
❑ Vectors to the Approach Course
❑ Approach Procedure to Straight-In or Circling Landing Minimums
❑ Circling Approach
❑ Missed Approach

Landing from an Instrument Approach

❑ Straight-In Landing
❑ Circling Approach
❑ Wake Turbulence Avoidance
❑ Wind Shear Avoidance
❑ Land and Hold Short Operations (LAHSO)

COMPLETION STANDARDS

- Demonstrate the ability to perform the correct holding procedures including the appropriate entry, timing, and wind correction procedures.
- While holding, maintain altitude ±100 feet, heading ±10°, airspeed ±15 knots, bank angles ±5°, and CDI within 3/4-scale deflection.
- When performing all full- and partial-panel approaches:
  - ◊ Prior to beginning the final approach segment: maintain altitude ±100 feet, selected heading ±10°, airspeed ±10 knots.
  - ◊ On final approach: maintain no more than a ¾-scale deflection of the CDI, and maintain airspeed ±10 knots.
  - ◊ Maintain altitude above the MDA, +100/-0 feet to the visual descent point (VDP) or missed approach point (MAP), as applicable; or maintain a stabilized final approach from the final approach fix (FAF) to the DA.

POSTFLIGHT DEBRIEFING

❑ Critique maneuvers/procedures and SRM.
❑ Create a plan for skills that need improvement.
❑ Update the record folder and logbook.

STUDY ASSIGNMENT

Ground Lesson 19

Stage II Exam.

Stage II Check

Prepare for the Stage II Check in Flight Lesson 23.

FLIGHT LESSON 23

DUAL — LOCAL
STAGE II CHECK

OBJECTIVE
Demonstrate to the chief instructor, the assistant chief instructor, or the designated check instructor:
- Proficiency in holding pattern entries and procedures.
- Proficiency in instrument approach procedures.

PREFLIGHT DISCUSSION
Conduct for the Stage II Check, including:
❑ Maneuvers and Procedures
❑ Acceptable Performance Criteria
❑ Applicable Rules

EVALUATE

AIR TRAFFIC CONTROL CLEARANCES AND PROCEDURES
Compliance with Air Traffic Control Clearances
❑ Approach Clearances
Holding Procedures
❑ VOR Holding
❑ GPS Holding
❑ Localizer Holding
❑ Intersection Holding

EMERGENCY OPERATIONS
Approaches with Loss of Primary Flight Instrument Indicators
❑ No-Gyro Radar Vectoring and Approach Procedures
❑ Partial-Panel Approach Procedures
❑ Partial-Panel Missed Approach Procedures

INSTRUMENT APPROACH PROCEDURES
Precision Approach (Full Panel and Partial Panel)
❑ ILS Approaches
❑ RNAV (GPS) Approaches (to LPV minimums with a DA less than 300 feet HAT)
Nonprecision Approach (Full Panel and Partial Panel)
❑ Localizer Approaches
❑ RNAV (GPS) Approaches
❑ VOR and VOR/DME Approaches
Approach Procedures
❑ Procedure Turn/Course Reversal
❑ Terminal Arrival Area (TAA)
❑ Vectors to the Approach Course
❑ Approach Procedure to Straight-In or Circling Landing Minimums
❑ Circling Approach
❑ Missed Approach

Landing from an Instrument Approach
❏ Straight-In Landing
❏ Circling Approach
❏ Wake Turbulence Avoidance
❏ Wind Shear Avoidance
❏ Land and Hold Short Operations (LAHSO)

COMPLETION STANDARDS

- Demonstrate the ability to perform the correct holding procedures including the appropriate entry, timing, and wind correction procedures.
- While holding, maintain altitude ±100 feet, heading ±10°, airspeed ±15 knots, bank angles ±5°, and CDI within 3/4-scale deflection.
- When performing all full- and partial-panel approaches:
  - ◊ Prior to beginning the final approach segment: maintain altitude ±100 feet, selected heading ±10°, airspeed ±10 knots.
  - ◊ On final approach: maintain no more than a ¾-scale deflection of the CDI, and maintain airspeed ±10 knots.
  - ◊ Maintain altitude above the MDA, +100/-0 feet to the visual descent point (VDP) or missed approach point (MAP), as applicable; or maintain a stabilized final approach from the final approach fix (FAF) to the DA.

POSTFLIGHT DEBRIEFING

❏ Critique maneuvers/procedures and SRM.
❏ Create a plan for skills that need improvement.
❏ Update the record folder and logbook.

STUDY ASSIGNMENT

Ground Lessons 20, 21 and 22

Weather Factors and Hazards
Analyzing Weather
IFR Flight Planning

IFR Cross-Country Briefing

Stage III

STAGE OBJECTIVES

During Stage III the student learns IFR cross-country procedures and increases proficiency to the level required of an instrument-rated pilot.

STAGE COMPLETION STANDARDS

This stage is complete when the student can demonstrate all IFR maneuvers and procedures at the proficiency level of an instrument-rated pilot, as outlined in the Instrument Rating Airman Certification Standards.

FLIGHT LESSON 24

DUAL — CROSS-COUNTRY

OBJECTIVES

- Become familiar with IFR cross-country flight operations by performing an IFR cross-country over 50 nautical miles from the original point of departure.
- Become familiar with the procedures for IFR cross-country flight planning, including filing IFR flight plans, and obtaining IFR clearances.
- Become familiar with IFR departure, enroute and arrival operations.

PREFLIGHT DISCUSSION

❏ Review of Enroute, Departure, Arrival, and Approach Charts
❏ RAIM Availability for GPS Navigation
❏ IFR Clearances, Clearance Void Times, and Hold-for-Release Times
❏ ATC Services
❏ Changes to IFR Clearances

INTRODUCE

IFR CROSS-COUNTRY FLIGHT

PREFLIGHT PREPARATION

Weather Information

❏ Departure, Enroute, Alternate, and Destination Meteorology
❏ Alternate Requirements

Cross-Country Flight Planning

❏ Route Planning and Alternate Selection
❏ Altitude Selection
❏ Weight and Balance
❏ Performance and Limitations
❏ Determining ETA
❏ Fuel Requirements
❏ Sources of Flight Information
❏ SIDs, ODPs, and STARs
❏ Navigation Log

- ❑ IFR Flight Plan
- ❑ Airframe Icing Considerations

ATC CLEARANCES AND PROCEDURES
- ❑ Clearance Copying and Readback
- ❑ Compliance with ATC Clearances—Departure, Enroute, Arrival, Approach
- ❑ Holding Procedures

PREFLIGHT PROCEDURES

Airplane Flight Instruments and Navigation Equipment
- ❑ GPS Programming
- ❑ VOR Equipment Operation

NAVIGATION SYSTEMS

Intercepting and Tracking Navigational Systems and Arcs (Full Panel and Partial Panel)
- ❑ GPS Course Interception and Tracking
- ❑ VOR Radial Interception and Tracking
- ❑ Localizer Course Interception and Tracking
- ❑ Intercepting and Tracking DME Arcs
- ❑ Autopilot Use for Navigation, if Equipped

Departure, Enroute, and Arrival Operations
- ❑ Standard Instrument Departure (SID)
- ❑ Obstacle Departure Procedure (ODP)
- ❑ Standard Terminal Arrival (STAR)
- ❑ Checklist Use
- ❑ Radio Communications
- ❑ ATC Services
- ❑ Use of Flight Deck Displays—Weather and Aeronautical Information

INSTRUMENT APPROACH PROCEDURES

Precision Approach
- ❑ ILS Approaches
- ❑ RNAV (GPS) Approaches (to LPV minimums with a DA less than 300 feet HAT)

Nonprecision Approach
- ❑ Localizer Approaches
- ❑ RNAV (GPS) Approaches
- ❑ VOR and VOR/DME Approaches

Approach Procedures
- ❑ Procedure Turn/Course Reversal
- ❑ Terminal Arrival Area (TAA)
- ❑ Vectors to the Approach Course
- ❑ Approach Procedure to Straight-In or Circling Landing Minimums
- ❑ Circling Approach
- ❑ Missed Approach

Landing from an Instrument Approach
- ❑ Straight-In Landing
- ❑ Circling Approach
- ❑ Wake Turbulence Avoidance
- ❑ Wind Shear Avoidance
- ❑ Land and Hold Short Operations (LAHSO)

NOTE: *Perform specific holding and approach procedures as needed.*

COMPLETION STANDARDS

- Demonstrate understanding of IFR cross-country flight operations by performing an IFR cross-country over 50 nautical miles from the original point of departure.
- Demonstrate understanding of the procedures for IFR cross-country flight planning, including filing IFR flight plans, and obtaining IFR clearances.
- Demonstrate understanding of IFR departure, enroute and arrival operations.

POSTFLIGHT DEBRIEFING

❑ Critique maneuvers/procedures and SRM.
❑ Create a plan for skills that need improvement.
❑ Update the record folder and logbook.

STUDY ASSIGNMENT

Ground Lessons 23 and 24

IFR Single-Pilot Resource Management
IFR Emergencies

FLIGHT LESSON 25

DUAL — CROSS-COUNTRY

OBJECTIVES

- Become familiar with emergency procedures in the IFR cross-country environment.
- Gain proficiency in IFR flight planning and IFR departure, enroute, and arrival procedures by performing an IFR cross-country flight over 50 nautical miles from the original point of departure.

PREFLIGHT DISCUSSION

❑ Alternate Airport Requirements Applying to GPS Approaches
❑ Emergency and Abnormal Procedures
❑ Loss of Communications Procedures
❑ Icing Operational Hazards
❑ Anti-Icing or Deicing Equipment on the Airplane
❑ Minimum Fuel
❑ Declaring an Emergency—Procedures, Frequencies, and Transponder Codes
❑ Diversion

INTRODUCE

IFR CROSS-COUNTRY FLIGHT

EMERGENCY OPERATIONS

❑ Loss of Communications
❑ Systems and Equipment Malfunctions
❑ Loss of Primary Flight Instrument Indicators
❑ Airframe and Powerplant Icing
❑ Low Fuel Supply
❑ Engine Failure

Approaches with Loss of Primary Flight Instrument Indicators
Precision Approach (Partial Panel)
- ❏ ILS Approaches
- ❏ RNAV (GPS) Approaches (to LPV minimums with a DA less than 300 feet HAT)

Nonprecision Approach (Partial Panel)
- ❏ Localizer Approaches
- ❏ RNAV (GPS) Approaches
- ❏ VOR and VOR/DME Approaches

REVIEW

IFR CROSS-COUNTRY FLIGHT

PREFLIGHT PREPARATION

Weather Information
- ❏ Departure, Enroute, Alternate, and Destination Meteorology
- ❏ Alternate Requirements

Cross-Country Flight Planning
- ❏ Route Planning and Alternate Selection
- ❏ Altitude Selection
- ❏ Weight and Balance
- ❏ Performance and Limitations
- ❏ Determining ETA
- ❏ Fuel Requirements
- ❏ Sources of Flight Information
- ❏ SIDs, ODPs, and STARs
- ❏ Navigation Log
- ❏ IFR Flight Plan
- ❏ Airframe Icing Considerations

ATC CLEARANCES AND PROCEDURES
- ❏ Clearance Copying and Readback
- ❏ Compliance with ATC Clearances—Departure, Enroute, Arrival, Approach
- ❏ Holding Procedures

PREFLIGHT PROCEDURES

Airplane Flight Instruments and Navigation Equipment
- ❏ GPS Programming
- ❏ VOR Equipment Operation

NAVIGATION SYSTEMS

Intercepting and Tracking Navigational Systems and Arcs (Full Panel and Partial Panel)
- ❏ GPS Course Interception and Tracking
- ❏ VOR Radial Interception and Tracking
- ❏ Localizer Course Interception and Tracking
- ❏ Intercepting and Tracking DME Arcs
- ❏ Autopilot Use for Navigation, if Equipped

Departure, Enroute, and Arrival Operations
- ❏ Standard Instrument Departure (SID)
- ❏ Obstacle Departure Procedure (ODP)
- ❏ Standard Terminal Arrival (STAR)

- ❑ Checklist Use
- ❑ Radio Communications
- ❑ ATC Services
- ❑ Use of Flight Deck Displays—Weather and Aeronautical Information

REVIEW

INSTRUMENT APPROACH PROCEDURES

Precision Approach
- ❑ ILS Approaches
- ❑ RNAV (GPS) Approaches (to LPV minimums with a DA less than 300 feet HAT)

Nonprecision Approach
- ❑ Localizer Approaches
- ❑ RNAV (GPS) Approaches
- ❑ VOR and VOR/DME Approaches

Approach Procedures
- ❑ Procedure Turn/Course Reversal
- ❑ Terminal Arrival Area (TAA)
- ❑ Vectors to the Approach Course
- ❑ Approach Procedure to Straight-In or Circling Landing Minimums
- ❑ Circling Approach
- ❑ Missed Approach

Landing from an Instrument Approach
- ❑ Straight-In Landing
- ❑ Circling Approach
- ❑ Wake Turbulence Avoidance
- ❑ Wind Shear Avoidance
- ❑ Land and Hold Short Operations (LAHSO)

NOTE: *Perform specific holding and approach procedures as needed.*

COMPLETION STANDARDS

- Demonstrate understanding of emergency operations in the IFR cross-country environment.
- Perform the proper procedures to plan and implement an IFR cross-country flight over 50 nautical miles from the original point of departure.
- Perform the proper procedures during IFR departure, enroute, and arrival operations.

POSTFLIGHT DEBRIEFING

- ❑ Critique maneuvers/procedures and SRM.
- ❑ Create a plan for skills that need improvement.
- ❑ Update the record folder and logbook.

STUDY ASSIGNMENT

Ground Lesson 24

IFR Emergencies

FLIGHT LESSON 26

DUAL — CROSS-COUNTRY

OBJECTIVES

- Increase proficiency in planning and performing an IFR cross-country flight.
- Increase proficiency in IFR departure, enroute, and arrival procedures.
- Increase proficiency in managing emergencies in the IFR cross-country environment.

NOTE: *The flight is designed to meet the cross-country requirements stated in Part 141, Appendix C. The flight must be conducted under IFR in the category and class of airplane for which the course is approved and must be at least 250 nautical miles in length along airways or ATC-directed routing. One leg of the flight must be at least a straight-line distance of 100 nautical miles between airports. The student must perform an instrument approach at each airport and perform a minimum of three different types of approaches using navigation systems.*

PREFLIGHT DISCUSSION

SINGLE-PILOT RESOURCE MANAGEMENT (SRM)

- ❑ Aeronautical Decision Making (ADM)
  - ◊ Using the ADM Process
  - ◊ Recognizing Hazardous Attitudes
- ❑ Risk Management
  - ◊ Using a Risk Management Tool (5Ps, PAVE)
  - ◊ Assessing Weather Risk
- ❑ Task Management
  - ◊ Planning and Prioritizing
  - ◊ Resource Use
- ❑ Situational Awareness
  - ◊ Dangers of Fixating on a Problem
  - ◊ Use of Navigation, Traffic, Terrain, and Weather Displays
- ❑ CFIT Awareness
  - ◊ Flight Planning to Avoid Terrain and Obstacles.
  - ◊ Use of Navigation, Terrain, and TAWS Displays
- ❑ Automation Management
  - ◊ Cross Checking Waypoint and Navaid Locations
  - ◊ Recognizing Mode or Status Changes of the Autopilot/FMS.

REVIEW

IFR CROSS-COUNTRY FLIGHT

PREFLIGHT PREPARATION

- ❑ Weather Information
- ❑ Cross-Country Flight Planning

ATC CLEARANCES AND PROCEDURES

- ❑ Clearance Copying and Readback
- ❑ Compliance with ATC Clearances—Departure, Enroute, Arrival, Approach
- ❑ Holding Procedures

PREFLIGHT PROCEDURES
- ❑ Airplane Flight Instruments and Navigation Equipment

NAVIGATION SYSTEMS

Intercepting and Tracking Navigational Systems and Arcs (Full Panel and Partial Panel)
- ❑ GPS Course Interception and Tracking
- ❑ VOR Radial Interception and Tracking
- ❑ Localizer Course Interception and Tracking
- ❑ Intercepting and Tracking DME Arcs
- ❑ Autopilot Use for Navigation, if Equipped

Departure, Enroute, and Arrival Operations
- ❑ Standard Instrument Departure (SID)
- ❑ Obstacle Departure Procedure (ODP)
- ❑ Standard Terminal Arrival (STAR)
- ❑ Checklist Use
- ❑ Radio Communications
- ❑ ATC Services
- ❑ Use of Flight Deck Displays—Weather and Aeronautical Information

INSTRUMENT APPROACH PROCEDURES

Precision Approach
- ❑ ILS Approaches
- ❑ RNAV (GPS) Approaches (to LPV minimums with a DA less than 300 feet HAT)

Nonprecision Approach
- ❑ Localizer Approaches
- ❑ RNAV (GPS) Approaches
- ❑ VOR and VOR/DME Approaches

Approach Procedures
- ❑ Procedure Turn/Course Reversal
- ❑ Terminal Arrival Area (TAA)
- ❑ Vectors to the Approach Course
- ❑ Approach Procedure to Straight-In or Circling Landing Minimums
- ❑ Circling Approach
- ❑ Missed Approach

Landing from an Instrument Approach
- ❑ Straight-In Landing
- ❑ Circling Approach
- ❑ Wake Turbulence Avoidance
- ❑ Wind Shear Avoidance
- ❑ Land and Hold Short Operations (LAHSO)

EMERGENCY OPERATIONS
- ❑ Loss of Communications
- ❑ Systems and Equipment Malfunctions
- ❑ Loss of Primary Flight Instrument Indicators
- ❑ Airframe and Powerplant Icing
- ❑ Low Fuel Supply
- ❑ Engine Failure

Approaches with Loss of Primary Flight Instrument Indicators

Precision Approach (Partial Panel)
- ❑ ILS Approaches
- ❑ RNAV (GPS) Approaches (to LPV minimums with a DA less than 300 feet HAT)

Nonprecision Approach (Partial Panel)
❏ Localizer Approaches
❏ RNAV (GPS) Approaches
❏ VOR and VOR/DME Approaches

NOTE: *Perform specific holding and approach procedures as needed.*

COMPLETION STANDARDS

- Demonstrate proficiency in planning and implementing an IFR cross-country flight at least 250 nautical miles in length along airways or ATC-directed routing with one leg at least a straight-line distance of 100 nautical miles between airports.
- Demonstrate proficiency in performing a minimum of three different types of approaches (at least one at each airport) using navigation systems.
- Demonstrate proficiency in managing emergency procedures in the IFR cross-country environment.
- Demonstrate proficiency in SRM skills by effectively managing risk and making decisions during IFR cross-country operations.

POSTFLIGHT DEBRIEFING

❏ Critique maneuvers/procedures and SRM.
❏ Create a plan for skills that need improvement.
❏ Update the record folder and logbook.

STUDY ASSIGNMENT

Instrument Rating Practical Test Briefing

FLIGHT LESSON 27

DUAL — CROSS-COUNTRY

OBJECTIVES

- Increase proficiency in planning and conducting all phases of the IFR cross-country flight to prepare for the Stage III Check.
- Increase proficiency in managing emergencies in the IFR cross-country environment.
- Increase proficiency in SRM skills by effectively managing risk and making decisions during IFR cross-country operations.

PREFLIGHT DISCUSSION

❏ SRM in the IFR Environment

REVIEW

IFR CROSS-COUNTRY FLIGHT

PREFLIGHT PREPARATION

❏ Weather Information
❏ Cross-Country Flight Planning

ATC CLEARANCES AND PROCEDURES
- ❑ Clearance Copying and Readback
- ❑ Compliance with ATC Clearances—Departure, Enroute, Arrival, Approach
- ❑ Holding Procedures

PREFLIGHT PROCEDURES
- ❑ Airplane Flight Instruments and Navigation Equipment

NAVIGATION SYSTEMS

Intercepting and Tracking Navigational Systems and Arcs (Full Panel and Partial Panel)
- ❑ GPS Course Interception and Tracking
- ❑ VOR Radial Interception and Tracking
- ❑ Localizer Course Interception and Tracking
- ❑ Intercepting and Tracking DME Arcs
- ❑ Autopilot Use for Navigation, if Equipped

Departure, Enroute, and Arrival Operations
- ❑ Standard Instrument Departure (SID)
- ❑ Obstacle Departure Procedure (ODP)
- ❑ Standard Terminal Arrival (STAR)
- ❑ Checklist Use
- ❑ Radio Communications
- ❑ ATC Services
- ❑ Use of Flight Deck Displays—Weather and Aeronautical Information

INSTRUMENT APPROACH PROCEDURES

Precision Approach
- ❑ ILS Approaches
- ❑ RNAV (GPS) Approaches (to LPV minimums with a DA less than 300 feet HAT)

Nonprecision Approach
- ❑ Localizer Approaches
- ❑ RNAV (GPS) Approaches
- ❑ VOR and VOR/DME Approaches

Approach Procedures
- ❑ Procedure Turn/Course Reversal
- ❑ Terminal Arrival Area (TAA)
- ❑ Vectors to the Approach Course
- ❑ Approach Procedure to Straight-In or Circling Landing Minimums
- ❑ Circling Approach
- ❑ Missed Approach

Landing from an Instrument Approach
- ❑ Straight-In Landing
- ❑ Circling Approach
- ❑ Wake Turbulence Avoidance
- ❑ Wind Shear Avoidance
- ❑ Land and Hold Short Operations (LAHSO)

EMERGENCY OPERATIONS
- ❑ Loss of Communications
- ❑ Systems and Equipment Malfunctions
- ❑ Loss of Primary Flight Instrument Indicators
- ❑ Airframe and Powerplant Icing
- ❑ Low Fuel Supply
- ❑ Engine Failure

Approaches with Loss of Primary Flight Instrument Indicators
Precision Approach (Partial Panel)
❏ ILS Approaches
❏ RNAV (GPS) Approaches (to LPV minimums with a DA less than 300 feet HAT)
Nonprecision Approach (Partial Panel)
❏ Localizer Approaches
❏ RNAV (GPS) Approaches
❏ VOR and VOR/DME Approaches

NOTE: *Perform specific holding and approach procedures as needed.*

COMPLETION STANDARDS

Demonstrate instrument pilot knowledge and proficiency in each of the listed tasks at the level required by the Instrument Rating Airman Certification Standards.

POSTFLIGHT DEBRIEFING

❏ Critique maneuvers/procedures and SRM.
❏ Create a plan for skills that need improvement.
❏ Update the record folder and logbook.

STUDY ASSIGNMENT

Ground Lesson 25

Stage III Exam

FLIGHT LESSON 28

DUAL — LOCAL
STAGE III CHECK

NOTE: *This flight may be conducted as a short cross-country or as a local flight in which the student establishes the airplane on a course for a planned cross-country flight to demonstrate proficiency in cross-country operations.*

OBJECTIVES

Demonstrate to the chief instructor, the assistant chief instructor, or the designated check instructor:

- Proficiency in planning and implementing an IFR cross-country flight.
- Proficiency in managing emergency procedures in the IFR cross-country environment.
- Proficiency in SRM skills by effectively managing risk and making decisions during IFR cross-country operations.

PREFLIGHT DISCUSSION

Conduct for the Stage III Check, including:
❏ Maneuvers and Procedures
❏ Acceptable Performance Criteria
❏ Applicable Rules

EVALUATE

IFR CROSS-COUNTRY FLIGHT

PREFLIGHT PREPARATION

Weather Information

- ❏ Departure, Enroute, Alternate, and Destination Meteorology
- ❏ Alternate Requirements

Cross-Country Flight Planning

- ❏ Route Planning and Alternate Selection
- ❏ Altitude Selection
- ❏ Weight and Balance
- ❏ Performance and Limitations
- ❏ Determining ETA
- ❏ Fuel Requirements
- ❏ Sources of Flight Information
- ❏ SIDs, ODPs, and STARs
- ❏ Navigation Log
- ❏ IFR Flight Plan
- ❏ Airframe Icing Considerations

IFR CROSS-COUNTRY FLIGHT

ATC CLEARANCES AND PROCEDURES

- ❏ Clearance Copying and Readback
- ❏ Compliance with ATC Clearances—Departure, Enroute, Arrival, Approach
- ❏ Holding Procedures

PREFLIGHT PROCEDURES

Airplane Flight Instruments and Navigation Equipment

- ❏ GPS Programming
- ❏ VOR Equipment Operation

NAVIGATION SYSTEMS

Intercepting and Tracking Navigational Systems and Arcs (Full Panel and Partial Panel)

- ❏ GPS Course Interception and Tracking
- ❏ VOR Radial Interception and Tracking
- ❏ Localizer Course Interception and Tracking
- ❏ Intercepting and Tracking DME Arcs
- ❏ Autopilot Use for Navigation, if Equipped

Departure, Enroute, and Arrival Operations

- ❏ Standard Instrument Departure (SID)
- ❏ Obstacle Departure Procedure (ODP)
- ❏ Standard Terminal Arrival (STAR)
- ❏ Checklist Use
- ❏ Radio Communications
- ❏ ATC Services
- ❏ Use of Flight Deck Displays—Weather and Aeronautical Information

INSTRUMENT APPROACH PROCEDURES

Precision Approach

❏ ILS Approaches
❏ RNAV (GPS) Approaches (to LPV minimums with a DA less than 300 feet HAT)

Nonprecision Approach

❏ Localizer Approaches
❏ RNAV (GPS) Approaches
❏ VOR and VOR/DME Approaches

Approach Procedures

❏ Procedure Turn/Course Reversal
❏ Terminal Arrival Area (TAA)
❏ Vectors to the Approach Course
❏ Approach Procedure to Straight-In or Circling Landing Minimums
❏ Circling Approach
❏ Missed Approach

Landing from an Instrument Approach

❏ Straight-In Landing
❏ Circling Approach
❏ Wake Turbulence Avoidance
❏ Wind Shear Avoidance
❏ Land and Hold Short Operations (LAHSO)

EMERGENCY OPERATIONS

❏ Loss of Communications
❏ Systems and Equipment Malfunctions
❏ Loss of Primary Flight Instrument Indicators
❏ Airframe and Powerplant Icing
❏ Low Fuel Supply
❏ Engine Failure

Approaches with Loss of Primary Flight Instrument Indicators

Precision Approach (Partial Panel)

❏ ILS Approaches
❏ RNAV (GPS) Approaches (to LPV minimums with a DA less than 300 feet HAT)

Nonprecision Approach (Partial Panel)

❏ Localizer Approaches
❏ RNAV (GPS) Approaches
❏ VOR and VOR/DME Approaches

NOTE: *Perform specific holding and approach procedures as needed.*

COMPLETION STANDARDS

- Demonstrate proficiency in all the listed tasks as required by the Instrument Rating Airman Certification Standards.
- Demonstrate proficiency in using SRM to make effective decisions, maintain situational awareness, prevent CFIT, and manage risk, tasks, and automation.

POSTFLIGHT DEBRIEFING

❏ Evaluate maneuvers/procedures and SRM.
❏ Plan additional instruction for skills not meeting Stage III completion standards.
❏ Update the record folder and logbook.

STUDY ASSIGNMENT

Ground Lesson 26

Instrument Rating End-of-Course Exam.

FLIGHT LESSON 29

DUAL — LOCAL

END-OF-COURSE FLIGHT CHECK FOR COURSE COMPLETION

OBJECTIVES

Demonstrate to the chief instructor, the assistant chief instructor, or the designated check instructor:

- Proficiency in all the listed tasks as required by the Instrument Rating Airman Certification Standards.
- Proficiency in SRM skills by effectively managing risk and making decisions.

PREFLIGHT DISCUSSION

Conduct for the End-of-Course Flight Check, including

❑ Maneuvers and Procedures
❑ Acceptable Performance Criteria
❑ Applicable Rules

EVALUATE

PREFLIGHT PREPARATION

❑ Pilot Qualifications
❑ Weather Information
❑ Cross-Country Flight Planning

PREFLIGHT PROCEDURES

❑ Airplane Systems Related to IFR Operations
❑ Airplane Flight Instruments and Navigation Equipment
❑ Instrument Flight Deck Check

AIR TRAFFIC CONTROL CLEARANCES AND PROCEDURES

❑ Clearance Copying and Readback
❑ Compliance with ATC Clearances—Departure, Enroute, Arrival, Approach

Holding Procedures

❑ VOR Holding
❑ GPS Holding
❑ Localizer Holding
❑ Intersection Holding

FLIGHT BY REFERENCE TO INSTRUMENTS

Instrument Flight (Full Panel and Partial Panel)

❑ Straight-and-Level Flight
❑ Standard-Rate Turns

- ❑ Constant Rate Climbs and Descents
- ❑ Constant Airspeed Climbs and Descents
- ❑ Timed Turns to Magnetic Compass Headings
- ❑ Magnetic Compass Turns
- ❑ Autopilot Use, if Equipped

Recovery From Unusual Flight Attitudes

- ❑ Nose- High Unusual Attitude
- ❑ Nose-Low Unusual Attitude

NAVIGATION SYSTEMS

Intercepting and Tracking Navigational Systems and Arcs (Full Panel and Partial Panel)

- ❑ GPS Course Interception and Tracking
- ❑ VOR Radial Interception and Tracking
- ❑ Localizer Course Interception and Tracking
- ❑ Intercepting and Tracking DME Arcs
- ❑ Autopilot Use for Navigation, if Equipped

Departure, Enroute, and Arrival Operations

- ❑ Standard Instrument Departure (SID)
- ❑ Obstacle Departure Procedure (ODP)
- ❑ Standard Terminal Arrival (STAR)
- ❑ Checklist Use
- ❑ Radio Communications
- ❑ ATC Services
- ❑ Use of Flight Deck Displays—Weather and Aeronautical Information

INSTRUMENT APPROACH PROCEDURES

Precision Approach

- ❑ ILS Approaches
- ❑ RNAV (GPS) Approaches (to LPV minimums with a DA less than 300 feet HAT)

Nonprecision Approach

- ❑ Localizer Approaches
- ❑ RNAV (GPS) Approaches
- ❑ VOR and VOR/DME Approaches

Approach Procedures

- ❑ Procedure Turn/Course Reversal
- ❑ Terminal Arrival Area (TAA)
- ❑ Vectors to the Approach Course
- ❑ Approach Procedure to Straight-In or Circling Landing Minimums
- ❑ Circling Approach
- ❑ Missed Approach

Landing from an Instrument Approach

- ❑ Straight-In Landing
- ❑ Circling Approach
- ❑ Wake Turbulence Avoidance
- ❑ Wind Shear Avoidance
- ❑ Land and Hold Short Operations (LAHSO)

EMERGENCY OPERATIONS

- ❑ Loss of Communications
- ❑ Systems and Equipment Malfunctions

- ❑ Loss of Primary Flight Instrument Indicators
- ❑ Airframe and Powerplant Icing
- ❑ Low Fuel Supply
- ❑ Engine Failure

Approaches with Loss of Primary Flight Instrument Indicators

Precision Approach (Partial Panel)

- ❑ ILS Approaches
- ❑ RNAV (GPS) Approaches (to LPV minimums with a DA less than 300 feet HAT)

Nonprecision Approach (Partial Panel)

- ❑ Localizer Approaches
- ❑ RNAV (GPS) Approaches
- ❑ VOR and VOR/DME Approaches

NOTE: *Perform specific holding and approach procedures as needed.*

POSTFLIGHT PROCEDURES

- ❑ Checking Instruments and Equipment

COMPLETION STANDARDS

- Demonstrate proficiency in all instrument rating tasks as required by the Instrument Rating Airman Certification Standards.
- Demonstrate the ability to use single-pilot resource management to make effective decisions, maintain situational awareness, prevent CFIT, and manage risk, tasks, and automation.

POSTFLIGHT DEBRIEFING

- ❑ Evaluate maneuvers/procedures and SRM.
- ❑ Plan additional instruction for skills not meeting course completion standards.
- ❑ Update the record folder and logbook.

Commercial Pilot Ground Training Syllabus

GROUND TRAINING COURSE OBJECTIVES

The student will obtain the aeronautical knowledge required by FAR Part 141 and Part 61 for commercial pilot certification and meet the prerequisites in Part 61 for the FAA Commercial Pilot Airman Knowledge Test.

GROUND TRAINING COURSE COMPLETION STANDARDS

Through knowledge exams and records, the student must demonstrate the aeronautical knowledge required by FAR Part 141 and Part 61 for commercial pilot certification. The student must also demonstrate the knowledge necessary to pass the FAA Commercial Pilot Airman Knowledge Test and show that the prerequisites specified in Part 61 have been met.

Stage I

STAGE OBJECTIVES

During this stage, the student increases knowledge of airports, airspace, flight information, and meteorology, as well as airplane performance, VFR cross-country flight planning, and navigation. In addition, the student gains a greater understanding of aviation physiology, single-pilot resource management (SRM) and the FARs applicable to commercial pilot operations.

STAGE COMPLETION STANDARDS

The student must pass the Stage I Exam with a minimum score of 80 percent, and review each incorrect response with the instructor to ensure complete understanding before starting Stage II.

NOTE: *Students should read Chapter 1, Section B — Commercial Pilot Requirements prior to Ground Lesson 27.*

GROUND LESSON 27

REFERENCES

Instrument/Commercial Textbook/e-Book
Chapter 1 — Building Professional Experience
Section B — Commercial Pilot Requirements

OBJECTIVES

Lesson Objective	Part 141/61 Aeronautical Knowledge	ACS Task
Recognize the certification requirements for a commercial certificate. Recognize the privileges and limitations of a commercial pilot certificate.	Applicable Federal Aviation Regulations for IFR flight operations	Pilot Qualifications

CONTENT

COURSE OVERVIEW

- ❑ Course Components
- ❑ Exams and Tests
- ❑ Policies and Procedures
- ❑ Student/Instructor Expectations

SECTION B — COMMERCIAL PILOT REQUIREMENTS

COMMERCIAL PILOT CAREERS

- ❑ Regional and Major Airline Qualifications
- ❑ Additional Job Qualifications

COMMERCIAL PILOT TRAINING

- ❑ Complex Airplane
- ❑ Technically Advanced Airplane (TAA)
- ❑ High Performance Airplane

COMMERCIAL PILOT PRIVILEGES

- ❑ Commercial Operations Regulations
- ❑ Medical Requirements
- ❑ Currency Requirements
- ❑ FAA WINGS—Pilot Proficiency Program

AIRWORTHINESS REQUIREMENTS

- ❑ Required Maintenance and Inspections
- ❑ Airworthiness Directives
- ❑ Aircraft Equipment Required for VFR
- ❑ Inoperative Instruments and Equipment
- ❑ Special Flight Permit

ADDITIONAL CERTIFICATES AND RATINGS

- ❑ Multi-Engine Rating
- ❑ Certificated Flight Instructor
- ❑ Airline Transport Pilot Certificate
- ❑ Additional Certificates and Ratings

COMPLETION STANDARDS

- Demonstrate understanding of commercial pilot training, and medical and currency requirements.
- Demonstrate understanding of airplane airworthiness requirements, including the required equipment and inspections, and the procedures for operating with inoperative equipment.

- Demonstrate understanding of additional certificates and ratings that apply to the commercial pilot.
- Complete with a minimum score of 80 percent: questions for Chapter 1B. Review each incorrect response with the instructor to ensure complete understanding before starting Ground Lesson 28.

STUDY ASSIGNMENT

Instrument/Commercial Textbook/e-Book

Chapter 3 — The Flight Environment

Section A — Airports, Airspace, and Flight Information

Commercial Pilot Online

GL — The Flight Environment

GROUND LESSON 28

REFERENCES

Instrument/Commercial Textbook/e-Book

Chapter 3 — The Flight Environment

Section A — Airports, Airspace, and Flight Information

Commercial Pilot Online

GL — The Flight Environment

***NOTE:** Students enrolled in the combined Instrument/Commercial Course are not required to accomplish the review of Chapter 3A or GL — The Flight Environment.*

OBJECTIVES

Lesson Objective	Part 141/61 Aeronautical Knowledge	ACS Task
Interpret airport markings, lighting, and signs. Identify procedures to avoid runway incursions and to perform land and hold short operations (LAHSO). Explain the structure and requirements of the National Airspace System. Recognize sources of flight information.	Procedures for operating within the National Airspace System	National Airspace System Communications, Light Signals, and Runway Lighting Systems

CONTENT

THE AIRPORT ENVIRONMENT

- ❑ Runway and Taxiway Markings and Signs
- ❑ Runway Incursion Avoidance
- ❑ Land and Hold Short Operations (LAHSO)
- ❑ Approach Light System
- ❑ Visual Glideslope Indicators
- ❑ Runway Lighting
- ❑ Airport Beacons and Obstruction Lights
- ❑ Aircraft Lighting
- ❑ Airport Security

AIRSPACE

- ❑ Uncontrolled Airspace (Class G)
- ❑ Controlled Airspace (Class A, B, C, D, and E)
- ❑ Special VFR
- ❑ Airspeed Limitations
- ❑ Special Use Airspace
- ❑ Other Airspace Areas
- ❑ Temporary Flight Restrictions (TFRs)
- ❑ Air Defense Identification Zone (ADIZ)
- ❑ Washington DC Special Flight Rules Area (SFRA)
- ❑ Intercept Procedures

FLIGHT INFORMATION

- ❑ Aeronautical Charts—VFR and IFR
- ❑ Chart Supplements
- ❑ Airport/Facility Directory
- ❑ Electronic Flight Bag (EFB)
- ❑ Notices to Airman (NOTAMs)
- ❑ Federal Aviation Regulations (FARs)
- ❑ *Aeronautical Information Manual* (AIM)
- ❑ Advisory Circulars

COMPLETION STANDARDS

- Demonstrate understanding of the airport environment, airspace, and flight information during oral quizzing by the instructor.
- Complete with a minimum score of 80 percent: questions for Chapter 3A; or GL — The Flight Environment. Review each incorrect response with the instructor to ensure complete understanding before starting Ground Lesson 29.

NOTE: *Students enrolled in the combined Instrument/Commercial Course are not required to complete the questions for Chapter 3A or online exam for GL — The Flight Environment .*

STUDY ASSIGNMENT

Instrument/Commercial Textbook/e-Book

Chapter 9 — Meteorology

Commercial Pilot Online

GL — Weather

GROUND LESSON 29

REFERENCES

Instrument/Commercial Textbook/EBook
Chapter 9 — Meteorology

Commercial Pilot Online — Jeppesen Learning Center
GL — Weather

NOTE: Students enrolled in the combined Instrument/Commercial Course are not required to accomplish the review of Chapter 9 or GL — Weather.

OBJECTIVES

Lesson Objective	Part 141/61 Aeronautical Knowledge	ACS Task
Explain the weather patterns and hazards related to flight operations. Recognize how to obtain and interpret aviation weather reports and forecasts, and graphic weather products for flight planning. Recognize how to obtain preflight and in-flight sources of weather information.	Meteorology to include recognition of critical weather situations, wind shear recognition and avoidance, and the use of aeronautical weather reports and forecasts	Weather Information

CONTENT

SECTION A — WEATHER FACTORS

GL — WEATHER

- ❑ The Atmosphere
- ❑ Atmospheric Circulation
- ❑ Moisture, Precipitation, and Stability
- ❑ Types of Clouds
- ❑ Air Mass
- ❑ Fronts
- ❑ High Altitude Weather

SECTION B — WEATHER HAZARDS AND ICE CONTROL SYSTEMS

GL — WEATHER

WEATHER HAZARDS

- ❑ Thunderstorms
- ❑ Hydroplaning
- ❑ Low Level Turbulence
- ❑ Wake Turbulence
- ❑ Clear Air Turbulence

- ❑ Mountain Wave Turbulence
- ❑ Reporting Turbulence
- ❑ Wind Shear
- ❑ Low Visibility
- ❑ Volcanic Ash
- ❑ Cold Weather Operations
- ❑ Icing

ICE CONTROL SYSTEMS

- ❑ Airfoil Ice Control
- ❑ Windshield Ice Control
- ❑ Propeller Ice Control
- ❑ Other Ice Control Systems

SECTION C — AVIATION WEATHER REPORTS AND FORECASTS

GL — WEATHER

OBSERVATIONS

- ❑ Aviation Routine Weather Report (METAR)
- ❑ Pilot Weather Reports (PIREPs)

FORECASTS

- ❑ Terminal Aerodrome Forecast (TAF)
- ❑ Winds and Temperatures Aloft Forecast
- ❑ AIRMETs and SIGMETs
- ❑ Severe Weather Reports and Forecasts

SECTION D — GRAPHIC WEATHER PRODUCTS

GL — WEATHER

OBSERVATIONS

- ❑ Radar Observations
- ❑ Satellite Imagery
- ❑ Graphic Depictions of METARs

ANALYSIS

- ❑ Surface Analysis Chart
- ❑ Ceiling and Visibility Analysis (CVA)

FORECASTS

- ❑ Aviation Forecasts
- ❑ Short-Range Surface Prognostic (Prog) Charts
- ❑ U.S. Low-Level Significant Weather (SIGWX) Chart
- ❑ Mid- and High Level SIGWX Charts
- ❑ Wind and Temperature Aloft Forecast
- ❑ Freezing-Level Graphics
- ❑ Current and Forecast Icing Products (CIP/FIP)
- ❑ G-AIRMET
- ❑ Graphical Forecast for Aviation (GFA) Tool

SECTION E — SOURCES OF WEATHER INFORMATION

GL — WEATHER

- ❑ Preflight Weather Sources
- ❑ Flight Service

- ❑ National Weather Service
- ❑ In-Flight Weather Sources
- ❑ Weather Radar Services
- ❑ Center Weather Advisory (CWA)
- ❑ Automated Weather Reporting Systems
- ❑ Data Link Weather
- ❑ Airborne Weather Radar

COMPLETION STANDARDS

- Demonstrate understanding of weather factors, weather hazards, aviation weather reports and forecasts, graphic weather products, and the sources of weather information during oral quizzing by the instructor.
- Complete with a minimum score of 80 percent: questions for Chapter 9; or online exams for GL — Weather. Review each incorrect response with the instructor to ensure complete understanding before starting Ground Lesson 30.

NOTE: *Students enrolled in the combined Instrument/Commercial Course are not required to complete the questions for Chapter 9 or online exams for GL — Weather.*

STUDY ASSIGNMENT

Review pilotage and dead reckoning methods for VFR cross-country flight planning and navigation.

Instrument/Commercial Textbook/e-Book

Chapter 2 — Principles of Instrument Flight
Section D — Instrument Navigation

GROUND LESSON 30

REFERENCES

Instrument/Commercial Textbook/e-Book
Chapter 2 — Principles of Instrument Flight
Section D — Instrument Navigation

OBJECTIVES

Lesson Objective	Part 141/61 Aeronautical Knowledge	ACS Task
Increase proficiency in using pilotage and dead reckoning for VFR cross-country flight planning and navigation. Increase proficiency in VFR flight planning, including selecting the proper VFR cruising altitudes, creating a route, and lost procedures.	Use of aeronautical charts and a magnetic compass for pilotage and dead reckoning Procedures for operating within the National Airspace System	Cross-Country Flight Planning National Airspace System
Explain the operation and limitations of VOR, DME, and GPS equipment. Explain how to navigate using VOR, DME, and GPS equipment.	Use of air navigation facilities	Pilotage and Dead Reckoning Navigation Systems and Radar Services

CONTENT

CROSS-COUNTRY FLIGHT PLANNING

- ❑ Route Planning
- ❑ Altitude Selection
- ❑ Weight and Balance
- ❑ Performance and Limitations
- ❑ Determining ETA
- ❑ Fuel Requirements
- ❑ Sources of Flight Information
- ❑ Navigation Log
- ❑ VFR Flight Plan

NAVIGATION

- ❑ Pilotage and Dead Reckoning
- ❑ Lost Procedures
- ❑ Diversion

SECTION D — INSTRUMENT NAVIGATION

VOR NAVIGATION

- ❑ Horizontal Situation Indicator
- ❑ Intercepting a Course
- ❑ Tracking
- ❑ Determining Your Progress
- ❑ Station Passage
- ❑ VOR Operational Considerations
- ❑ VOR Checks
- ❑ Distance Measuring Equipment
- ❑ DME Arcs

AREA NAVIGATION (RNAV)

- ❑ Required Navigation Performance (RNP)
- ❑ Inertial Navigation System (INS)
- ❑ Flight Management Systems (FMS)

SATELLITE NAVIGATION — GPS

- ❑ Trilateration
- ❑ Wide Area Augmentation System (WAAS)
- ❑ Ground-Based Augmentation System (GBAS)
- ❑ Requirements for IFR GPS Navigation
- ❑ Navigating with GPS

COMPLETION STANDARDS

- Demonstrate understanding of the pilotage and dead reckoning methods for VFR cross-country flight planning and navigation and navigating with VOR and GPS equipment during oral quizzing by the instructor before starting Ground Lesson 31.
- Complete with a minimum score of 80 percent: questions for Chapter 2D. With the instructor, review each incorrect response to ensure complete understanding before starting Ground Lesson 5.

NOTE: *Students enrolled in the combined Instrument/Commercial Course are not required to complete the questions for Chapter 2D.*

STUDY ASSIGNMENT

Instrument/Commercial Textbook/e-Book

Chapter 1 — Building Professional Experience
Section C — Aviation Physiology

Commercial Pilot Online

GL — Advanced Human Factors

GROUND LESSON 31

REFERENCES

Instrument/Commercial Textbook/e-Book

Chapter 1 — Building Professional Experience
Section C — Aviation Physiology
Section D — SRM Concepts

Commercial Pilot Online

GL — Advanced Human Factors

OBJECTIVES

Lesson Objective	Part 141/61 Aeronautical Knowledge	ACS Task
Explain the causes, symptoms, and prevention of aviation physiology factors, including disorientation, hypoxia, and hyperventilation. Explain how aviation physiology factors apply to operations in the commercial flight environment, including night vision and high-altitude operations.	Night and high-altitude operations	Human Factors
Become familiar with the human factors concepts that affect aeronautical decision making and judgment. Become familiar with the single-pilot resource management (SRM) techniques that increase flight safety.	Aeronautical decision making and judgment	Human Factors

CONTENT

SECTION C — AVIATION PHYSIOLOGY

GL — ADVANCED HUMAN FACTORS

VISION IN FLIGHT

- ❑ Night Vision
- ❑ Dark Adaptation
- ❑ Visual Illusions

SPATIAL DISORIENTATION

- ❑ Vestibular System
- ❑ Motion Sickness

HYPOXIA

- ❑ Hypoxic Hypoxia
- ❑ Hypoxia—Hypemic, Stagnant, Histotoxic
- ❑ Prevention of Hypoxia
- ❑ Supplemental Oxygen
- ❑ High Altitude Training

PRESSURE EFFECTS

- ❑ Ear and Sinus Block
- ❑ Decompression Sickness

HYPERVENTILATION

- ❑ Cause and Symptoms
- ❑ Prevention

FITNESS FOR FLIGHT
- ❑ Stress
- ❑ Fatigue
- ❑ Dehydration
- ❑ Alcohol and Drugs
- ❑ Hypothermia

SECTION D — SRM CONCEPTS
- ❑ Aeronautical Decision Making
- ❑ Risk Management
- ❑ Task Management
- ❑ Situational Awareness
- ❑ CFIT Awareness
- ❑ Automation Management

COMPLETION STANDARDS
- Demonstrate understanding of the causes, symptoms, and prevention of physiological factors affecting flight operations and SRM concepts during oral quizzing by the instructor before starting Ground Lesson 32.
- Complete with a minimum score of 80 percent: questions for Chapter 1C and 1D; or online exam for GL — Advanced Human Factors. With the instructor, review each incorrect response to ensure complete understanding before starting Ground Lesson 32.

NOTE: *Students enrolled in the combined Instrument/Commercial Course are not required to complete the questions for Chapter 1C.*

STUDY ASSIGNMENT
FAR/AIM
Commercial FARs

Commercial Pilot Online
GL — Commercial FARs

GROUND LESSON 32

REFERENCES
FAR/AIM
Commercial FARs

Commercial Pilot Online
GL — Commercial FARs

OBJECTIVES

Lesson Objective	Part 141/61 Aeronautical Knowledge	ACS Task
Explain the regulations that apply to the requirements for commercial pilot certification and operations in FAR Part 61 and FAR Part 119. Explain the general operating and flight rules that apply to commercial flight operations in FAR Part 91.	Applicable Federal Aviation Regulations of this chapter that relate to commercial pilot privileges, limitations, and flight operations	Pilot Qualifications Airworthiness Requirements
Define the terms used in NTSB 830. List the incidents and accidents that require NTSB notification and the information that must be given in notification.	Accident reporting requirements of the National Transportation Safety Board	Communications, Light Signals, and Runway Lighting Systems

CONTENT

FAR/AIM

GL — COMMERCIAL FARS

COMMERCIAL FARS

- ❑ FAR Part 1
- ❑ FAR Part 61
- ❑ FAR Part 91
- ❑ FAR Part 119
- ❑ NTSB Part 830

COMPLETION STANDARDS

- Demonstrate understanding of the FARs that apply to commercial operations and NTSB Part 830 during oral quizzing by the instructor.
- Complete with a minimum score of 80 percent: online exams for GL — Commercial FARs. Review each incorrect response with the instructor to ensure complete understanding before taking the Stage I Exam in Ground Lesson 33.

STUDY ASSIGNMENT

Review the content of Ground Lessons 28 – 32 to prepare for the Stage I Exam.

GROUND LESSON 33
STAGE I EXAM

REFERENCES

Ground Lessons 28 – 32

OBJECTIVE

Demonstrate knowledge of the subjects covered in Ground Lessons 28 – 32 by passing the Stage I Exam.

CONTENT

STAGE I EXAM

❑ Commercial Pilot Requirements
❑ Airports, Airspace, and Flight Information
❑ Meteorology
❑ Cross-Country Flight Planning and Instrument Navigation
❑ Aviation Physiology and SRM Concepts
❑ Commercial FARs and NTSB Part 830

COMPLETION STANDARDS

To complete the lesson and stage, pass the Stage I Exam with a minimum score of 80 percent. With the instructor, review each incorrect response to ensure complete understanding before starting Stage II.

STUDY ASSIGNMENT

Instrument/Commercial Textbook/e-Book

Chapter 11 — Advanced Systems
Section A — High-Performance Powerplants

Commercial Pilot Online

GL — High-Performance Powerplants

Stage II

STAGE OBJECTIVES

During this stage, the student learns about the operation of complex airplane systems and electronic flight instrument displays, determines airplane performance and weight and balance, and explores advanced aerodynamics concepts. The student increases knowledge of emergency procedures and using single-pilot resource management (SRM) and crew resource management (CRM) skills to help make effective decisions. In addition, the student learns the steps to perform the flight maneuvers required for commercial pilot certification.

STAGE COMPLETION STANDARDS

The student must pass the Stage II Exam and the Commercial Pilot End-of-Course Exam with a minimum score of 80 percent, and review each incorrect response with the instructor to ensure complete understanding.

GROUND LESSON 34

REFERENCES

Instrument/Commercial Textbook/e-Book
Chapter 11 — Advanced Systems
Section A — High-Performance Powerplants

Commercial Pilot Online — Jeppesen Learning Center
GL — High-Performance Powerplants

OBJECTIVES

Lesson Objective	Part 141/61 Aeronautical Knowledge	ACS Task
Explain the components and operation of a fuel injection system. Describe how a turbocharging system operates. Explain the principles of propeller pitch control and the components and operation of a constant-speed propeller.	Safe and efficient operation of aircraft Principles and functions of aircraft systems	Operation of Systems

CONTENT

FUEL INJECTION SYSTEMS

- ❑ Comparison to Carbureted Systems
- ❑ Fuel Injection System Design and Operation
- ❑ Mixture Control
- ❑ Fuel Pumps
- ❑ Operating Procedures
- ❑ Normal, Hot, and Flooded Starts
- ❑ Engine Shutdown
- ❑ Engine Monitoring
- ❑ Oil Temperature and Pressure Gauges
- ❑ Exhaust Gas Temperature Gauge
- ❑ Cylinder Head Temperature Gauge
- ❑ Abnormal Combustion
- ❑ Induction Icing

TURBOCHARGING SYSTEMS

- ❑ Turbocharging Principles
- ❑ System Operation
- ❑ High Altitude Performance

CONSTANT-SPEED PROPELLERS

- ❑ Propeller Principles
- ❑ Constant-Speed Propeller Operation
- ❑ Power Controls
- ❑ FADEC

COMPLETION STANDARDS

- Demonstrate understanding of fuel injection systems, turbocharging systems, and constant-speed propellers during oral quizzing by the instructor.
- Complete with a minimum score of 80 percent: questions for Chapter 11A or online exam for GL — High-Performance Powerplants. With the instructor, review each incorrect response to ensure complete understanding before starting Ground Lesson 35.

STUDY ASSIGNMENT

Instrument/Commercial Textbook/e-Book

Chapter 11 — Advanced Systems

Section B — Supplemental Oxygen and Pressurization

Commercial Pilot Online

GL — Environmental Systems

GROUND LESSON 35

REFERENCES

Instrument/Commercial Textbook/e-Book
Chapter 11 — Advanced Systems
Section B — Supplemental Oxygen and Pressurization

Commercial Pilot Online
GL — Environmental Systems

OBJECTIVES

Lesson Objective	Part 141/61 Aeronautical Knowledge	ACS Task
Explain the components and operation of aircraft oxygen systems. Describe the components and operation of cabin pressurization systems.	Safe and efficient operation of aircraft Principles and functions of aircraft systems Night and high-altitude operations	Operation of Systems

CONTENT

OXYGEN SYSTEMS

- ❑ Continuous-Flow
- ❑ Connecting and Using Oxygen Equipment
- ❑ Diluter-Demand
- ❑ Pressure-Demand
- ❑ Pulse-Demand
- ❑ Oxygen Storage
- ❑ Oxygen Servicing

CABIN PRESSURIZATION

- ❑ Pressurization Principles
- ❑ Pressurization Components
- ❑ Pressurization Emergencies

COMPLETION STANDARDS

- Demonstrate understanding of oxygen and cabin pressurization systems during oral quizzing by the instructor.
- Complete with a minimum score of 80 percent: questions for Chapter 11B or online exam for GL — Environmental Systems. With the instructor, review each incorrect response to ensure complete understanding before starting Ground Lesson 36.

STUDY ASSIGNMENT

Instrument/Commercial Textbook/e-Book

Chapter 11 — Advanced Systems
Section C — Retractable Landing Gear

Commercial Pilot Online

GL — Retractable Landing Gear

TAA Option

Chapter 2 — Principles of Instrument Flight
Section B — Electronic Flight Displays

GROUND LESSON 36

***NOTE:** If you selected the technically advanced airplane (TAA) option by checking the appropriate box in the Preface and are not enrolled in the combined Instrument/Commercial Course; include the lesson content indicated as TAA Option in Ground Lesson 36.*

REFERENCES

Instrument/Commercial Textbook/e-Book

Chapter 11 — Advanced Systems
Section C — Retractable Landing Gear

TAA Option

Chapter 2 — Principles of Instrument Flight
Section B — Electronic Flight Displays

Commercial Pilot Online

GL — Retractable Landing Gear

OBJECTIVES

Lesson Objective	Part 141/61 Aeronautical Knowledge	ACS Task
Explain the components and operation of retractable landing gear systems.	Safe and efficient operation of aircraft	Operation of Systems
Describe gear system malfunctions and the operation of the emergency gear extension system.	Principles and functions of aircraft systems	
TAA Option		
Explain the function and operation of electronic flight instruments and components.		
Recognize the limitations and common errors of electronic flight instrument displays.		

CONTENT

CHAPTER 11, SECTION C — RETRACTABLE LANDING GEAR

GL — RETRACTABLE LANDING GEAR

LANDING GEAR SYSTEMS
- ❑ Electrical Gear Systems
- ❑ Hydraulic Gear Systems

GEAR SYSTEM SAFETY
- ❑ Gear Position Indicators
- ❑ Gear Warning Horn
- ❑ Safety Switches
- ❑ Airspeed Limitations

OPERATING PROCEDURES
- ❑ Gear System Malfunctions
- ❑ Emergency Gear Extension

TAA OPTION

CHAPTER 2, SECTION B — ELECTRONIC FLIGHT DISPLAYS

PRIMARY FLIGHT DISPLAY (PFD)
- ❑ Attitude and Heading Reference System (AHRS)
- ❑ Attitude Indicator
- ❑ Horizontal Situation Indicator (HSI)
- ❑ Air Data Computer (ADC)
- ❑ Airspeed Indicator
- ❑ Altimeter
- ❑ Vertical Speed Indicator (VSI)
- ❑ PFD Failure

MULTIFUNCTION DISPLAY (MFD)
- ❑ Features
- ❑ Map Display

AUTOMATION
- ❑ Operation
- ❑ Flight Director

COMPLETION STANDARDS
- Demonstrate understanding of the components and operation of retractable landing gear systems during oral quizzing by the instructor.
- Complete with a minimum score of 80 percent: questions for Chapter 11C or online exam for GL — Retractable Landing Gear. With the instructor, review each incorrect response to ensure complete understanding before starting Ground Lesson 37.

TAA OPTION

- Demonstrate understanding of electronic flight displays during oral quizzing by the instructor.
- Complete with a minimum score of 80 percent: questions for Chapter 2B. With the instructor, review each incorrect response to ensure complete understanding before starting Ground Lesson 37.

STUDY ASSIGNMENT

Instrument/Commercial Textbook/e-Book

Chapter 12 — Aerodynamics and Performance Limitations
  Section A — Advanced Aerodynamics
Chapter 14 — Commercial Maneuvers
  Section A — Accelerated Stalls

Commercial Pilot Online

GL — Aerodynamic Principles
GL — Aerodynamic Considerations
ML — Accelerated Stalls

GROUND LESSON 37

REFERENCES

Instrument/Commercial Textbook/e-Book

Chapter 12 — Aerodynamics and Performance Limitations
  Section A — Advanced Aerodynamics
Chapter 14 — Commercial Maneuvers
  Section A — Accelerated Stalls

Commercial Pilot Online

GL — Aerodynamic Principles
GL — Aerodynamic Considerations
ML — Accelerated Stalls

OBJECTIVES

Lesson Objective	Part 141/61 Aeronautical Knowledge	ACS Task
Explain how airplane design and operation affect the forces of lift, weight, thrust, and drag. Describe how weight and load factor affect the airplane's flight characteristics. Explain how airplane design and operation affect longitudinal, lateral, and directional stability. Recognize the aerodynamic characteristics of the airplane in maneuvering flight. Identify the causes of and recovery procedures for stalls and spins. Recognize the procedures and performance considerations necessary to perform and recover from accelerated stalls.	Basic aerodynamics and the principles of flight Significance and effects of exceeding aircraft performance limitations	Performance and Limitations **Aerodynamics associated with:** Steep Turns Chandelles Lazy Eights Eights on Pylons Maneuvering During Slow Flight Power-Off Stalls Power-On Stalls Accelerated Stalls Spin Awareness

CONTENT

CHAPTER 12, SECTION A — ADVANCED AERODYNAMICS

GL — AERODYNAMIC PRINCIPLES

LIFT
- ❑ Lift Equation
- ❑ Controlling Lift
- ❑ High-Lift Devices

DRAG
- ❑ Induced Drag
- ❑ Ground Effect
- ❑ Parasite Drag
- ❑ Total Drag
- ❑ Maximum Range
- ❑ High-Drag Devices

THRUST
- ❑ Propeller Efficiency
- ❑ Maximum Level Flight Speed

WEIGHT AND LOAD FACTOR
- ❑ Load Factor
- ❑ Maneuvering Speed
- ❑ V-g Diagram

AIRFRAME ICING
- ❑ Aerodynamic Effects

AIRCRAFT STABILITY
- ❑ Static Stability
- ❑ Dynamic Stability
- ❑ Longitudinal Stability
- ❑ Lateral Stability
- ❑ Directional Stability

CHAPTER 12, SECTION A — ADVANCED AERODYNAMICS

GL — AERODYNAMIC CONSIDERATIONS

MANEUVERING FLIGHT
- ❑ Straight-and-Level Flight
- ❑ Climbs
- ❑ Glides
- ❑ Turns

STALL AND SPIN AWARENESS
- ❑ Boundary Layer
- ❑ Causes and Types of Stalls
- ❑ Stall Recognition and Recovery
- ❑ Spin Causes and Phases
- ❑ Spin Recovery

HIGH SPEED FLIGHT
- ❑ Subsonic Versus Supersonic Flow
- ❑ Speed Ranges
- ❑ Shock Waves
- ❑ Maximum Operating Limit Speed
- ❑ Vortex Generators
- ❑ Sweepback

CHAPTER 14, SECTION A — ACCELERATED STALLS

ML — ACCELERATED STALLS

ACCELERATED STALLS
- ❑ Description
- ❑ Procedure

COMPLETION STANDARDS

- Demonstrate understanding of the four forces of flight, aircraft stability, the aerodynamics of flight maneuvers, stall and spin awareness, and high speed flight during oral quizzing by the instructor.
- Complete with a minimum score of 80 percent: questions for Chapter 12A and 14A; or online exams for GL — Aerodynamic Principles and GL — Aerodynamic Considerations. With the instructor, review each incorrect response to ensure complete understanding before starting Ground Lesson 39.

STUDY ASSIGNMENT

Instrument/Commercial Textbook/e-Book

Chapter 12 — Aerodynamics and Performance Limitations

Section B — Predicting Performance

Commercial Pilot Online

GL — Predicting Performance

GROUND LESSON 38

REFERENCES

Instrument/Commercial Textbook/e-Book
Chapter 12 — Aerodynamics and Performance Limitations
Section B — Predicting Performance

Commercial Pilot Online
GL — Predicting Performance

OBJECTIVES

Lesson Objective	Part 141/61 Aeronautical Knowledge	ACS Task
Identify the factors that affect airplane performance. Determine airplane performance using performance charts in the Pilot's Operating Handbook (POH) or Airplane Flight Manual (AFM).	Use of performance charts Significance and effects of exceeding aircraft performance limitations	Performance and Limitations

CONTENT

FACTORS AFFECTING PERFORMANCE

- ❑ Density Altitude
- ❑ Surface Winds
- ❑ Weight
- ❑ Runway Conditions

PILOT'S OPERATING HANDBOOK

- ❑ Performance Charts
- ❑ Takeoff Charts
- ❑ Climb Performance Charts
- ❑ Cruise Performance Charts
- ❑ Descent Charts
- ❑ Landing Distance Charts
- ❑ Glide Distance
- ❑ Stall Speeds

COMPLETION STANDARDS

- Demonstrate understanding of the factors that affect airplane performance and be able to determine airplane performance using charts during oral quizzing by the instructor.
- Complete with a minimum score of 80 percent: questions for Chapter 12B or online exam for GL — Predicting Performance. With the instructor, review each incorrect response to ensure complete understanding before starting Ground Lesson 39.

STUDY ASSIGNMENT

Instrument/Commercial Textbook/e-Book
Chapter 12 — Aerodynamics and Performance Limitations
Section C — Controlling Weight and Balance

Commercial Pilot Online
GL — Weight and Balance

GROUND LESSON 39

REFERENCES

Instrument/Commercial Textbook/e-Book
Chapter 12 — Aerodynamics and Performance Limitations
Section C — Controlling Weight and Balance

Commercial Pilot Online
GL — Weight and Balance

OBJECTIVES

Lesson Objective	Part 141/61 Aeronautical Knowledge	ACS Task
Recognize how the weight and balance condition affects airplane performance. Determine the airplane's weight and balance condition using the computation, graph, and table methods.	Weight and balance computations	Performance and Limitations

CONTENT

WEIGHT AND BALANCE LIMITATIONS
- ❑ Maximum Weight Limits
- ❑ Center of Gravity (CG) Limits
- ❑ Forward CG Effects
- ❑ Aft CG Effects
- ❑ Lateral CG Effects

WEIGHT AND BALANCE DOCUMENTS
- ❏ Weight and Balance Report
- ❏ Equipment List

WEIGHT AND BALANCE COMPUTATIONS
- ❏ Moment Computations
- ❏ Determining Center of Gravity Position

WEIGHT AND BALANCE CONDITION CHECKS
- ❏ Computation Method
- ❏ Graph Method
- ❏ Table Method
- ❏ Weight Shift Computation

COMPLETION STANDARDS

- Demonstrate understanding of how weight and balance affects airplane performance and determine the airplane's weight and balance condition using the computation, graph, and table methods during oral quizzing by the instructor.
- Complete with a minimum score of 80 percent: questions for Chapter 12C or online exam for GL — Weight and Balance. With the instructor, review each incorrect response to ensure complete understanding before starting Ground Lesson 40.

STUDY ASSIGNMENT

Instrument/Commercial Textbook/e-Book
Chapter 13 — Commercial Flight Considerations
Section A — Emergency Operations

Commercial Pilot Online
GL — Emergency Situations

GROUND LESSON 40

REFERENCES

Instrument/Commercial Textbook/e-Book
Chapter 13 — Commercial Flight Considerations
Section A — Emergency Operations

Commercial Pilot Online
GL — Emergency Situations

OBJECTIVES

Lesson Objective	Part 141/61 Aeronautical Knowledge	ACS Task
Explain the procedures used to manage systems and equipment malfunctions and emergency situations. Identify the reasons for an emergency descent and explain how to perform this procedure. Describe emergency landing procedures and the items that should be included with emergency equipment and survival gear.	Safe and efficient operation of aircraft Maneuvers, procedures, and emergency operations appropriate to the aircraft	Systems and Equipment Malfunctions Emergency Descent Emergency Approach and Landing (Simulated) Emergency Equipment and Survival Gear

CONTENT

❑ Partial Power Loss

SYSTEMS AND EQUIPMENT MALFUNCTIONS

❑ Electrical System Malfunction
❑ Gyroscopic Instrument Malfunction
❑ Pitot-Static System Malfunction
❑ Electronic Flight Deck Display Malfunction
❑ Flap Malfunction
❑ Landing Gear Malfunction
❑ Loss of Elevator Control
❑ Inoperative Trim
❑ Oxygen System Malfunction

OTHER ABNORMAL/EMERGENCY SITUATIONS

❑ Inadvertent Icing Encounter
❑ Smoke and Fire
❑ Door Opening in Flight
❑ Decompression

EMERGENCY DESCENT

❑ Description
❑ Procedure Steps

EMERGENCY APPROACH AND LANDING

❑ Landing After an Engine Failure—Procedure Steps
❑ Engine Failure After Takeoff—Procedure Steps
❑ Emergency Equipment and Survival Gear

NTSB 830

❑ Accident and Incident Reporting Requirements

COMPLETION STANDARDS

- Demonstrate understanding of emergency operations during oral quizzing by the instructor.
- Complete with a minimum score of 80 percent: questions for Chapter 13A or online exam for GL — Emergency Situations. With the instructor, review each incorrect response to ensure complete understanding before starting Ground Lesson 44.

STUDY ASSIGNMENT

Instrument/Commercial Textbook/e-Book

Chapter 14 — Commercial Maneuvers

Section B — Soft-Field and Short-Field Takeoffs and Landings

Commercial Pilot Online

ML — Maximum Performance Takeoffs and Landings

GROUND LESSON 41

REFERENCES

Instrument/Commercial Textbook/e-Book

Chapter 14 — Commercial Maneuvers

Section B — Soft-Field and Short-Field Takeoffs and Landings

Commercial Pilot Online

ML — Maximum Performance Takeoffs and Landings

OBJECTIVES

Lesson Objective	Part 141/61 Aeronautical Knowledge	ACS Task
Recognize the procedures and performance considerations necessary to perform: • Soft-field takeoffs and climbs. • Soft-field approaches and landings. • Short-field takeoffs and maximum performance climbs. • Short-field approaches, and landings.	Maneuvers, procedures, and emergency operations appropriate to the aircraft	Soft-Field Takeoff and Climb Soft-Field Approach and Landing Short-Field Takeoff and Maximum Performance Climb Short-Field Approach and Landing

CONTENT

SOFT FIELD

- ❑ Takeoff and Climb
- ❑ Approach and Landing

SHORT FIELD

- ❑ Takeoff and Maximum Performance Climb
- ❑ Approach and Landing

COMPLETION STANDARDS

- Demonstrate understanding of soft-field and short-field takeoffs and landings during oral quizzing by the instructor.

- Complete the questions for Chapter 14B with a minimum score of 80 percent. With the instructor, review each incorrect response to ensure complete understanding before starting Ground Lesson 42.

STUDY ASSIGNMENT

Instrument/Commercial Textbook/e-Book

Chapter 14 — Commercial Maneuvers
  Section C — Steep Turns
  Section D — Chandelles
  Section E — Lazy Eights

Commercial Pilot Online

ML — Steep Turns
ML — Chandelles
ML — Lazy Eights

GROUND LESSON 42

REFERENCES

Instrument/Commercial Textbook/e-Book

Chapter 14 — Commercial Maneuvers
  Section C — Steep Turns
  Section D — Chandelles
  Section E — Lazy Eights

Commercial Pilot Online

ML — Steep Turns
ML — Chandelles
ML — Lazy Eights

OBJECTIVES

Lesson Objective	Part 141/61 Aeronautical Knowledge	ACS Task
Recognize the procedures and performance considerations necessary to perform: • Steep turns. • Chandelles. • Lazy Eights.	Maneuvers, procedures, and emergency operations appropriate to the aircraft	Steep Turns Chandelles Lazy Eights

CONTENT

STEEP TURNS
- ❑ Description
- ❑ Procedure

CHANDELLES
- ❑ Description
- ❑ Procedure

LAZY EIGHTS
- ❑ Description
- ❑ Procedure

COMPLETION STANDARDS

- Demonstrate understanding of steep turns, chandelles, and lazy eights during oral quizzing by the instructor.
- Complete the questions for Chapter 14, Sections C, D, and E with a minimum score of 80 percent. With the instructor, review each incorrect response to ensure complete understanding before starting Ground Lesson 43.

STUDY ASSIGNMENT

Instrument/Commercial Textbook/e-Book

Chapter 14 — Commercial Maneuvers
- Section F — Eights-on-Pylons
- Section G — Steep Spiral
- Section H — Power-Off 180° Accuracy Approach and Landing

Commercial Pilot Online

- ML — Eights-on-Pylons
- ML — Steep Spirals
- ML — Power-Off 180° Accuracy Approach and Landing

GROUND LESSON 43

REFERENCES

Instrument/Commercial Textbook/e-Book

Chapter 14 — Commercial Maneuvers
- Section F — Eights-on-Pylons
- Section G — Steep Spiral
- Section H — Power-Off 180° Accuracy Approach and Landing

Commercial Pilot Online

- ML — Eights-on-Pylons
- ML — Steep Spirals
- ML — Power-Off 180° Accuracy Approach and Landing

OBJECTIVES

Lesson Objective	Part 141/61 Aeronautical Knowledge	ACS Task
Recognize the procedures and performance considerations necessary to perform: • Eights-on-pylons. • Steep spirals. • Power-off 180° accuracy approach and landing.	Maneuvers, procedures, and emergency operations appropriate to the aircraft	Eights-on-Pylons Steep Spirals Power-off 180° Accuracy Approach and Landing

CONTENT

EIGHTS-ON-PYLONS
- ❏ Description
- ❏ Procedure

STEEP SPIRAL
- ❏ Description
- ❏ Procedure

POWER-OFF 180° ACCURACY APPROACH AND LANDING
- ❏ Description
- ❏ Procedure

COMPLETION STANDARDS

- Demonstrate understanding of eights-on-pylons, steep spirals, and power-off 180° accuracy approaches and landings during oral quizzing by the instructor.
- Complete the questions for Chapter 14, Sections F, G, and H with a minimum score of 80 percent. With the instructor, review each incorrect response to ensure complete understanding before starting Ground Lesson 44.

STUDY ASSIGNMENT

Instrument/Commercial Textbook/e-Book

Chapter 13 — Commercial Flight Considerations

Section B — Commercial Pilot SRM

Commercial Pilot Online

GL — Commercial Pilot SRM

GROUND LESSON 44

REFERENCES

Instrument/Commercial Textbook/e-Book
Chapter 13 — Commercial Flight Considerations
Section B — Commercial Pilot SRM

Commercial Pilot Online
GL — Commercial Pilot SRM

OBJECTIVES

Lesson Objective	Part 141/61 Aeronautical Knowledge	ACS Task
Recognize how single-pilot resources management (SRM) and crew resource management (CRM) skills can enhance flight safety in the commercial flight environment. Explain how to use the aeronautical decision-making (ADM) process during commercial flight operations.	Aeronautical decision making and judgment	Human Factors

CONTENT

- ❏ Commercial Operations
- ❏ Crew Resource Management
- ❏ Aeronautical Decision Making
- ❏ Risk Management
- ❏ Task Management
- ❏ Situational Awareness
- ❏ Controlled Flight Into Terrain Awareness
- ❏ Automation Management

COMPLETION STANDARDS

- Demonstrate understanding of using SRM and CRM skills and the ADM process to make effective decisions in the commercial environment during oral quizzing by the instructor.
- Complete with a minimum score of 80 percent: questions for Chapter 13B or online exams for GL — Commercial Pilot SRM. With the instructor, review each incorrect response to ensure complete understanding before starting Ground Lesson 45.

STUDY ASSIGNMENT

Review the content of Ground Lessons 35 – 44 to prepare for the Stage II Exam.

GROUND LESSON 45
STAGE II EXAM

REFERENCES

Ground Lessons 34 – 44

OBJECTIVE

Demonstrate knowledge of the subjects covered in Ground Lessons 34 – 44 by passing the Stage II Exam.

CONTENT

STAGE II EXAM

- ❏ High Performance Powerplants
- ❏ Supplemental Oxygen and Pressurization
- ❏ Retractable Landing Gear
- ❏ Advanced Aerodynamics
- ❏ Predicting Performance
- ❏ Controlling Weight and Balance
- ❏ Emergency Operations
- ❏ Commercial Maneuvers
- ❏ Commercial Pilot SRM

COMPLETION STANDARDS

To complete the lesson and stage, pass the Stage II Exam with a minimum score of 80 percent. Review each incorrect response with the instructor to ensure complete understanding before taking the End-of-Course Exam in Ground Lesson 46.

STUDY ASSIGNMENT

Review the references for Ground Lessons 28 – 45 to prepare for the Commercial Pilot End-of-Course Exam.

GROUND LESSON 46
END-OF-COURSE EXAM

REFERENCES

Ground Lessons 28 – 45

OBJECTIVE

Demonstrate comprehension of the material covered in Ground Lessons 28 – 45 by passing the Commercial Pilot End-of-Course Exam to prepare for the FAA Commercial Pilot Airman Knowledge Test.

CONTENT

❑ Commercial Pilot End-of-Course Exam

COMPLETION STANDARDS

To complete the lesson and the Commercial Pilot Ground Training, pass the Commercial Pilot End-of-Course Exam with a minimum score of 80 percent. With the instructor, review each incorrect response to ensure complete understanding before taking the FAA Commercial Pilot Airman Knowledge Test.

STUDY ASSIGNMENT

Review the content of Ground Lessons 28 – 45 to prepare for the FAA Commercial Pilot Airman Knowledge Test.

Commercial Pilot Flight Training Syllabus

FLIGHT TRAINING COURSE OBJECTIVES

The student will obtain the aeronautical skill and experience required by FAR Part 141 and Part 61 for a commercial pilot certificate with an airplane category rating and single-engine class rating.

FLIGHT TRAINING COURSE COMPLETION STANDARDS

Through flight tests and school records, the student must demonstrate that the necessary aeronautical skill and experience required by FAR Part 141 and Part 61 for a commercial pilot certificate with an airplane category rating and single-engine class rating have been met.

NOTE: *Throughout the flight training course, the student must apply and be evaluated on single-pilot resource management (SRM) skills, including aeronautical decision-making (ADM), and risk management. The student must be able to counteract hazardous attitudes, apply the ADM process to make effective decisions, identify hazards and mitigate risks. In addition, the student must demonstrate the ability to manage tasks and automation, maintain situational awareness, and take actions to prevent controlled flight into terrain (CFIT).*

Stage I

STAGE OBJECTIVES

During Stage I, the student increases proficiency in cross-country procedures by planning and performing extended cross-country flights. The student also increases proficiency in performing night operations.

STAGE COMPLETION STANDARDS

This stage is complete when the student can demonstrate proficiency in planning and implementing cross-country flights using pilotage, dead reckoning, and navigation systems. In addition, the student must demonstrate proficiency in safe night flight operations.

NOTE: *Completion of the specific instrument tasks listed in each lesson must be based on:*

- *The available airplane equipment.*
- *Whether the student is concurrently enrolled in the instrument course or has an instrument rating.*
- *Whether the cross-country is conducted under VFR or IFR.*

NOTE: *Preflight Procedures and Postflight Procedures are not listed for every flight lesson because these tasks are performed on every flight.*

FLIGHT LESSON 30

DUAL — CROSS-COUNTRY

NOTE: *As indicated in the Allocation Tables, complete Ground Lessons 27, 28, 29, and 30 and the Cross-Country Procedures Briefing prior to this flight.*

OBJECTIVES

- Complete a cross-country flight that includes a straight-line distance of more than 100 nautical miles from the original departure point.
- Increase proficiency in cross-country skills, including emergency operations, in preparation for solo cross-country flights.

PREFLIGHT DISCUSSION

❑ Positive Exchange of Flight Controls
❑ Emergency Operations
❑ Operating at Unfamiliar Airports
❑ Wire Strike Avoidance
❑ Airport Security
❑ Runway Incursion Avoidance
❑ Temporary Flight Restrictions (TFRs)
❑ NOTAMs
❑ Weather Briefing
❑ Density Altitude Considerations
❑ Risk Management (5Ps, PAVE)
❑ Single-Pilot Resource Management (SRM)
❑ Crew Resource Management (CRM)

INTRODUCE

CROSS-COUNTRY FLIGHT

PREFLIGHT PREPARATION

❑ Pilot Qualifications
❑ Airworthiness Requirements
❑ Weather Information
❑ National Airspace System
❑ Operation of Systems
❑ Human Factors

Cross-Country Flight Planning

❑ Route Planning
❑ Altitude Selection
❑ Weight and Balance
❑ Performance and Limitations
❑ Determining ETA
❑ Fuel Requirements
❑ Sources of Flight Information
❑ Navigation Log
❑ VFR Flight Plan

PREFLIGHT PROCEDURES
- ❑ Self-Assessment
- ❑ Preflight Inspection
- ❑ Flight Deck Management
- ❑ Engine Starting
- ❑ Taxiing
- ❑ Before Takeoff Check/Runup

NAVIGATION
- ❑ Pilotage and Dead Reckoning
- ❑ Lost Procedures
- ❑ Diversion

Navigation Systems and Radar Services
- ❑ VOR Orientation
- ❑ VOR Radial Interception and Tracking
- ❑ GPS Programming
- ❑ GPS Orientation
- ❑ GPS Course Interception and Tracking
- ❑ Use of ATC Services
- ❑ Autopilot Use for Navigation, if Equipped

CROSS-COUNTRY PROCEDURES
- ❑ Collision Avoidance
- ❑ Flight Deck Management
- ❑ Power Settings and Mixture Control
- ❑ CFIT Avoidance
- ❑ Estimating Visibility in Flight
- ❑ Flight on Federal Airways
- ❑ Opening and Closing Flight Plan

AIRPORT OPERATIONS
- ❑ Radio Communications
- ❑ Lost Communication Procedures/ATC Light Signals
- ❑ Airport, Runway, and Taxiway Signs, Markings, and Lighting
- ❑ Traffic Patterns
- ❑ Runway Incursion Avoidance
- ❑ Wake Turbulence Avoidance
- ❑ Wind Shear Avoidance
- ❑ Land and Hold Short Operations (LAHSO)

TAKEOFFS, LANDINGS, AND GO-AROUNDS
(Includes operations in crosswinds)
- ❑ Rejected Takeoff
- ❑ Normal Takeoff and Climb
- ❑ Normal Approach and Landing
- ❑ Go-Around/Rejected Landing

EMERGENCY OPERATIONS
- ❑ Systems and Equipment Malfunctions
- ❑ Emergency Descent
- ❑ Emergency Approach and Landing (Simulated)
- ❑ Emergency Equipment and Survival Gear

FLIGHT BY REFERENCE TO INSTRUMENTS

Instrument Flight (Full Panel and Partial Panel)

- ❑ Straight-and-Level Flight, Turns, Climbs, and Descents
- ❑ Intercepting and Tracking Navigational Systems

NOTE: *The instrument portion of this lesson should be accomplished on an "as required" basis depending on an assessment of the student's capabilities. Students enrolled in the Commercial Pilot Certification Course only must complete 10 hours of instrument training to meet the requirements of Part 141, Appendix D.*

POSTFLIGHT PROCEDURES

- ❑ After Landing, Parking, and Securing

COMPLETION STANDARDS

- Demonstrate the ability to make effective decisions as pilot in command on a cross-country flight that includes a straight-line distance of more than 100 nautical miles from the original departure point.
- Arrive at the enroute checkpoints within three minutes of the initial or revised ETA.
- Maintain positive aircraft control with the appropriate altitude ±100 feet and heading ±10°.

POSTFLIGHT DEBRIEFING

- ❑ Critique maneuvers/procedures and SRM.
- ❑ Create a plan for skills that need improvement.
- ❑ Update the record folder and logbook.

FLIGHT LESSON 31

SOLO — CROSS-COUNTRY

OBJECTIVES

- Increase proficiency in cross-country operations during a flight assigned by the instructor.
- Increase proficiency in single-pilot resource management (SRM).

PREFLIGHT DISCUSSION

- ❑ Cross-Country Flight Planning
- ❑ Risk Management (5Ps, PAVE)

REVIEW

CROSS-COUNTRY FLIGHT

PREFLIGHT PREPARATION

- ❑ Pilot Qualifications
- ❑ Airworthiness Requirements
- ❑ Weather Information
- ❑ National Airspace System

- ❑ Operation of Systems
- ❑ Human Factors

Cross-Country Flight Planning

- ❑ Route Planning
- ❑ Altitude Selection
- ❑ Weight and Balance
- ❑ Performance and Limitations
- ❑ Determining ETA
- ❑ Fuel Requirements
- ❑ Sources of Flight Information
- ❑ Navigation Log
- ❑ VFR Flight Plan

PREFLIGHT PROCEDURES

- ❑ Self-Assessment
- ❑ Preflight Inspection
- ❑ Flight Deck Management
- ❑ Engine Starting
- ❑ Taxiing
- ❑ Before Takeoff Check/Runup

NAVIGATION

- ❑ Pilotage and Dead Reckoning

Navigation Systems and Radar Services

- ❑ VOR Orientation
- ❑ VOR Radial Interception and Tracking
- ❑ GPS Programming
- ❑ GPS Orientation
- ❑ GPS Course Interception and Tracking
- ❑ Use of ATC Services
- ❑ Autopilot Use for Navigation, if Equipped

CROSS-COUNTRY PROCEDURES

- ❑ Collision Avoidance
- ❑ Flight Deck Management
- ❑ Power Settings and Mixture Control
- ❑ CFIT Avoidance
- ❑ Estimating Visibility in Flight
- ❑ Flight on Federal Airways
- ❑ Opening and Closing Flight Plan

AIRPORT OPERATIONS

- ❑ Radio Communications
- ❑ Airport, Runway, and Taxiway Signs, Markings, and Lighting
- ❑ Traffic Patterns
- ❑ Runway Incursion Avoidance
- ❑ Wake Turbulence Avoidance
- ❑ Wind Shear Avoidance
- ❑ Land and Hold Short Operations (LAHSO)

TAKEOFFS, LANDINGS, AND GO-AROUNDS

(Includes operations in crosswinds)

- ❑ Normal Takeoff and Climb
- ❑ Normal Approach and Landing

POSTFLIGHT PROCEDURES
- ❑ After Landing, Parking, and Securing

COMPLETION STANDARDS

- Increase proficiency in cross-country flight planning by selecting optimum cruising altitudes and appropriate checkpoints for a flight with a landing at a point more than 50 nautical miles from the original departure point.
- Accurately calculate fuel consumption and provisions for an adequate reserve upon landing.
- Make effective decisions as pilot in command on a cross-country flight.

POSTFLIGHT DEBRIEFING

- ❑ Critique maneuvers/procedures and SRM.
- ❑ Create a plan for skills that need improvement.
- ❑ Update the record folder and logbook.

STUDY ASSIGNMENT

Ground Lesson 31

Aviation Physiology

SRM Concepts

FLIGHT LESSON 32

DUAL — LOCAL, NIGHT

OBJECTIVES

- Prepare for a night flight—use techniques to maintain visual adaptation to the dark, verify the required airplane equipment is onboard, and obtain the necessary personal equipment.
- Interpret airport lighting and properly activate pilot controlled lighting.
- Perform night operations—scan for traffic using off-center viewing, interpret aircraft lighting, maintain orientation, navigate, and effectively read charts.
- Gain proficiency in performing takeoffs and landings and emergency procedures at night.

PREFLIGHT DISCUSSION

- ❑ Aviation Physiology
- ❑ CFIT Avoidance
- ❑ Wire Strike Avoidance
- ❑ Visual Illusions and Disorientation
- ❑ Night Vision and Night Scanning/Collision Avoidance
- ❑ Airplane Equipment and Lighting Requirements for Night Operation
- ❑ Airport and Obstruction Lighting
- ❑ Pilot-Controlled Lighting
- ❑ Personal Equipment

INTRODUCE

PREFLIGHT PREPARATION—NIGHT
- ❏ Pilot Qualifications
- ❏ Airworthiness Requirements
- ❏ Weather Information
- ❏ Operation of Systems
- ❏ Human Factors

PREFLIGHT PROCEDURES—NIGHT
- ❏ Self-Assessment
- ❏ Preflight Inspection
- ❏ Flight Deck Management
- ❏ Engine Starting
- ❏ Taxiing
- ❏ Before Takeoff Check/Runup

NIGHT FLIGHT
- ❏ Night Preparation—Visual Adaptation, Lighting, Equipment
- ❏ Night Operations—Orientation, Navigation, Chart Reading
- ❏ Collision Avoidance—Night

AIRPORT OPERATIONS
- ❏ Radio Communications
- ❏ Lost Communication Procedures/ATC Light Signals
- ❏ Airport, Runway, and Taxiway Signs, Markings, and Lighting
- ❏ Traffic Patterns
- ❏ Runway Incursion Avoidance
- ❏ Wake Turbulence Avoidance
- ❏ Wind Shear Avoidance
- ❏ Land and Hold Short Operations (LAHSO)

SLOW FIGHT AND STALLS
- ❏ Maneuvering During Slow Flight
- ❏ Power-Off Stalls
- ❏ Power-On Stalls
- ❏ Spin Awareness

PERFORMANCE MANEUVERS
- ❏ Steep Turns

TAKEOFFS, LANDINGS, AND GO-AROUNDS
(Includes operations in crosswinds)
- ❏ Rejected Takeoff
- ❏ Normal Takeoff and Climb
- ❏ Normal Approach and Landing
- ❏ Go-Around/Rejected Landing

POSTFLIGHT PROCEDURES
- ❏ After Landing, Parking, and Securing

COMPLETION STANDARDS
- Prepare for a night flight—use techniques to maintain visual adaptation to the dark, verify the required airplane equipment is onboard, and obtain the necessary personal equipment.

- Interpret airport lighting and properly activate pilot controlled lighting.
- Perform night operations—scan for traffic using off-center viewing, interpret aircraft lighting, maintain orientation, navigate, and effectively read charts.
- Gain proficiency in performing takeoffs and landings at night.
- Demonstrate the ability to make effective decisions as pilot in command on a night flight.

POSTFLIGHT DEBRIEFING

❑ Critique maneuvers/procedures and SRM.
❑ Create a plan for skills that need improvement.
❑ Update the record folder and logbook.

FLIGHT LESSON 33

DUAL — CROSS-COUNTRY, NIGHT

OBJECTIVES

- Gain proficiency in night cross-country procedures, including preflight planning, navigation, emergencies, and operating at unfamiliar airports.
- Complete a flight that includes a straight-line distance of more than 100 nautical miles from the original departure point.

PREFLIGHT DISCUSSION

❑ Airspace Requirements
❑ Weather Briefing
❑ NOTAMs
❑ Night Orientation, Navigation, and Chart Reading Techniques
❑ Emergency Operations
❑ CFIT Avoidance
❑ Wire Strike Avoidance
❑ Runway Incursion Avoidance

INTRODUCE

CROSS-COUNTRY FLIGHT

PREFLIGHT PREPARATION—NIGHT

❑ Pilot Qualifications
❑ Airworthiness Requirements
❑ Weather Information
❑ National Airspace System
❑ Operation of Systems
❑ Human Factors

Cross-Country Flight Planning

❑ Route Planning
❑ Altitude Selection
❑ Weight and Balance
❑ Performance and Limitations
❑ Determining ETA

- ❑ Fuel Requirements
- ❑ Sources of Flight Information
- ❑ Navigation Log
- ❑ VFR Flight Plan

PREFLIGHT PROCEDURES—NIGHT

- ❑ Self-Assessment
- ❑ Preflight Inspection
- ❑ Flight Deck Management
- ❑ Engine Starting
- ❑ Taxiing
- ❑ Before Takeoff Check/Runup

NIGHT FLIGHT

- ❑ Night Preparation—Visual Adaptation, Lighting, Equipment
- ❑ Night Operations—Orientation, Navigation, Chart Reading
- ❑ Collision Avoidance—Night

NAVIGATION

- ❑ Pilotage and Dead Reckoning
- ❑ Lost Procedures
- ❑ Diversion

Navigation Systems and Radar Services

- ❑ VOR Orientation
- ❑ VOR Radial Interception and Tracking
- ❑ GPS Programming
- ❑ GPS Orientation
- ❑ GPS Course Interception and Tracking
- ❑ Use of ATC Services
- ❑ Autopilot Use for Navigation, if Equipped

CROSS-COUNTRY PROCEDURES

- ❑ Collision Avoidance
- ❑ Flight Deck Management
- ❑ Power Settings and Mixture Control
- ❑ CFIT Avoidance
- ❑ Estimating Visibility in Flight
- ❑ Flight on Federal Airways
- ❑ Opening and Closing Flight Plan

AIRPORT OPERATIONS

- ❑ Radio Communications
- ❑ Lost Communication Procedures/ATC Light Signals
- ❑ Airport, Runway, and Taxiway Signs, Markings, and Lighting
- ❑ Traffic Patterns
- ❑ Runway Incursion Avoidance
- ❑ Wake Turbulence Avoidance
- ❑ Wind Shear Avoidance
- ❑ Land and Hold Short Operations (LAHSO)

TAKEOFFS, LANDINGS, AND GO-AROUNDS

(Includes operations in crosswinds)

- ❑ Rejected Takeoff
- ❑ Normal Takeoff and Climb

- ❑ Normal Approach and Landing
- ❑ Go-Around/Rejected Landing

EMERGENCY OPERATIONS
- ❑ Systems and Equipment Malfunctions
- ❑ Emergency Descent
- ❑ Emergency Approach and Landing (Simulated)
- ❑ Emergency Equipment and Survival Gear

FLIGHT BY REFERENCE TO INSTRUMENTS
Instrument Flight (Full Panel and Partial Panel)
- ❑ Straight-and-Level Flight, Turns, Climbs, and Descents
- ❑ Intercepting and Tracking Navigational Systems

NOTE: *The instrument portion of this lesson should be accomplished on an "as required" basis depending on an assessment of the student's capabilities. Students enrolled in the Commercial Pilot Certification Course only must complete 10 hours of instrument training to meet the requirements of Part 141, Appendix D.*

POSTFLIGHT PROCEDURES
- ❑ After Landing, Parking, and Securing

COMPLETION STANDARDS
- Demonstrate the ability to make effective decisions as pilot in command on a night cross-country flight that includes a straight-line distance of more than 100 nautical miles from the original departure point.
- Arrive at the enroute checkpoints within three minutes of the initial or revised ETA.
- Maintain positive aircraft control with altitude ±100 feet and heading ±10°.

POSTFLIGHT DEBRIEFING
- ❑ Critique maneuvers/procedures and SRM.
- ❑ Create a plan for skills that need improvement.
- ❑ Update the record folder and logbook.

STUDY ASSIGNMENT
Ground Lesson 33
Commercial FARs

FLIGHT LESSONS 34 AND 35

SOLO — LOCAL, NIGHT

OBJECTIVE
Increase proficiency and confidence in performing maneuvers and procedures in the night environment at an airport with an operating control tower.

PREFLIGHT DISCUSSION
- ❑ Night Flight Operations
- ❑ Single-Pilot Resource Management

REVIEW

PREFLIGHT PREPARATION—NIGHT

- ❑ Pilot Qualifications
- ❑ Airworthiness Requirements
- ❑ Weather Information
- ❑ Operation of Systems
- ❑ Human Factors

PREFLIGHT PROCEDURES—NIGHT

- ❑ Self-Assessment
- ❑ Preflight Inspection
- ❑ Flight Deck Management
- ❑ Engine Starting
- ❑ Taxiing
- ❑ Before Takeoff Check/Runup

NIGHT FLIGHT

- ❑ Night Preparation—Visual Adaptation, Lighting, Equipment
- ❑ Night Operations—Orientation, Navigation, Chart Reading
- ❑ Collision Avoidance—Night

AIRPORT OPERATIONS

- ❑ Radio Communications
- ❑ Airport, Runway, and Taxiway Signs, Markings, and Lighting
- ❑ Traffic Patterns
- ❑ Runway Incursion Avoidance
- ❑ Wake Turbulence Avoidance
- ❑ Wind Shear Avoidance
- ❑ Land and Hold Short Operations (LAHSO)

TAKEOFFS, LANDINGS, AND GO-AROUNDS

(Includes operations in crosswinds)

- ❑ Normal Takeoff and Climb
- ❑ Normal Approach and Landing

POSTFLIGHT PROCEDURES

- ❑ After Landing, Parking, and Securing

NOTE: *The 10 night takeoffs and landings with each involving flight in the traffic pattern at an airport with an operating control tower are a Part 141 requirement. Five should be completed in Flight Lesson 33 and the other five in Flight Lesson 34. However, this requirement may be accomplished with fewer than five per flight, as long as the total of 10 is completed.*

COMPLETION STANDARDS

Successfully complete two night flights with a total of at least 10 takeoffs and landings at an airport with an operating control tower.

POSTFLIGHT DEBRIEFING

- ❑ Critique maneuvers/procedures and SRM.
- ❑ Create a plan for skills that need improvement.
- ❑ Update the record folder and logbook.

FLIGHT LESSON 36

SOLO — CROSS-COUNTRY, NIGHT

NOTE: *The night solo training time requirements for this lesson may be completed in more than one flight.*

OBJECTIVES

- Increase proficiency and confidence in night operations by planning and performing a night cross-country flight that includes a landing at a point more than 50 nautical miles from the original departure point.
- Increase proficiency in navigating during cross-country flights at night.

PREFLIGHT DISCUSSION

- ❑ Night Cross-Country Flight Planning
- ❑ Night Flight Operations
- ❑ Single-Pilot Resource Management

REVIEW

CROSS-COUNTRY FLIGHT

PREFLIGHT PREPARATION—NIGHT

- ❑ Pilot Qualifications
- ❑ Airworthiness Requirements
- ❑ Weather Information
- ❑ National Airspace System
- ❑ Operation of Systems
- ❑ Human Factors

Cross-Country Flight Planning

- ❑ Route Planning
- ❑ Altitude Selection
- ❑ Weight and Balance
- ❑ Performance and Limitations
- ❑ Determining ETA
- ❑ Fuel Requirements
- ❑ Sources of Flight Information
- ❑ Navigation Log
- ❑ VFR Flight Plan

PREFLIGHT PROCEDURES—NIGHT

- ❑ Self-Assessment
- ❑ Preflight Inspection
- ❑ Flight Deck Management
- ❑ Engine Starting
- ❑ Taxiing
- ❑ Before Takeoff Check/Runup

NIGHT FLIGHT

- ❑ Night Preparation—Visual Adaptation, Lighting, Equipment
- ❑ Night Operations—Orientation, Navigation, Chart Reading
- ❑ Collision Avoidance—Night

NAVIGATION
- ❑ Pilotage and Dead Reckoning

Navigation Systems and Radar Services
- ❑ VOR Radial Interception and Tracking
- ❑ GPS Course Interception and Tracking
- ❑ Use of ATC Services
- ❑ Autopilot Use for Navigation, if Equipped

CROSS-COUNTRY PROCEDURES
- ❑ Collision Avoidance
- ❑ Flight Deck Management
- ❑ Power Settings and Mixture Control
- ❑ CFIT Avoidance
- ❑ Estimating Visibility in Flight
- ❑ Flight on Federal Airways
- ❑ Opening and Closing `Flight Plan

AIRPORT OPERATIONS
- ❑ Radio Communications
- ❑ Airport, Runway, and Taxiway Signs, Markings, and Lighting
- ❑ Traffic Patterns
- ❑ Runway Incursion Avoidance
- ❑ Wake Turbulence Avoidance
- ❑ Wind Shear Avoidance
- ❑ Land and Hold Short Operations (LAHSO)

TAKEOFFS, LANDINGS, AND GO-AROUNDS
(Includes operations in crosswinds)
- ❑ Normal Takeoff and Climb
- ❑ Normal Approach and Landing

POSTFLIGHT PROCEDURES
- ❑ After Landing, Parking, and Securing

COMPLETION STANDARDS

- Increase skill in cross-country flight planning by selecting optimum cruising altitudes and appropriate checkpoints for a flight with a landing at a point more than 50 nautical miles from the original departure point.
- Increase proficiency in cross-country and night operations.
- During the postflight briefing, explain the operational and safety considerations associated with night cross-country flying.

POSTFLIGHT DEBRIEFING

- ❑ Critique maneuvers/procedures and SRM.
- ❑ Create a plan for skills that need improvement.
- ❑ Update the record folder and logbook.

STUDY ASSIGNMENT

Ground Lesson 33

Stage I Exam

FLIGHT LESSONS 37 AND 38

SOLO (DUAL) — CROSS-COUNTRY

OBJECTIVES

- Increase proficiency in cross-country flights with a focus on pilotage, dead-reckoning, and operating at unfamiliar airports by performing a flight that includes a landing at a point more than 50 nautical miles from the original departure point.
- If the lesson is used for dual instruction, increase proficiency in planning and conducting all phases of cross-country flight to prepare for the Stage I Check.

PREFLIGHT DISCUSSION

❏ Cross-Country Flight Planning
❏ Risk Management (5Ps, PAVE)

REVIEW

CROSS-COUNTRY FLIGHT

PREFLIGHT PREPARATION

❏ Pilot Qualifications
❏ Airworthiness Requirements
❏ Weather Information
❏ National Airspace System
❏ Operation of Systems
❏ Human Factors

Cross-Country Flight Planning

❏ Route Planning
❏ Altitude Selection
❏ Weight and Balance
❏ Performance and Limitations
❏ Determining ETA
❏ Fuel Requirements
❏ Sources of Flight Information
❏ Navigation Log
❏ VFR Flight Plan

NAVIGATION

❏ Pilotage and Dead Reckoning

Navigation Systems and Radar Services

❏ VOR Radial Interception and Tracking
❏ GPS Course Interception and Tracking
❏ Use of ATC Services
❏ Autopilot Use for Navigation, if Equipped

CROSS-COUNTRY PROCEDURES

❏ Collision Avoidance
❏ Flight Deck Management
❏ Power Settings and Mixture Control
❏ CFIT Avoidance
❏ Estimating Visibility in Flight
❏ Flight on Federal Airways
❏ Opening and Closing Flight Plan

AIRPORT OPERATIONS
- ❑ Radio Communications
- ❑ Airport, Runway, and Taxiway Signs, Markings, and Lighting
- ❑ Traffic Patterns
- ❑ Runway Incursion Avoidance
- ❑ Wake Turbulence Avoidance
- ❑ Wind Shear Avoidance
- ❑ Land and Hold Short Operations (LAHSO)

TAKEOFFS, LANDINGS, AND GO-AROUNDS
(Includes operations in crosswinds)
- ❑ Normal Takeoff and Climb
- ❑ Normal Approach and Landing

COMPLETION STANDARDS

- Demonstrate proficiency in cross-country flight planning by selecting optimum cruising altitudes and appropriate checkpoints and accurately calculating fuel consumption.
- Complete a flight with a landing at a point more than 50 nautical miles from the original departure point to increase proficiency in cross-country operations, especially pilotage, dead reckoning, and operating at unfamiliar airports.
- Demonstrate proficiency in using SRM to make effective decisions, maintain situational awareness, prevent CFIT, and manage risk, tasks, and automation.
- If the lesson is used for dual instruction, demonstrate proficiency in all the listed tasks as required by the Commercial Pilot Airman Certification Standards.

FLIGHT LESSONS 39, 40, AND 41

SOLO (DUAL) — CROSS-COUNTRY

OBJECTIVES

- Increase proficiency in cross-country flights with a focus on VOR and/or GPS navigation by performing a flight that includes a landing at a point more than 50 nautical miles from the original departure point.
- If the lesson is used for dual instruction, increase proficiency in planning and conducting all phases of cross-country flight to prepare for the Stage I Check.

PREFLIGHT DISCUSSION

- ❑ Cross-Country Flight Planning
- ❑ Risk Management (5Ps, PAVE)

REVIEW

CROSS-COUNTRY FLIGHT

PREFLIGHT PREPARATION
- ❑ Pilot Qualifications
- ❑ Airworthiness Requirements
- ❑ Weather Information
- ❑ National Airspace System
- ❑ Operation of Systems
- ❑ Human Factors

Cross-Country Flight Planning
- ❏ Route Planning
- ❏ Altitude Selection
- ❏ Weight and Balance
- ❏ Performance and Limitations
- ❏ Determining ETA
- ❏ Fuel Requirements
- ❏ Sources of Flight Information
- ❏ Navigation Log
- ❏ VFR Flight Plan

NAVIGATION
- ❏ Pilotage and Dead Reckoning

Navigation Systems and Radar Services
- ❏ VOR Radial Interception and Tracking
- ❏ GPS Course Interception and Tracking
- ❏ Use of ATC Services
- ❏ Autopilot Use for Navigation, if Equipped

CROSS-COUNTRY PROCEDURES
- ❏ Collision Avoidance
- ❏ Flight Deck Management
- ❏ Power Settings and Mixture Control
- ❏ CFIT Avoidance
- ❏ Estimating Visibility in Flight
- ❏ Flight on Federal Airways
- ❏ Opening and Closing Flight Plan

AIRPORT OPERATIONS
- ❏ Radio Communications
- ❏ Airport, Runway, and Taxiway Signs, Markings, and Lighting
- ❏ Traffic Patterns
- ❏ Runway Incursion Avoidance
- ❏ Wake Turbulence Avoidance
- ❏ Wind Shear Avoidance
- ❏ Land and Hold Short Operations (LAHSO)

TAKEOFFS, LANDINGS, AND GO-AROUNDS
(Includes operations in crosswinds)
- ❏ Normal Takeoff and Climb
- ❏ Normal Approach and Landing

COMPLETION STANDARDS

- Demonstrate proficiency in cross-country flight planning by selecting optimum cruising altitudes and appropriate checkpoints and accurately calculating fuel consumption.
- Complete a flight with a landing at a point more than 50 nautical miles from the original departure point to increase proficiency in cross-country operations, especially VOR and/or GPS navigation.
- Demonstrate proficiency in using SRM to make effective decisions, maintain situational awareness, prevent CFIT, and manage risk, tasks, and automation.
- If the lesson is used for dual instruction, demonstrate proficiency in all the listed tasks as required by the Commercial Pilot Airman Certification Standards.

POSTFLIGHT DEBRIEFING

- ❏ Critique maneuvers/procedures and SRM.
- ❏ Create a plan for skills that need improvement.
- ❏ Update the record folder and logbook.

FLIGHT LESSON 42

DUAL — CROSS-COUNTRY

OBJECTIVES

- Demonstrate proficiency in cross-country flight planning; pilotage and dead reckoning; VOR, and GPS navigation; and operating at unfamiliar airports.
- Demonstrate proficiency in managing emergency situations during a cross-country flight
- Perform a flight that includes a landing at a point more than 50 nautical miles from the original departure point.
- Demonstrate proficiency in planning and conducting all phases of cross-country flight to prepare for the Stage I Check.

PREFLIGHT DISCUSSION

- ❏ Cross-Country Flight Planning
- ❏ Emergency Operations
- ❏ Risk Management (5Ps, PAVE)

REVIEW

CROSS-COUNTRY FLIGHT

PREFLIGHT PREPARATION

- ❏ Pilot Qualifications
- ❏ Airworthiness Requirements
- ❏ Weather Information
- ❏ National Airspace System
- ❏ Operation of Systems
- ❏ Human Factors

Cross-Country Flight Planning

- ❏ Route Planning
- ❏ Altitude Selection
- ❏ Weight and Balance
- ❏ Performance and Limitations
- ❏ Determining ETA
- ❏ Fuel Requirements
- ❏ Sources of Flight Information
- ❏ Navigation Log
- ❏ VFR Flight Plan

NAVIGATION

- ❏ Pilotage and Dead Reckoning
- ❏ Lost Procedures

❑ Diversion

Navigation Systems and Radar Services
❑ VOR Radial Interception and Tracking
❑ GPS Course Interception and Tracking
❑ Use of ATC Services
❑ Autopilot Use for Navigation, if Equipped

CROSS-COUNTRY PROCEDURES
❑ Collision Avoidance
❑ Flight Deck Management
❑ Power Settings and Mixture Control
❑ CFIT Awareness
❑ Estimating Visibility in Flight
❑ Flight on Federal Airways
❑ Opening and Closing Flight Plan

AIRPORT OPERATIONS
❑ Radio Communications
❑ Lost Communication Procedures/ATC Light Signals
❑ Airport, Runway, and Taxiway Signs, Markings, and Lighting
❑ Traffic Patterns
❑ Runway Incursion Avoidance
❑ Wake Turbulence Avoidance
❑ Wind Shear Avoidance
❑ Land and Hold Short Operations (LAHSO)

TAKEOFFS, LANDINGS, AND GO-AROUNDS
(Includes operations in crosswinds)
❑ Rejected Takeoff
❑ Normal Takeoff and Climb
❑ Normal Approach and Landing
❑ Go-Around/Rejected Landing

EMERGENCY OPERATIONS
❑ Systems and Equipment Malfunctions
❑ Emergency Descent
❑ Emergency Approach and Landing (Simulated)
❑ Emergency Equipment and Survival Gear

FLIGHT BY REFERENCE TO INSTRUMENTS
Instrument Flight (Full and Partial Panel)
❑ Straight-and-Level Flight, Turns, Climbs, and Descents
❑ Intercepting and Tracking Navigational Systems

NOTE: *The instrument portion of this lesson should be accomplished on an "as required" basis depending on an assessment of the student's capabilities. Students enrolled in the Commercial Pilot Certification Course only must complete 10 hours of instrument training to meet the requirements of Part 141, Appendix D.*

COMPLETION STANDARDS

- Demonstrate proficiency in all the listed tasks as required by the Commercial Pilot Airman Certification Standards.
- Demonstrate proficiency in using SRM to make effective decisions, maintain situational awareness, prevent CFIT, and manage risk, tasks, and automation.

POSTFLIGHT DEBRIEFING

- ❑ Critique maneuvers/procedures and SRM.
- ❑ Create a plan for skills that need improvement.
- ❑ Update the record folder and logbook.

FLIGHT LESSON 43

SOLO — CROSS-COUNTRY

OBJECTIVE

Gain cross-country experience by completing a flight that meets the long cross-country requirements: landings at a minimum of three points, one of which is at least a straight-line distance of 250 nautical miles from the original departure point. If the flight is conducted in Hawaii, the alternate provisions of FAR 141, Appendix D, apply.

PREFLIGHT DISCUSSION

- ❑ Cross-Country Flight Planning
- ❑ Risk Management (5Ps, PAVE)

REVIEW

CROSS-COUNTRY FLIGHT

PREFLIGHT PREPARATION

- ❑ Pilot Qualifications
- ❑ Airworthiness Requirements
- ❑ Weather Information
- ❑ National Airspace System
- ❑ Operation of Systems
- ❑ Human Factors

Cross-Country Flight Planning

- ❑ Route Planning
- ❑ Altitude Selection
- ❑ Weight and Balance
- ❑ Performance and Limitations
- ❑ Determining ETA
- ❑ Fuel Requirements
- ❑ Sources of Flight Information
- ❑ Navigation Log
- ❑ VFR Flight Plan

NAVIGATION

- ❑ Pilotage and Dead Reckoning

Navigation Systems and Radar Services

- ❑ VOR Radial Interception and Tracking
- ❑ GPS Course Interception and Tracking
- ❑ Use of ATC Services
- ❑ Autopilot Use for Navigation, if Equipped

CROSS-COUNTRY PROCEDURES
- ❑ Collision Avoidance
- ❑ Flight Deck Management
- ❑ Power Settings and Mixture Control
- ❑ CFIT Avoidance
- ❑ Estimating Visibility in Flight
- ❑ Flight on Federal Airways
- ❑ Opening and Closing Flight Plan

AIRPORT OPERATIONS
- ❑ Radio Communications
- ❑ Airport, Runway, and Taxiway Signs, Markings, and Lighting
- ❑ Traffic Patterns
- ❑ Runway Incursion Avoidance
- ❑ Wake Turbulence Avoidance
- ❑ Wind Shear Avoidance
- ❑ Land and Hold Short Operations (LAHSO)

TAKEOFFS, LANDINGS, AND GO-AROUNDS
(Includes operations in crosswinds)
- ❑ Normal Takeoff and Climb
- ❑ Normal Approach and Landing

COMPLETION STANDARDS

- Demonstrate proficiency in cross-country flight planning by selecting optimum cruising altitudes and appropriate checkpoints and accurately calculating fuel consumption.
- Demonstrate proficiency in using SRM to make effective decisions, maintain situational awareness, prevent CFIT, and manage risk, tasks, and automation.
- Complete a solo cross-country with landings at a minimum of three points, one of which is at least a straight-line distance of 250 nautical miles from the original departure point.

POSTFLIGHT DEBRIEFING

- ❑ Critique maneuvers/procedures and SRM.
- ❑ Create a plan for skills that need improvement.
- ❑ Update the record folder and logbook.

FLIGHT LESSON 44

DUAL — CROSS-COUNTRY

STAGE I CHECK

OBJECTIVE

Demonstrate to the chief instructor, the assistant chief instructor, or the designated check instructor:
- Proficiency in planning and implementing a cross-country flight.
- Proficiency in managing emergency procedures.
- Proficiency in SRM skills by effectively managing risk and making decisions during cross-country operations.

PREFLIGHT DISCUSSION

Conduct for the Stage I Check, including:

- ❑ Maneuvers and Procedures
- ❑ Acceptable Performance Criteria
- ❑ Applicable Rules

EVALUATE

CROSS-COUNTRY FLIGHT

PREFLIGHT PREPARATION

- ❑ Pilot Qualifications
- ❑ Airworthiness Requirements
- ❑ Weather Information
- ❑ National Airspace System
- ❑ Operation of Systems
- ❑ Human Factors

Cross-Country Flight Planning

- ❑ Route Planning
- ❑ Altitude Selection
- ❑ Weight and Balance
- ❑ Performance and Limitations
- ❑ Determining ETA
- ❑ Fuel Requirements
- ❑ Sources of Flight Information
- ❑ Navigation Log
- ❑ VFR Flight Plan

PREFLIGHT PROCEDURES

- ❑ Self-Assessment
- ❑ Preflight Inspection
- ❑ Flight Deck Management
- ❑ Engine Starting
- ❑ Taxiing
- ❑ Before Takeoff Check/Runup

NAVIGATION

- ❑ Pilotage and Dead Reckoning
- ❑ Lost Procedures
- ❑ Diversion

Navigation Systems and Radar Services

- ❑ VOR Radial Interception and Tracking
- ❑ GPS Course Interception and Tracking
- ❑ Use of ATC Services
- ❑ Autopilot Use for Navigation, if Equipped

CROSS-COUNTRY PROCEDURES

- ❑ Collision Avoidance
- ❑ Flight Deck Management

- ❑ Power Settings and Mixture Control
- ❑ CFIT Awareness
- ❑ Estimating Visibility in Flight
- ❑ Flight on Federal Airways
- ❑ Opening and Closing Flight Plan

AIRPORT OPERATIONS
- ❑ Radio Communications
- ❑ Lost Communication Procedures/ATC Light Signals
- ❑ Airport, Runway, and Taxiway Signs, Markings, and Lighting
- ❑ Traffic Patterns
- ❑ Runway Incursion Avoidance
- ❑ Wake Turbulence Avoidance
- ❑ Wind Shear Avoidance
- ❑ Land and Hold Short Operations (LAHSO)

TAKEOFFS, LANDINGS, AND GO-AROUNDS
(Includes operations in crosswinds)
- ❑ Rejected Takeoff
- ❑ Normal Takeoff and Climb
- ❑ Normal Approach and Landing
- ❑ Go-Around/Rejected Landing

EMERGENCY OPERATIONS
- ❑ Systems and Equipment Malfunctions
- ❑ Emergency Descent
- ❑ Emergency Approach and Landing (Simulated)
- ❑ Emergency Equipment and Survival Gear

POSTFLIGHT PROCEDURES
- ❑ After Landing, Parking, and Securing

COMPLETION STANDARDS

- Demonstrate commercial pilot proficiency in each of the listed procedures at the level required by the Commercial Pilot Airman Certification Standards.
- Demonstrate the ability to use single-pilot resource management to make effective decisions, maintain situational awareness, prevent CFIT, and manage risk, tasks, and automation.

POSTFLIGHT DEBRIEFING

- ❑ Evaluate maneuvers/procedures and SRM.
- ❑ Plan additional instruction for skills not meeting Stage I completion standards.
- ❑ Update the record folder and logbook.

Stage II Complex Airplane

The Commercial Pilot Certification Course included in this syllabus provides flight lessons that cover a transition to a complex airplane or to a technically advanced airplane (TAA). If you selected the TAA option by checking the appropriate box in the Preface, refer to the Stage II TAA Option. You may conduct the lessons included in Stage II TAA Option in place of the same numbered flight lessons included in this section—Stage II Complex Airplane Transition. Lessons in Stage II that are not specifically identified as complex or TAA, such as dual and solo lessons focused on introducing and practicing commercial maneuvers, may be performed in a complex airplane, TAA, or other training airplane.

STAGE OBJECTIVES

During this stage, the student gains proficiency in operating a complex aircraft. The student learns the procedures to operate the complex airplane's systems and manage equipment malfunctions and failures. In addition, the student gains skills to perform the flight maneuvers required for commercial pilot certification.

STAGE COMPLETION STANDARDS

This stage is complete when the student can demonstrate commercial pilot proficiency in the operation of the complex aircraft and can correctly perform the steps for each commercial maneuver.

FLIGHT LESSON 45

SOLO — LOCAL

OBJECTIVE

Increase proficiency in performing stalls, slow flight, normal takeoffs and landings, and ground reference maneuvers to enhance coordination and airplane control.

PREFLIGHT DISCUSSION

- ❑ Stall Indications and Recovery
- ❑ Spin Awareness
- ❑ Situational Awareness

REVIEW

SLOW FLIGHT AND STALLS

- ❑ Maneuvering During Slow Flight
- ❑ Power-Off Stalls
- ❑ Power-On Stalls

PERFORMANCE AND GROUND REFERENCE MANEUVERS

- ❑ Steep Turns

Ground Reference Maneuvers (as assigned by the instructor)

- ❏ S-Turns
- ❏ Turns Around a Point

TAKEOFFS, LANDINGS, AND GO-AROUNDS
(Includes operations in crosswinds)
- ❏ Normal Takeoff and Climb
- ❏ Normal Approach and Landing

COMPLETION STANDARDS

Perform each maneuver to the level required by the Private Pilot Airman Certification Standards.

POSTFLIGHT DEBRIEFING

- ❏ Critique maneuvers/procedures and SRM.
- ❏ Create a plan for skills that need improvement.
- ❏ Update the record folder and logbook.

STUDY ASSIGNMENT

Ground Lessons 34, 35, and 36
High Performance Powerplants
Environmental and Ice Control Systems
Retractable Landing Gear

Complex Airplane Transition Briefing

FLIGHT LESSON 46

DUAL — LOCAL, COMPLEX AIRPLANE

OBJECTIVES

- Become familiar with operating complex airplane systems and equipment during ground and flight operations.
- Become familiar with high altitude operations, including the use of supplemental oxygen and pressurization equipment as applicable to the airplane.
- Properly configure the airplane and apply wind correction in the traffic pattern to perform takeoffs and landings.

PREFLIGHT DISCUSSION

- ❏ Pilot's Operating Handbook
- ❏ Complex Airplane Systems and Equipment
- ❏ Airplane Performance and Limitations

INTRODUCE

PREFLIGHT PREPARATION
- ❏ Pilot Qualifications
- ❏ Airworthiness Requirements
- ❏ Weather Information
- ❏ Performance and Limitations

- ❑ Operation of Systems
- ❑ Human Factors

PREFLIGHT PROCEDURES
- ❑ Self-Assessment
- ❑ Preflight Inspection
- ❑ Flight Deck Management
- ❑ Engine Starting
- ❑ Taxiing
- ❑ Before Takeoff Check/Runup

BASIC MANEUVERS
- ❑ Straight-and-Level Flight
- ❑ Climbs and Descents
- ❑ Use of Retractable Landing Gear and Flaps
- ❑ Use of Constant-Speed Propeller
- ❑ Power Settings and Mixture Control

HIGH ALTITUDE OPERATIONS
- ❑ Supplemental Oxygen Use
- ❑ Pressurization System Operation

NOTE: *If high altitude systems are not applicable to the airplane to be used for the practical test, the student must still demonstrate knowledge of high altitude operations sufficient to meet the requirements specified in the FAA Commercial Pilot Airman Certification Standards.*

AIRPORT OPERATIONS
- ❑ Radio Communications
- ❑ Airport, Runway, and Taxiway Signs, Markings, and Lighting
- ❑ Traffic Patterns

TAKEOFFS, LANDINGS, AND GO-AROUNDS
(Includes operations in crosswinds)
- ❑ Rejected Takeoff
- ❑ Normal Takeoff and Climb
- ❑ Normal Approach and Landing
- ❑ Go-Around/Rejected Landing

POSTFLIGHT PROCEDURES
- ❑ After Landing, Parking, and Securing

COMPLETION STANDARDS

- Demonstrate understanding of the complex airplane systems and operations.
- Demonstrate understanding of supplemental oxygen use and pressurization system operation.
- Perform takeoffs and landings using the proper configuration, airspeed, and wind correction.

POSTFLIGHT DEBRIEFING

- ❑ Critique maneuvers/procedures and SRM.
- ❑ Create a plan for skills that need improvement.
- ❑ Update the record folder and logbook.

STUDY ASSIGNMENT

Ground Lessons 37, 38, and 39

Advanced Aerodynamics and Accelerated Stalls
Predicting Performance
Controlling Weight and Balance

FLIGHT LESSON 47

DUAL — LOCAL, COMPLEX AIRPLANE

OBJECTIVES

- Become familiar with recognizing and recovering from power-off, power-on, and accelerated stalls.
- Become familiar with attitude instrument flying in the complex airplane.
- Become familiar with using the navigation system and autopilot (if so equipped) in the complex airplane.
- Increase proficiency in performing basic flight maneuvers and takeoffs and landings in the complex airplane.

PREFLIGHT DISCUSSION

❏ Stall Characteristics of Airplane
❏ Spin Awareness

INTRODUCE

SLOW FLIGHT AND STALLS

❏ Maneuvering During Slow Flight
❏ Power-Off Stalls
❏ Power-On Stalls
❏ Accelerated Stalls
❏ Spin Awareness

FLIGHT BY REFERENCE TO INSTRUMENTS

Instrument Flight (Full Panel and Partial Panel)
❏ Straight-and-Level Flight, Turns, Climbs, and Descents
❏ Recovery From Unusual Flight Attitudes

NOTE: *The instrument portion of this lesson should be accomplished on an "as required" basis depending on an assessment of the student's capabilities. Students enrolled in the Commercial Pilot Certification Course only must complete 10 hours of instrument training to meet the requirements of Part 141, Appendix D.*

NAVIGATION

Navigation Systems and Radar Services
❏ VOR Radial Interception and Tracking
❏ GPS Course Interception and Tracking
❏ Autopilot Use for Navigation, if Equipped

REVIEW

PREFLIGHT PREPARATION
- ❑ Pilot Qualifications
- ❑ Airworthiness Requirements
- ❑ Weather Information
- ❑ Performance and Limitations
- ❑ Operation of Systems
- ❑ Human Factors

PREFLIGHT PROCEDURES
- ❑ Self-Assessment
- ❑ Preflight Inspection
- ❑ Flight Deck Management
- ❑ Engine Starting
- ❑ Taxiing
- ❑ Before Takeoff Check/Runup

BASIC MANEUVERS
- ❑ Straight-and-Level Flight
- ❑ Climbs and Descents
- ❑ Use of Retractable Landing Gear and Flaps
- ❑ Use of Constant-Speed Propeller
- ❑ Power Settings and Mixture Control

HIGH ALTITUDE OPERATIONS
- ❑ Supplemental Oxygen Use
- ❑ Pressurization System Operation

NOTE: *If high altitude systems are not applicable to the airplane to be used for the practical test, the student must still demonstrate knowledge of high altitude operations sufficient to meet the requirements specified in the FAA Commercial Pilot Airman Certification Standards.*

AIRPORT OPERATIONS
- ❑ Radio Communications
- ❑ Airport, Runway, and Taxiway Signs, Markings, and Lighting
- ❑ Traffic Patterns

TAKEOFFS, LANDINGS, AND GO-AROUNDS
(Includes operations in crosswinds)
- ❑ Rejected Takeoff
- ❑ Normal Takeoff and Climb
- ❑ Normal Approach and Landing
- ❑ Go-Around/Rejected Landing

POSTFLIGHT PROCEDURES
- ❑ After Landing, Parking, and Securing

COMPLETION STANDARDS
- Demonstrate understanding of power-off, power-on, and accelerated stall indications and recovery procedures.
- Demonstrate pilot-in-command proficiency while operating complex airplane systems and using navigation systems and the autopilot (if so equipped).

- Demonstrate proficiency in performing the traffic pattern, takeoffs, landings, and go-arounds.

POSTFLIGHT DEBRIEFING

❏ Critique maneuvers/procedures and SRM.
❏ Create a plan for skills that need improvement.
❏ Update the record folder and logbook.

STUDY ASSIGNMENT

Ground Lesson 40

Emergency Operations

FLIGHT LESSON 48

DUAL — LOCAL, COMPLEX AIRPLANE

OBJECTIVES

- Become familiar with emergency procedures, including landing gear malfunctions and the emergency descent.
- Become familiar with performing soft-field and short-field takeoffs and landings in the complex airplane.
- Increase proficiency in performing basic flight maneuvers, navigation, and takeoffs and landings in the complex airplane.

PREFLIGHT DISCUSSION

❏ System and Equipment Malfunctions
❏ Emergency Procedures
❏ Airplane Configuration for Soft-Field and Short-Field Takeoffs and Landings

INTRODUCE

EMERGENCY OPERATIONS

Systems and Equipment Malfunctions

❏ Partial Power Loss
❏ Electrical Malfunction
❏ Instrument Malfunction
❏ Landing Gear Malfunction
❏ Flap Malfunction
❏ Inoperative Trim
❏ Smoke and Fire
❏ Airplane Specific Malfunctions
❏ Door Opening in Flight

Emergency Procedures

❏ Emergency Descent
❏ Emergency Approach and Landing (Simulated)
❏ Emergency Equipment and Survival Gear

FLIGHT BY REFERENCE TO INSTRUMENTS

Instrument Flight (Full Panel and Partial Panel)

❑ GPS Course Interception and Tracking
❑ VOR Radial Interception and Tracking

NOTE: *The instrument portion of this lesson should be accomplished on an "as required" basis depending on an assessment of the student's capabilities. Students enrolled in the Commercial Pilot Certification Course only must complete 10 hours of instrument training to meet the requirements of Part 141, Appendix D.*

TAKEOFFS, LANDINGS, AND GO-AROUNDS

(Includes operations in crosswinds)

❑ Soft-Field Takeoff and Climb
❑ Soft-Field Approach and Landing
❑ Short-Field Takeoff and Maximum Performance Climb
❑ Short-Field Approach and Landing

REVIEW

PREFLIGHT PREPARATION

❑ Pilot Qualifications
❑ Airworthiness Requirements
❑ Weather Information
❑ Performance and Limitations
❑ Operation of Systems
❑ Human Factors

PREFLIGHT PROCEDURES

❑ Self-Assessment
❑ Preflight Inspection
❑ Flight Deck Management
❑ Engine Starting
❑ Taxiing
❑ Before Takeoff Check/Runup

HIGH ALTITUDE OPERATIONS

❑ Supplemental Oxygen Use
❑ Pressurization System Operation

NOTE: *If high altitude systems are not applicable to the airplane to be used for the practical test, the student must still demonstrate knowledge of high altitude operations sufficient to meet the requirements specified in the FAA Commercial Pilot Airman Certification Standards.*

SLOW FLIGHT AND STALLS

❑ Maneuvering During Slow Flight
❑ Power-Off Stalls
❑ Power-On Stalls
❑ Accelerated Stalls
❑ Spin Awareness

FLIGHT BY REFERENCE TO INSTRUMENTS

Instrument Flight (Full and Partial Panel)

❑ Straight-and-Level Flight, Turns, Climbs, and Descents
❑ Recovery From Unusual Flight Attitudes

❑ GPS Course Interception and Tracking
❑ VOR Radial Interception and Tracking
❑ Autopilot Use for Navigation, if Equipped

TAKEOFFS, LANDINGS, AND GO-AROUNDS
(Includes operations in crosswinds)
❑ Rejected Takeoff
❑ Normal Takeoff and Climb
❑ Normal Approach and Landing
❑ Go-Around/Rejected Landing

POSTFLIGHT PROCEDURES
❑ After Landing, Parking, and Securing

COMPLETION STANDARDS

- Demonstrate understanding of how to manage systems and equipment malfunctions and perform the emergency procedures associated with the complex airplane.
- Demonstrate understanding of the proper airplane configurations to perform soft-field and short-field takeoffs and landings in the complex airplane.
- Demonstrate pilot-in-command proficiency while operating complex airplane systems, navigating, and performing basic maneuvers.
- Demonstrate proficiency in recognizing and recovering from power-off, power-on, and accelerated stalls.
- Demonstrate proficiency in performing the traffic pattern, takeoffs, landings, and go-arounds.

POSTFLIGHT DEBRIEFING

❑ Critique maneuvers/procedures and SRM.
❑ Create a plan for skills that need improvement.
❑ Update the record folder and logbook.

STUDY ASSIGNMENT

Ground Lesson 41

Soft-Field and Short-Field Takeoffs and Landings

FLIGHT LESSONS 49 AND 50

DUAL — LOCAL OR CROSS-COUNTRY, COMPLEX AIRPLANE

NOTE: *These lessons may be conducted as two separate flights to airports in the local area or the flight hours may be combined to accommodate a cross-country flight with at least one stop over 50 nautical miles from the original point of departure.*

OBJECTIVES

- Increase proficiency in using the airplane's navigation system and using the autopilot (if equipped) for navigation.
- Gain proficiency in soft-field and short-field takeoffs and landings in the complex airplane.
- Increase proficiency in performing slow flight and recognizing and recovering from stalls in the complex airplane.

PREFLIGHT DISCUSSION

❑ Navigation System
❑ Workload Management

INTRODUCE

❑ Cross-Country Flight Planning
❑ National Airspace System

REVIEW

NAVIGATION SYSTEMS AND RADAR SERVICES

❑ GPS Course Interception and Tracking
❑ VOR Radial Interception and Tracking
❑ Autopilot Use for Navigation, if Equipped

SLOW FLIGHT AND STALLS

❑ Maneuvering During Slow Flight
❑ Power-Off Stalls
❑ Power-On Stalls
❑ Accelerated Stalls
❑ Spin Awareness

EMERGENCY OPERATIONS

Systems and Equipment Malfunctions

❑ Partial Power Loss
❑ Electrical Malfunction
❑ Instrument Malfunction
❑ Landing Gear Malfunction
❑ Flap Malfunction
❑ Inoperative Trim
❑ Smoke and Fire

- ❑ Airplane Specific Malfunctions
- ❑ Door Opening in Flight

Emergency Procedures

- ❑ Emergency Descent
- ❑ Emergency Approach and Landing (Simulated)
- ❑ Emergency Equipment and Survival Gear

FLIGHT BY REFERENCE TO INSTRUMENTS

Instrument Flight (Full and Partial Panel)

- ❑ GPS Course Interception and Tracking
- ❑ VOR Radial Interception and Tracking

NOTE: *The instrument portion of this lesson should be accomplished on an "as required" basis depending on an assessment of the student's capabilities. Students enrolled in the Commercial Pilot Certification Course only must complete 10 hours of instrument training to meet the requirements of Part 141, Appendix D.*

TAKEOFFS, LANDINGS, AND GO-AROUNDS

(Includes operations in crosswinds)

- ❑ Soft-Field Takeoff and Climb
- ❑ Soft-Field Approach and Landing
- ❑ Short-Field Takeoff and Maximum Performance Climb
- ❑ Short-Field Approach and Landing

COMPLETION STANDARDS

- Demonstrate understanding of short-field and soft-field takeoff and landing configurations and procedures.
- Demonstrate proficiency in managing systems and equipment malfunctions and performing the emergency procedures associated with the complex airplane.
- Demonstrate the ability to use single-pilot resource management to make effective decisions as pilot in command of a complex airplane.

POSTFLIGHT DEBRIEFING

- ❑ Critique maneuvers/procedures and SRM.
- ❑ Create a plan for skills that need improvement.
- ❑ Update the record folder and logbook.

FLIGHT LESSON 51

DUAL — LOCAL

OBJECTIVES

- Increase knowledge of the causes and recovery procedures that apply to secondary stalls, cross-control stalls, and elevator trim stalls.
- Increase proficiency in recognizing and recovering from power-off, power-on, and accelerated stalls.
- Increase proficiency in correctly configuring the airplane and applying wind correction soft-field and short-field takeoffs and landings.

PREFLIGHT DISCUSSION

- ❑ Stall/Spin Awareness
- ❑ Demonstrated Stalls Causes and Recovery Procedures
- ❑ Situational Awareness

INTRODUCE

DEMONSTRATED STALLS

- ❑ Secondary Stall
- ❑ Cross-Control Stall
- ❑ Elevator Trim Stall

NOTE: *The demonstrated stalls are not a proficiency requirement for commercial pilot certification. The purpose of the demonstrations is to reinforce private pilot knowledge of these stalls and help the student recognize, prevent, and if necessary, recover before the stall develops into a spin. These stalls should be practiced with a qualified flight instructor. Some stalls may be prohibited in some airplanes.*

REVIEW

SLOW FLIGHT AND STALLS

- ❑ Maneuvering During Slow Flight
- ❑ Power-Off Stalls
- ❑ Power-On Stalls
- ❑ Accelerated Stalls
- ❑ Spin Awareness

EMERGENCY OPERATIONS

Systems and Equipment Malfunctions

- ❑ Partial Power Loss
- ❑ Electrical Malfunction
- ❑ Instrument Malfunction
- ❑ Landing Gear Malfunction
- ❑ Flap Malfunction
- ❑ Inoperative Trim
- ❑ Smoke and Fire
- ❑ Airplane Specific Malfunctions
- ❑ Door Opening in Flight

Emergency Procedures

- ❑ Emergency Descent
- ❑ Emergency Approach and Landing (Simulated)
- ❑ Emergency Equipment and Survival Gear

TAKEOFFS, LANDINGS, AND GO-AROUNDS

(Includes operations in crosswinds)

- ❑ Soft-Field Takeoff and Climb
- ❑ Soft-Field Approach and Landing
- ❑ Short-Field Takeoff and Maximum Performance Climb
- ❑ Short-Field Approach and Landing

COMPLETION STANDARDS

- Demonstrate understanding of stall and spin aerodynamics, including recognition of and recovery procedures for the demonstrated stalls.
- Demonstrate proficiency in recognizing and recovering from power-off, power-on, and accelerated stalls.
- Demonstrate proficiency in managing systems and equipment malfunctions and performing the emergency procedures associated with the complex airplane.
- Demonstrate proficiency in performing soft-field and short-field takeoffs and landings. During short-field landings, select a point on the runway and land not more than 100 feet beyond the point.

POSTFLIGHT DEBRIEFING

❑ Critique maneuvers/procedures and SRM.
❑ Create a plan for skills that need improvement.
❑ Update the record folder and logbook.

STUDY ASSIGNMENT

Commercial Maneuvers Briefing

Ground Lesson 41

Steep Turns
Chandelles
Lazy Eights

FLIGHT LESSON 52

DUAL — LOCAL

OBJECTIVES

- Become familiar with the steps to perform steep turns, chandelles, and lazy eights.
- Increase proficiency in stall recognition and recovery and spin awareness.
- Increase proficiency in soft-field and short-field takeoff and landings.

PREFLIGHT DISCUSSION

❑ Steps to Perform Listed Maneuvers
❑ Listed Maneuvers – Common Errors
❑ Situational Awareness

INTRODUCE

PERFORMANCE AND GROUND REFERENCE MANEUVERS

❑ Steep Turns
❑ Chandelles
❑ Lazy Eights

REVIEW

DEMONSTRATED STALLS

❏ Secondary Stall
❏ Cross-Control Stall
❏ Elevator Trim Stall

NOTE: *The demonstrated stalls are not a proficiency requirement for commercial pilot certification. The purpose of the demonstrations is to reinforce private pilot knowledge of these stalls and help the student recognize, prevent, and if necessary, recover before the stall develops into a spin. These stalls should be practiced with a qualified flight instructor. Some stalls may be prohibited in some airplanes.*

TAKEOFFS, LANDINGS, AND GO-AROUNDS
(Includes operations in crosswinds)

❏ Soft-Field Takeoff and Climb
❏ Soft-Field Approach and Landing
❏ Short-Field Takeoff and Maximum Performance Climb
❏ Short-Field Approach and Landing

COMPLETION STANDARDS

- Demonstrate understanding of the entry, performance, and recovery techniques for steep turns, chandelles, and lazy eights.
- Demonstrate proficiency in stall and spin recognition and recovery.
- Demonstrate proficiency in soft-field and short-field takeoffs and landings.

POSTFLIGHT DEBRIEFING

❏ Critique maneuvers/procedures and SRM.
❏ Create a plan for skills that need improvement.
❏ Update the record folder and logbook.

STUDY ASSIGNMENT

Ground Lesson 42
Eights-on-Pylons
Steep Spirals
Power-Off 180° Accuracy Approach and Landing

FLIGHT LESSON 53

DUAL — LOCAL

OBJECTIVES

- Become familiar with the steps to perform eights-on-pylons, steep spirals, and power-off 180° accuracy approaches and landings.
- Gain proficiency in performing steep turns, lazy eights, and chandelles.

PREFLIGHT DISCUSSION

- ❏ Steps to Perform Listed Maneuvers
- ❏ Listed Maneuvers – Common Errors
- ❏ Situational Awareness

INTRODUCE

PERFORMANCE AND GROUND REFERENCE MANEUVERS

- ❏ Eights-On-Pylons
- ❏ Steep Spiral

TAKEOFFS, LANDINGS, AND GO-AROUNDS

- ❏ Power-Off 180° Accuracy Approach and Landing

REVIEW

- ❏ Steep Turns
- ❏ Chandelles
- ❏ Lazy Eights

COMPLETION STANDARDS

- Demonstrate understanding of the steps to perform eights-on-pylons, steep spirals, and power-off 180° accuracy approaches and landings.
- Demonstrate increased proficiency in performing steep turns, chandelles, and lazy eights—use the correct entry and recovery procedures and display increased coordination.

POSTFLIGHT DEBRIEFING

- ❏ Critique maneuvers/procedures and SRM.
- ❏ Create a plan for skills that need improvement.
- ❏ Update the record folder and logbook.

FLIGHT LESSON 54

DUAL — LOCAL

OBJECTIVE

- Gain proficiency in performing steep turns, chandelles, lazy eights, eights-on-pylons, steep spirals, and power-off 180° accuracy approaches and landings.
- Use single-pilot resource management to effectively manage risk and make decisions.

PREFLIGHT DISCUSSION

- ❏ Maneuver Performance and Aerodynamic Considerations
- ❏ Commercial ACS Requirements
- ❏ Single-Pilot Resource Management

REVIEW

PERFORMANCE AND GROUND REFERENCE MANEUVERS

- ❑ Steep Turns
- ❑ Chandelles
- ❑ Lazy Eights
- ❑ Eights-On-Pylons
- ❑ Steep Spiral

TAKEOFFS, LANDINGS, AND GO-AROUNDS

(Includes operations in crosswinds)

- ❑ Power-Off 180° Accuracy Approach and Landing

COMPLETION STANDARDS

- Demonstrate increased proficiency in performing the commercial maneuvers to the level required by the Commercial Pilot Airman Certification Standards.
- Demonstrate the ability to use single-pilot resource management to manage risk and make effective decisions.

POSTFLIGHT DEBRIEFING

- ❑ Critique maneuvers/procedures and SRM.
- ❑ Create a plan for skills that need improvement.
- ❑ Update the record folder and logbook.

STUDY ASSIGNMENT

Ground Lesson 44

Commercial Pilot SRM

FLIGHT LESSONS 55, 56, AND 57

SOLO — LOCAL

OBJECTIVES

- Gain proficiency in precise airplane control by operating near the performance limits of the airplane during steep turns, chandelles, lazy eights, eights-on-pylons, steep spirals, and power-off 180° accuracy approaches and landings.
- Increase proficiency in performing slow flight and stalls and soft-field and short-field takeoffs and landings.

PREFLIGHT DISCUSSION

- ❑ Steps to Perform Listed Maneuvers
- ❑ Listed Maneuvers – Common Errors
- ❑ Situational Awareness
- ❑ Single-Pilot Resource Management

REVIEW

PERFORMANCE AND GROUND REFERENCE MANEUVERS
- ❑ Steep Turns
- ❑ Chandelles
- ❑ Lazy Eights
- ❑ Eights-on-Pylons
- ❑ Steep Spiral

SLOW FLIGHT AND STALLS
- ❑ Maneuvering During Slow Flight
- ❑ Power-Off Stalls
- ❑ Power-On Stalls
- ❑ Accelerated Stalls
- ❑ Spin Awareness

TAKEOFFS, LANDINGS, AND GO-AROUNDS
(Includes operations in crosswinds)
- ❑ Soft-Field Takeoff and Climb
- ❑ Soft-Field Approach and Landing
- ❑ Short-Field Takeoff and Maximum Performance Climb
- ❑ Short-Field Approach and Landing
- ❑ Power-Off 180° Accuracy Approach and Landing

COMPLETION STANDARDS

- Increase proficiency in the entry, performance, and recovery techniques for each maneuver.
- Increase proficiency in precise airplane control by operating near the performance limits of the airplane when performing commercial maneuvers.
- Use single-pilot resource management techniques to make effective decisions during flight operations.

POSTFLIGHT DEBRIEFING

- ❑ Critique maneuvers/procedures and SRM.
- ❑ Create a plan for skills that need improvement.
- ❑ Update the record folder and logbook.

FLIGHT LESSON 58

DUAL — LOCAL

OBJECTIVE

Increase proficiency in performing emergency operations to the level required by the Commercial Pilot Airman Certification Standards.

PREFLIGHT DISCUSSION

- ❑ Emergency Procedures
- ❑ Aeronautical Decision Making (ADM)

REVIEW

EMERGENCY OPERATIONS

Systems and Equipment Malfunctions

❏ Partial Power Loss
❏ Electrical Malfunction
❏ Instrument Malfunction
❏ Landing Gear Malfunction
❏ Flap Malfunction
❏ Inoperative Trim
❏ Smoke and Fire
❏ Airplane Specific Malfunctions
❏ Door Opening in Flight

Emergency Procedures

❏ Emergency Descent
❏ Emergency Approach and Landing (Simulated)
❏ Emergency Equipment and Survival Gear

FLIGHT BY REFERENCE TO INSTRUMENTS

Instrument Flight (Full Panel and Partial Panel)

❏ Straight-and-Level Flight, Turns, Climbs, and Descents
❏ Recovery From Unusual Flight Attitudes

NOTE: *The instrument portion of this lesson should be accomplished on an "as required" basis depending on an assessment of the student's capabilities. Students enrolled in the Commercial Pilot Certification Course only must complete 10 hours of instrument training to meet the requirements of Part 141, Appendix D.*

COMPLETION STANDARDS

- Demonstrate increased proficiency in managing systems and equipment malfunctions and performing emergency procedures to the level required by the Commercial Pilot Airman Certification Standards.
- Display competency in the instrument maneuvers to the level required by the Instrument Rating Airman Certification Standards.
- Demonstrate the ability to use single-pilot resource management to manage risk and make effective decisions.

POSTFLIGHT DEBRIEFING

❏ Critique maneuvers/procedures and SRM.
❏ Create a plan for skills that need improvement.
❏ Update the record folder and logbook.

STUDY ASSIGNMENT

Ground Lesson 44

Commercial Pilot SRM

FLIGHT LESSONS 59, 60, AND 61

SOLO — LOCAL

OBJECTIVES

- Increase proficiency and confidence in performing slow flight, stalls, and commercial maneuvers.
- Increase proficiency in single-pilot resource management and aeronautical decision making skills.
- Increase proficiency in flight deck management skills.

NOTE: *The instructor may decide to assign practice specific maneuvers and/or procedures based on student proficiency level.*

PREFLIGHT DISCUSSION

❏ Steps to Perform Listed Maneuvers
❏ Listed Maneuvers – Common Errors
❏ Single-Pilot Resource Management

REVIEW

PERFORMANCE AND GROUND REFERENCE MANEUVERS

❏ Steep Turns
❏ Chandelles
❏ Lazy Eights
❏ Eights-On-Pylons
❏ Steep Spiral

SLOW FLIGHT AND STALLS

❏ Maneuvering During Slow Flight
❏ Power-Off Stalls
❏ Power-On Stalls
❏ Accelerated Stalls
❏ Spin Awareness

COMPLETION STANDARDS

Gain the ability to use single-pilot resource management, make effective decisions, and manage the cockpit while performing each maneuver to the level required by the Commercial Pilot Airman Certification Standards.

POSTFLIGHT DEBRIEFING

❏ Critique maneuvers/procedures and SRM.
❏ Create a plan for skills that need improvement.
❏ Update the record folder and logbook.

FLIGHT LESSONS 62 AND 63

SOLO — LOCAL

OBJECTIVES

- Increase proficiency and confidence in performing soft-field and short-field takeoffs and landings and the power-off 180° accuracy approach and landing.
- Increase proficiency in single-pilot resource management and aeronautical decision making skills.
- Increase proficiency in flight deck management skills.

NOTE: *The instructor may decide to assign practice specific maneuvers and/or procedures based on student proficiency level.*

PREFLIGHT DISCUSSION

❑ Takeoff and Landing Configurations
❑ Common Errors
❑ Single-Pilot Resource Management

REVIEW

TAKEOFFS AND LANDINGS

❑ Soft-Field Takeoff and Climb
❑ Soft-Field Approach and Landing
❑ Short-Field Takeoff and Maximum Performance Climb
❑ Short-Field Approach and Landing
❑ Power-Off 180° Accuracy Approach and Landing

COMPLETION STANDARDS

Be proficient in using single-pilot resource management, making effective decisions, and managing the cockpit while performing each maneuver to the level required by the Commercial Pilot Airman Certification Standards.

POSTFLIGHT DEBRIEFING

❑ Critique maneuvers/procedures and SRM.
❑ Create a plan for skills that need improvement.
❑ Update the record folder and logbook.

FLIGHT LESSONS 64 AND 65

DUAL — LOCAL

OBJECTIVE

Perform the listed maneuvers and procedures to the level required by the Commercial Pilot Airman Certification Standards in preparation for the Stage II Check.

PREFLIGHT DISCUSSION

- ❏ Single-Pilot Resource Management
- ❏ Commercial Pilot Airman Certification Standards

REVIEW

SLOW FLIGHT AND STALLS

- ❏ Maneuvering During Slow Flight
- ❏ Power-Off Stalls
- ❏ Power-On Stalls
- ❏ Accelerated Stalls
- ❏ Spin Awareness

PERFORMANCE AND GROUND REFERENCE MANEUVERS

- ❏ Steep Turns
- ❏ Chandelles
- ❏ Lazy Eights
- ❏ Eights-On-Pylons
- ❏ Steep Spiral

TAKEOFFS, LANDINGS, AND GO-AROUNDS

(Includes operations in crosswinds)

- ❏ Soft-Field Takeoff and Climb
- ❏ Soft-Field Approach and Landing
- ❏ Short-Field Takeoff and Maximum Performance Climb
- ❏ Short-Field Approach and Landing
- ❏ Power-Off 180° Accuracy Approach and Landing
- ❏ Go-Around/Rejected Landing

POSTFLIGHT PROCEDURES

- ❏ After Landing, Parking, and Securing

COMPLETION STANDARDS

- Demonstrate proficiency in the listed maneuvers and procedures to the level required by the Commercial Pilot Airman Certification Standards.
- Demonstrate proficiency in using single-pilot resource management to manage risks and make effective decisions.

POSTFLIGHT DEBRIEFING

- ❏ Critique maneuvers/procedures and SRM.
- ❏ Create a plan for skills that need improvement.
- ❏ Update the record folder and logbook.

FLIGHT LESSON 66

DUAL — LOCAL, COMPLEX AIRPLANE

OBJECTIVES

To prepare for the Stage II Check:

- Review complex airplane operations and use of the navigation system.
- Review slow flight and stalls, commercial maneuvers, and takeoffs and landings.
- Review emergency operations.
- Correct any deficient knowledge and skill areas.

PREFLIGHT DISCUSSION

❑ Complex Airplane Systems and Equipment
❑ Single-Pilot Resource Management
❑ Commercial Pilot Airman Certification Standards

REVIEW

PREFLIGHT PREPARATION

❑ Pilot Qualifications
❑ Airworthiness Requirements
❑ Weather Information
❑ Cross-Country Flight Planning
❑ National Airspace System
❑ Performance and Limitations
❑ Operation of Systems
❑ Human Factors

PREFLIGHT PROCEDURES

❑ Self-Assessment
❑ Preflight Inspection
❑ Flight Deck Management
❑ Engine Starting
❑ Taxiing
❑ Before Takeoff Check/Runup

HIGH ALTITUDE OPERATIONS

❑ Supplemental Oxygen Use
❑ Pressurization System Operation

NOTE: *If high altitude systems are not applicable to the airplane to be used for the practical test, the student must still demonstrate knowledge of high altitude operations sufficient to meet the requirements specified in the FAA Commercial Pilot Airman Certification Standards.*

EMERGENCY OPERATIONS

Systems and Equipment Malfunctions

❑ Partial Power Loss
❑ Electrical Malfunction
❑ Instrument Malfunction
❑ Landing Gear Malfunction

- ❏ Flap Malfunction
- ❏ Inoperative Trim
- ❏ Smoke and Fire
- ❏ Airplane Specific Malfunctions
- ❏ Door Opening in Flight

Emergency Procedures

- ❏ Emergency Descent
- ❏ Emergency Approach and Landing (Simulated)
- ❏ Emergency Equipment and Survival Gear

SLOW FLIGHT AND STALLS

- ❏ Maneuvering During Slow Flight
- ❏ Power-Off Stalls
- ❏ Power-On Stalls
- ❏ Accelerated Stalls
- ❏ Spin Awareness

PERFORMANCE AND GROUND REFERENCE MANEUVERS

- ❏ Steep Turns
- ❏ Chandelles
- ❏ Lazy Eights
- ❏ Eights-On-Pylons
- ❏ Steep Spiral

NAVIGATION SYSTEMS AND RADAR SERVICES

- ❏ VOR Radial Interception and Tracking
- ❏ GPS Course Interception and Tracking
- ❏ Autopilot Use for Navigation, if Equipped

AIRPORT OPERATIONS

- ❏ Radio Communications
- ❏ Airport, Runway, and Taxiway Signs, Markings, and Lighting
- ❏ Traffic Patterns
- ❏ Runway Incursion Avoidance
- ❏ Wake Turbulence Avoidance
- ❏ Wind Shear Avoidance
- ❏ Land and Hold Short Operations (LAHSO)

TAKEOFFS, LANDINGS, AND GO-AROUNDS

(Includes operations in crosswinds)

- ❏ Rejected Takeoff
- ❏ Normal Takeoff and Climb
- ❏ Normal Approach and Landing
- ❏ Soft-Field Takeoff and Climb
- ❏ Soft-Field Approach and Landing
- ❏ Short-Field Takeoff and Maximum Performance Climb
- ❏ Short-Field Approach and Landing
- ❏ Power-Off 180° Accuracy Approach and Landing
- ❏ Go-Around/Rejected Landing

FLIGHT BY REFERENCE TO INSTRUMENTS

Instrument Flight (Full Panel and Partial Panel)

- ❏ Straight-and-Level Flight, Turns, Climbs, and Descents
- ❏ Recovery From Unusual Flight Attitudes

- ❏ GPS Course Interception and Tracking
- ❏ VOR Radial Interception and Tracking

NOTE: *The instrument portion of this lesson should be accomplished on an "as required" basis depending on an assessment of the student's capabilities. Students enrolled in the Commercial Pilot Certification Course only must complete 10 hours of instrument training to meet the requirements of Part 141, Appendix D.*

POSTFLIGHT PROCEDURES

- ❏ After Landing, Parking, and Securing

COMPLETION STANDARDS

- Demonstrates the ability to safely act as pilot in command of the complex airplane.
- Perform the listed maneuvers and procedures to the level required by the Commercial Pilot Airman Certification Standards in preparation for the Stage II Check.

POSTFLIGHT DEBRIEFING

- ❏ Critique maneuvers/procedures and SRM.
- ❏ Create a plan for skills that need improvement.
- ❏ Update the record folder and logbook.

STUDY ASSIGNMENT

Ground Lessons 45 and 46

Stage II Exam

Commercial Pilot End-Of-Course Exam

FLIGHT LESSON 67

DUAL — LOCAL, COMPLEX AIRPLANE

STAGE II CHECK

OBJECTIVE

Demonstrate proficiency as pilot in command of a complex airplane to the chief instructor, assistant chief, or a designated check instructor during the Stage II Check.

PREFLIGHT DISCUSSION

Conduct for the Stage II Check, including:

- ❏ Maneuvers and Procedures
- ❏ Acceptable Performance Criteria
- ❏ Applicable Rules

EVALUATE

PREFLIGHT PREPARATION

- ❏ Pilot Qualifications
- ❏ Airworthiness Requirements

- ❑ Weather Information
- ❑ Cross-Country Flight Planning
- ❑ National Airspace System
- ❑ Performance and Limitations
- ❑ Operation of Systems
- ❑ Human Factors

PREFLIGHT PROCEDURES

- ❑ Self-Assessment
- ❑ Preflight Inspection
- ❑ Flight Deck Management
- ❑ Engine Starting
- ❑ Taxiing
- ❑ Before Takeoff Check/Runup

HIGH ALTITUDE OPERATIONS

- ❑ Supplemental Oxygen Use
- ❑ Pressurization System Operation

***NOTE:** If high altitude systems are not applicable to the airplane to be used for the practical test, the student must still demonstrate knowledge of high altitude operations sufficient to meet the requirements specified in the FAA Commercial Pilot Airman Certification Standards.*

EMERGENCY OPERATIONS

Systems and Equipment Malfunctions

- ❑ Partial Power Loss
- ❑ Electrical Malfunction
- ❑ Instrument Malfunction
- ❑ Landing Gear Malfunction
- ❑ Flap Malfunction
- ❑ Inoperative Trim
- ❑ Smoke and Fire
- ❑ Airplane Specific Malfunctions
- ❑ Door Opening in Flight

Emergency Procedures

- ❑ Emergency Descent
- ❑ Emergency Approach and Landing (Simulated)
- ❑ Emergency Equipment and Survival Gear

SLOW FLIGHT AND STALLS

- ❑ Maneuvering During Slow Flight
- ❑ Power-Off Stalls
- ❑ Power-On Stalls
- ❑ Accelerated Stalls
- ❑ Spin Awareness

PERFORMANCE AND GROUND REFERENCE MANEUVERS

- ❑ Steep Turns
- ❑ Chandelles
- ❑ Lazy Eights
- ❑ Eights-On-Pylons
- ❑ Steep Spiral

AIRPORT OPERATIONS
❑ Radio Communications
❑ Lost Communication Procedures/ATC Light Signals
❑ Airport, Runway, and Taxiway Signs, Markings, and Lighting

TAKEOFFS, LANDINGS, AND GO-AROUNDS
(Includes operations in crosswinds)
❑ Rejected Takeoff
❑ Normal Takeoff and Climb
❑ Normal Approach and Landing
❑ Soft-Field Takeoff and Climb
❑ Soft-Field Approach and Landing
❑ Short-Field Takeoff and Maximum Performance Climb
❑ Short-Field Approach and Landing
❑ Power-Off 180° Accuracy Approach and Landing
❑ Go-Around/Rejected Landing

FLIGHT BY REFERENCE TO INSTRUMENTS
Instrument Flight (Full and Partial Panel)
❑ Straight-and-Level Flight, Turns, Climbs, and Descents
❑ Recovery From Unusual Flight Attitudes
❑ GPS Course Interception and Tracking
❑ VOR Radial Interception and Tracking

NOTE: *The instrument portion of this lesson should be accomplished on an "as required" basis depending on an assessment of the student's capabilities. Students enrolled in the Commercial Pilot Certification Course only must complete 10 hours of instrument training to meet the requirements of Part 141, Appendix D.*

POSTFLIGHT PROCEDURES
❑ After Landing, Parking, and Securing

COMPLETION STANDARDS

- Demonstrate commercial pilot proficiency as pilot in command of a complex airplane as outlined in the Commercial Pilot Airman Certification Standards.
- Demonstrate the ability to use single-pilot resource management to make effective decisions, maintain situational awareness, prevent CFIT, and manage risk, tasks, and automation.

POSTFLIGHT DEBRIEFING

❑ Critique maneuvers/procedures and SRM.
❑ Create a plan for skills that need improvement.
❑ Update the record folder and logbook.

Stage III
Complex Airplane

The Commercial Pilot Certification Course included in this syllabus provides flight lessons that cover a transition to a complex airplane or to a technically advanced airplane (TAA). If you selected the TAA option by checking the appropriate box in the Preface, refer to the Stage III TAA Option. You may conduct the lessons included in Stage III TAA Option in place of the same numbered flight lessons included in this section—Stage III Complex Airplane. Lessons in Stage III that are not specifically identified as complex or TAA, such as dual and solo lessons focused on practicing commercial maneuvers, may be performed in a complex airplane, TAA, or other training airplane.

STAGE OBJECTIVES

During this stage, the student performs maneuvers and procedures to attain the proficiency level required of a commercial pilot with an instrument rating.

STAGE COMPLETION STANDARDS

This stage is complete when the student can demonstrate all flight maneuvers and procedures at the level required by the Commercial Pilot Airman Certification Standards for a commercial pilot with an instrument rating. The student also successfully completes the Stage III and End-of-Course Flight Checks.

NOTE: *Completion of the instrument navigation, holding, and approach tasks listed in specific lessons must be based on the available aircraft equipment.*

FLIGHT LESSONS 68 AND 69

DUAL — LOCAL

OBJECTIVES

- Increase proficiency in instrument scanning and interpretation while reviewing full and partial-panel navigation and approach procedures.
- Increase proficiency in performing emergency procedures and commercial maneuvers.

PREFLIGHT DISCUSSION

❑ Instrument Malfunctions—Gyroscopic, Pitot-Static, Electronic Flight Display
❑ Task Management

REVIEW

PERFORMANCE AND GROUND REFERENCE MANEUVERS

❏ Steep Turns
❏ Chandelles
❏ Lazy Eights
❏ Eights-On-Pylons
❏ Steep Spiral

EMERGENCY OPERATIONS

Systems and Equipment Malfunctions

❏ Partial Power Loss
❏ Electrical Malfunction
❏ Instrument Malfunction
❏ Landing Gear Malfunction
❏ Flap Malfunction
❏ Inoperative Trim
❏ Smoke and Fire
❏ Airplane Specific Malfunctions
❏ Door Opening in Flight

Emergency Procedures

❏ Emergency Descent
❏ Emergency Approach and Landing (Simulated)
❏ Emergency Equipment and Survival Gear

FLIGHT BY REFERENCE TO INSTRUMENTS

Instrument Flight (Full Panel and Partial Panel)

❏ Straight-and-Level Flight, Turns, Climbs, and Descents
❏ Recovery From Unusual Flight Attitudes
❏ GPS Course Interception and Tracking
❏ VOR Radial Interception and Tracking
❏ Holding Procedures

INSTRUMENT APPROACH PROCEDURES

Precision Approach (Full Panel and Partial Panel)

❏ ILS Approaches
❏ RNAV (GPS) Approaches (to LPV minimums with a DA less than 300 feet HAT)

Nonprecision Approach (Full Panel and Partial Panel)

❏ Localizer Approaches
❏ RNAV (GPS) Approaches
❏ VOR and VOR/DME Approaches

NOTE: *The instrument portion of this lesson should be accomplished on an "as required" basis depending on an assessment of the student's capabilities. Students enrolled in the Commercial Pilot Certification Course only must complete 10 hours of instrument training to meet the requirements of Part 141, Appendix D.*

COMPLETION STANDARDS

- Demonstrate proficiency in steep turns, chandelles, lazy eights, eights-on-pylons, and steep spirals to the level required by the Commercial Pilot Airman Certification Standards.

- Demonstrate proficiency in full- and partial-panel instrument flight, including VOR and GPS navigation and instrument approach procedures.

POSTFLIGHT DEBRIEFING

❑ Critique maneuvers/procedures and SRM.
❑ Create a plan for skills that need improvement.
❑ Update the record folder and logbook.

FLIGHT LESSONS 70 AND 71

SOLO — LOCAL

OBJECTIVES

- Increase proficiency in any commercial maneuvers that do not yet meet the requirements of the Commercial Pilot Airman Certification Standards.
- Increase proficiency in using single-pilot resource management techniques to maintain flight safety.

PREFLIGHT DISCUSSION

❑ Steps to Perform Listed Maneuvers
❑ Listed Maneuvers – Common Errors
❑ Single-Pilot Resource Management

REVIEW

PERFORMANCE AND GROUND REFERENCE MANEUVERS

❑ Steep Turns
❑ Chandelles
❑ Lazy Eights
❑ Eights-On-Pylons
❑ Steep Spiral

COMPLETION STANDARDS

- Perform the commercial maneuvers with smoothness and coordination to meet the requirements of the Commercial Pilot Airman Certification Standards.
- Use single-pilot resource management techniques to make effective decisions during flight operations.

POSTFLIGHT DEBRIEFING

❑ Critique maneuvers/procedures and SRM.
❑ Create a plan for skills that need improvement.
❑ Update the record folder and logbook.

FLIGHT LESSON 72

DUAL — LOCAL

OBJECTIVES

- Demonstrate proficiency in any commercial maneuvers to meet the requirements of the Commercial Pilot Airman Certification Standards.
- Correct any areas of faulty performance.

PREFLIGHT DISCUSSION

❏ Commercial Pilot Airman Certification Standards
❏ Single-Pilot Resource Management

REVIEW

PERFORMANCE AND GROUND REFERENCE MANEUVERS

❏ Steep Turns
❏ Chandelles
❏ Lazy Eights
❏ Eights-On-Pylons
❏ Steep Spiral

COMPLETION STANDARDS

- Demonstrate an understanding of the important performance elements of each maneuver including the correct entry, execution, and recovery techniques.
- Demonstrate proficiency in each maneuver at the level required by the Commercial Pilot Airman Certification Standards.
- Use single-pilot resource management techniques to make effective decisions during flight operations.

POSTFLIGHT DEBRIEFING

❏ Critique maneuvers/procedures and SRM.
❏ Create a plan for skills that need improvement.
❏ Update the record folder and logbook.

FLIGHT LESSONS 73, 74, AND 75

SOLO — LOCAL

NOTE: *If the student does not require additional practice of commercial maneuvers, at the student's and instructor's discretion, these flight lessons may be performed as cross-country flights.*

OBJECTIVES

- Practice each flight maneuver assigned with emphasis on those maneuvers that were poorly or inaccurately performed during the previous dual flight.
- Increase proficiency in any commercial maneuvers that do not yet meet the requirements of the Commercial Pilot Airman Certification Standards.

- Increase proficiency in using single-pilot resource management techniques to maintain flight safety.

PREFLIGHT DISCUSSION

- ❑ Steps to Perform Listed Maneuvers
- ❑ Listed Maneuvers – Common Errors
- ❑ Single-Pilot Resource Management

REVIEW

PREFLIGHT PREPARATION

- ❑ Weather Information
- ❑ Cross-Country Flight Planning

NAVIGATION

- ❑ Pilotage and Dead Reckoning
- ❑ Navigation Systems and Radar Services

PERFORMANCE AND GROUND REFERENCE MANEUVERS

- ❑ Steep Turns
- ❑ Chandelles
- ❑ Lazy Eights
- ❑ Eights-On-Pylons
- ❑ Steep Spiral

TAKEOFFS, LANDINGS, AND GO-AROUNDS

(Includes operations in crosswinds)

- ❑ Normal Takeoff and Climb
- ❑ Normal Approach and Landing
- ❑ Soft-Field Takeoff and Climb
- ❑ Soft-Field Approach and Landing
- ❑ Short-Field Takeoff and Maximum Performance Climb
- ❑ Short-Field Approach and Landing
- ❑ Power-Off 180° Accuracy Approach and Landing

COMPLETION STANDARDS

- Perform the commercial maneuvers with smoothness and coordination to meet the requirements of the Commercial Pilot Airman Certification Standards.
- Use single-pilot resource management techniques to make effective decisions during flight operations.

POSTFLIGHT DEBRIEFING

- ❑ Critique maneuvers/procedures and SRM.
- ❑ Create a plan for skills that need improvement.
- ❑ Update the record folder and logbook.

FLIGHT LESSONS 76 AND 77

DUAL — LOCAL

NOTE; *At the instructor's discretion, these flight lessons may be performed as cross-country flights.*

OBJECTIVES

- Increase proficiency in all commercial maneuvers and procedures to identify areas where improved performance is necessary.
- Increase proficiency in instrument procedures on an "as required" basis.

PREFLIGHT DISCUSSION

❏ Commercial Pilot Airman Certification Standards
❏ Single-Pilot Resource Management

REVIEW

PREFLIGHT PREPARATION

❏ Weather Information
❏ Cross-Country Flight Planning

NAVIGATION

❏ Pilotage and Dead Reckoning
❏ Navigation Systems and Radar Services
❏ Diversion
❏ Lost Procedures

SLOW FLIGHT AND STALLS

❏ Maneuvering During Slow Flight
❏ Power-Off Stalls
❏ Power-On Stalls
❏ Accelerated Stalls
❏ Spin Awareness

PERFORMANCE AND GROUND REFERENCE MANEUVERS

❏ Steep Turns
❏ Chandelles
❏ Lazy Eights
❏ Eights-On-Pylons
❏ Steep Spiral

FLIGHT BY REFERENCE TO INSTRUMENTS

Instrument Flight (Full Panel and Partial Panel)

❏ GPS Course Interception and Tracking
❏ VOR Radial Interception and Tracking
❏ Holding Procedures

INSTRUMENT APPROACH PROCEDURES

Precision Approach (Full Panel and Partial Panel)

❏ ILS Approaches
❏ RNAV (GPS) Approaches (to LPV minimums with a DA less than 300 feet HAT)

Nonprecision Approach (Full Panel and Partial Panel)
- ❑ Localizer Approaches
- ❑ RNAV (GPS) Approaches
- ❑ VOR and VOR/DME Approaches

NOTE: *The instrument portion of this lesson should be accomplished on an "as required" basis depending on an assessment of the student's capabilities. Students enrolled in the Commercial Pilot Certification Course only must complete 10 hours of instrument training to meet the requirements of Part 141, Appendix D.*

TAKEOFFS, LANDINGS, AND GO-AROUNDS
(Includes operations in crosswinds)
- ❑ Soft-Field Takeoff and Climb
- ❑ Soft-Field Approach and Landing
- ❑ Short-Field Takeoff and Maximum Performance Climb
- ❑ Short-Field Approach and Landing
- ❑ Power-Off 180° Accuracy Approach and Landing
- ❑ Go-Around/Rejected Landing

COMPLETION STANDARDS

- Demonstrate proficiency in each maneuver at the level required by the Commercial Pilot Airman Certification Standards.
- Use single-pilot resource management techniques to make effective decisions during flight operations.
- Demonstrate proficiency at the level required by the Instrument Rating Airman Certification Standards in all instrument procedures on an "as required" basis.

POSTFLIGHT DEBRIEFING

- ❑ Critique maneuvers/procedures and SRM.
- ❑ Create a plan for skills that need improvement.
- ❑ Update the record folder and logbook.

FLIGHT LESSON 78

DUAL — LOCAL, COMPLEX AIRPLANE

OBJECTIVES

- Increase proficiency in all commercial maneuvers and procedures in the complex airplane to the level required by the Commercial Pilot Airman Certification Standards.
- Operate airplane systems and equipment and perform normal and emergency procedures in the complex airplane to the level required by the Commercial Pilot Airman Certification Standards.

PREFLIGHT DISCUSSION

- ❑ Complex Airplane Systems and Equipment
- ❑ Complex Airplane Normal and Emergency Procedures
- ❑ Commercial Pilot Airman Certification Standards
- ❑ Single-Pilot Resource Management

REVIEW

PREFLIGHT PREPARATION

- ❑ Pilot Qualifications
- ❑ Airworthiness Requirements
- ❑ Weather Information
- ❑ Performance and Limitations
- ❑ Operation of Systems
- ❑ Human Factors

PREFLIGHT PROCEDURES

- ❑ Self-Assessment
- ❑ Preflight Inspection
- ❑ Flight Deck Management
- ❑ Engine Starting
- ❑ Taxiing
- ❑ Before Takeoff Check/Runup

HIGH ALTITUDE OPERATIONS

- ❑ Supplemental Oxygen Use
- ❑ Pressurization System Operation

NOTE: *If high altitude systems are not applicable to the airplane to be used for the practical test, the student must still demonstrate knowledge of high altitude operations sufficient to meet the requirements specified in the FAA Commercial Pilot Airman Certification Standards.*

EMERGENCY OPERATIONS

Systems and Equipment Malfunctions

- ❑ Partial Power Loss
- ❑ Electrical Malfunction
- ❑ Instrument Malfunction
- ❑ Landing Gear Malfunction
- ❑ Flap Malfunction
- ❑ Inoperative Trim

- ❑ Smoke and Fire
- ❑ Airplane Specific Malfunctions
- ❑ Door Opening in Flight

Emergency Procedures

- ❑ Emergency Descent
- ❑ Emergency Approach and Landing (Simulated)
- ❑ Emergency Equipment and Survival Gear

SLOW FLIGHT AND STALLS

- ❑ Maneuvering During Slow Flight
- ❑ Power-Off Stalls
- ❑ Power-On Stalls
- ❑ Accelerated Stalls
- ❑ Spin Awareness

PERFORMANCE AND GROUND REFERENCE MANEUVERS

- ❑ Steep Turns
- ❑ Chandelles
- ❑ Lazy Eights
- ❑ Eights-On-Pylons
- ❑ Steep Spiral

INSTRUMENT APPROACH PROCEDURES

Precision Approach (Full Panel and Partial Panel)

- ❑ ILS Approaches
- ❑ RNAV (GPS) Approaches (to LPV minimums with a DA less than 300 feet HAT)

Nonprecision Approach (Full and Partial Panel)

- ❑ Localizer Approaches
- ❑ RNAV (GPS) Approaches
- ❑ VOR and VOR/DME Approaches

NOTE: *The instrument portion of this lesson should be accomplished on an "as required" basis depending on an assessment of the student's capabilities. Students enrolled in the Commercial Pilot Certification Course only must complete 10 hours of instrument training to meet the requirements of Part 141, Appendix D.*

TAKEOFFS, LANDINGS, AND GO-AROUNDS

(Includes operations in crosswinds)

- ❑ Rejected Takeoff
- ❑ Normal Takeoff and Climb
- ❑ Normal Approach and Landing
- ❑ Soft-Field Takeoff and Climb
- ❑ Soft-Field Approach and Landing
- ❑ Short-Field Takeoff and Maximum Performance Climb
- ❑ Short-Field Approach and Landing
- ❑ Power-Off 180° Accuracy Approach and Landing
- ❑ Go-Around/Rejected Landing

POSTFLIGHT PROCEDURES

- ❑ After Landing, Parking, and Securing

COMPLETION STANDARDS

- Demonstrate proficiency in all commercial maneuvers and procedures in the complex airplane to the level required by the Commercial Pilot Airman Certification Standards.
- Demonstrate understanding of the complex airplane flight characteristics, systems, equipment, and emergency procedures by performing all operations to the level required by the Commercial Pilot Airman Certification Standards.

POSTFLIGHT DEBRIEFING

- ❑ Critique maneuvers/procedures and SRM.
- ❑ Create a plan for skills that need improvement.
- ❑ Update the record folder and logbook.

FLIGHT LESSONS 79, 80, AND 81

SOLO — LOCAL

NOTE: *If the student does not require additional practice of commercial maneuvers, at the student's and instructor's discretion, these flight lessons may be performed as cross-country flights.*

OBJECTIVE

Practice slow flight and stalls, commercial maneuvers, and takeoffs and landings to correct any faulty performance areas from the previous dual flight.

PREFLIGHT DISCUSSION

- ❑ Steps to Perform Listed Maneuvers
- ❑ Listed Maneuvers – Common Errors
- ❑ Single-Pilot Resource Management

OBJECTIVES

- Practice each flight maneuver assigned with emphasis on those maneuvers that were poorly or inaccurately performed during the previous dual flight.
- Increase proficiency in any commercial maneuvers that do not yet meet the requirements of the Commercial Pilot Airman Certification Standards.
- Increase proficiency in using single-pilot resource management techniques to maintain flight safety.

PREFLIGHT DISCUSSION

- ❑ Steps to Perform Listed Maneuvers
- ❑ Listed Maneuvers – Common Errors
- ❑ Single-Pilot Resource Management

REVIEW

PREFLIGHT PREPARATION

- ❑ Weather Information
- ❑ Cross-Country Flight Planning

NAVIGATION
- ❑ Pilotage and Dead Reckoning
- ❑ Navigation Systems and Radar Services

SLOW FLIGHT AND STALLS
- ❑ Maneuvering During Slow Flight
- ❑ Power-Off Stalls
- ❑ Power-On Stalls
- ❑ Accelerated Stalls
- ❑ Spin Awareness

PERFORMANCE AND GROUND REFERENCE MANEUVERS
- ❑ Steep Turns
- ❑ Chandelles
- ❑ Lazy Eights
- ❑ Eights-On-Pylons
- ❑ Steep Spiral

TAKEOFFS, LANDINGS, AND GO-AROUNDS
(Includes operations in crosswinds)
- ❑ Normal Takeoff and Climb
- ❑ Normal Approach and Landing
- ❑ Soft-Field Takeoff and Climb
- ❑ Soft-Field Approach and Landing
- ❑ Short-Field Takeoff and Maximum Performance Climb
- ❑ Short-Field Approach and Landing
- ❑ Power-Off 180° Accuracy Approach and Landing

COMPLETION STANDARDS

Perform all commercial maneuvers and procedures to the level required by the Commercial Pilot Airman Certification Standards by correcting any areas of faulty performance.

POSTFLIGHT DEBRIEFING

- ❑ Critique maneuvers/procedures and SRM.
- ❑ Create a plan for skills that need improvement.
- ❑ Update the record folder and logbook.

FLIGHT LESSON 82

DUAL — CROSS-COUNTRY, COMPLEX AIRPLANE

OBJECTIVES

- Increase proficiency in flight planning and cross-country operations in a complex airplane by performing a cross-country flight over 50 nautical miles from the original point of departure.
- Increase proficiency in using single-pilot resources management skills to make effective decisions during a cross-country flight in a complex airplane.

PREFLIGHT DISCUSSION

❏ Cross-Country Flight Planning
❏ Risk Management (5Ps, PAVE)

REVIEW

CROSS-COUNTRY FLIGHT

PREFLIGHT PREPARATION

❏ Pilot Qualifications
❏ Airworthiness Requirements
❏ Weather Information
❏ National Airspace System
❏ Operation of Systems
❏ Human Factors

Cross-Country Flight Planning

❏ Route Planning
❏ Altitude Selection
❏ Weight and Balance
❏ Performance and Limitations
❏ Determining ETA
❏ Fuel Requirements
❏ Sources of Flight Information
❏ Navigation Log
❏ VFR Flight Plan

PREFLIGHT PROCEDURES

❏ Self-Assessment
❏ Preflight Inspection
❏ Flight Deck Management
❏ Engine Starting
❏ Taxiing
❏ Before Takeoff Check/Runup

NAVIGATION

❏ Pilotage and Dead Reckoning
❏ Diversion
❏ Lost Procedures

Navigation Systems and Radar Services

❏ VOR Radial Interception and Tracking

- ❑ GPS Course Interception and Tracking
- ❑ Use of ATC Services
- ❑ Autopilot Use for Navigation, if Equipped

CROSS-COUNTRY PROCEDURES
- ❑ Collision Avoidance
- ❑ Flight Deck Management
- ❑ Power Settings and Mixture Control
- ❑ CFIT Avoidance
- ❑ Estimating Visibility in Flight
- ❑ Flight on Federal Airways
- ❑ Opening and Closing Flight Plan

EMERGENCY OPERATIONS

Systems and Equipment Malfunctions
- ❑ Partial Power Loss
- ❑ Electrical Malfunction
- ❑ Instrument Malfunction
- ❑ Landing Gear Malfunction
- ❑ Flap Malfunction
- ❑ Inoperative Trim
- ❑ Smoke and Fire
- ❑ Airplane Specific Malfunctions
- ❑ Door Opening in Flight

Emergency Procedures
- ❑ Emergency Descent
- ❑ Emergency Approach and Landing (Simulated)
- ❑ Emergency Equipment and Survival Gear

INSTRUMENT APPROACH PROCEDURES

Precision Approach (Full Panel and Partial Panel)
- ❑ ILS Approaches
- ❑ RNAV (GPS) Approaches (to LPV minimums with a DA less than 300 feet HAT)

Nonprecision Approach (Full Panel and Partial Panel)
- ❑ Localizer Approaches
- ❑ RNAV (GPS) Approaches
- ❑ VOR and VOR/DME Approaches

***NOTE:** The instrument portion of this lesson should be accomplished on an "as required" basis depending on an assessment of the student's capabilities. Students enrolled in the Commercial Pilot Certification Course only must complete 10 hours of instrument training to meet the requirements of Part 141, Appendix D.*

AIRPORT OPERATIONS
- ❑ Radio Communications
- ❑ Lost Communication Procedures/ATC Light Signals
- ❑ Airport, Runway, and Taxiway Signs, Markings, and Lighting
- ❑ Traffic Patterns
- ❑ Runway Incursion Avoidance
- ❑ Wake Turbulence Avoidance
- ❑ Wind Shear Avoidance
- ❑ Land and Hold Short Operations (LAHSO)

TAKEOFFS, LANDINGS, AND GO-AROUNDS
(Includes operations in crosswinds)
- ❑ Normal Takeoff and Climb
- ❑ Normal Approach and Landing

COMPLETION STANDARDS

- Demonstrate the ability to safely act as pilot in command of the complex airplane during cross-country flights.
- Demonstrate proficiency in managing systems and equipment malfunctions and performing emergency procedures in a complex airplane during a cross-country flight.
- Demonstrate proficiency in using single-pilot resources management skills to make effective decisions during a cross-country flight in a TAA.

POSTFLIGHT DEBRIEFING

- ❑ Critique maneuvers/procedures and SRM.
- ❑ Create a plan for skills that need improvement.
- ❑ Update the record folder and logbook.

STUDY ASSIGNMENT

Prepare for the Stage III Check in Flight Lesson 86.

FLIGHT LESSON 83

DUAL — LOCAL, COMPLEX AIRPLANE

OBJECTIVE

Perform all maneuvers and procedures at the level required in the Commercial Pilot Airman Certification Standards in preparation for the Stage III Flight Check and the FAA Commercial Pilot Practical Test.

PREFLIGHT DISCUSSION

- ❑ Complex Airplane Systems and Equipment
- ❑ Commercial Pilot Airman Certification Standards
- ❑ Single-Pilot Resource Management

REVIEW

PREFLIGHT PREPARATION
- ❑ Pilot Qualifications
- ❑ Airworthiness Requirements
- ❑ Weather Information
- ❑ Cross-Country Flight Planning
- ❑ National Airspace System
- ❑ Performance and Limitations
- ❑ Operation of Systems
- ❑ Human Factors

PREFLIGHT PROCEDURES
- ❏ Self-Assessment
- ❏ Preflight Inspection
- ❏ Flight Deck Management
- ❏ Engine Starting
- ❏ Taxiing
- ❏ Before Takeoff Check/Runup

PERFORMANCE AND GROUND REFERENCE MANEUVERS
- ❏ Steep Turns
- ❏ Chandelles
- ❏ Lazy Eights
- ❏ Eights-On-Pylons
- ❏ Steep Spiral

TAKEOFFS, LANDINGS, AND GO-AROUNDS
(Includes operations in crosswinds)
- ❏ Rejected Takeoff
- ❏ Normal Takeoff and Climb
- ❏ Normal Approach and Landing
- ❏ Soft-Field Takeoff and Climb
- ❏ Soft-Field Approach and Landing
- ❏ Short-Field Takeoff and Maximum Performance Climb
- ❏ Short-Field Approach and Landing
- ❏ Power-Off 180° Accuracy Approach and Landing
- ❏ Go-Around

COMPLETION STANDARDS
Demonstrate proficiency in performing each of the listed maneuvers and procedures to the level required by the Commercial Pilot Airman Certification Standards.

POSTFLIGHT DEBRIEFING
- ❏ Critique maneuvers/procedures and SRM.
- ❏ Create a plan for skills that need improvement.
- ❏ Update the record folder and logbook.

STUDY ASSIGNMENT
Commercial Pilot Practical Test Briefing

FLIGHT LESSONS 84 AND 85

DUAL — LOCAL

OBJECTIVE
Perform all maneuvers and procedures at the level required in the Commercial Pilot Airman Certification Standards in preparation for the Stage III Flight Check and the FAA Commercial Pilot Practical Test.

PREFLIGHT DISCUSSION

- ❑ Commercial Pilot Airman Certification Standards
- ❑ Single-Pilot Resource Management

REVIEW

PREFLIGHT PREPARATION

- ❑ Pilot Qualifications
- ❑ Airworthiness Requirements
- ❑ Weather Information
- ❑ National Airspace System
- ❑ Performance and Limitations
- ❑ Operation of Systems
- ❑ Human Factors

PREFLIGHT PROCEDURES

- ❑ Self-Assessment
- ❑ Preflight Inspection
- ❑ Flight Deck Management
- ❑ Engine Starting
- ❑ Taxiing
- ❑ Before Takeoff Check/Runup

SLOW FLIGHT AND STALLS

- ❑ Maneuvering During Slow Flight
- ❑ Power-Off Stalls
- ❑ Power-On Stalls
- ❑ Accelerated Stalls
- ❑ Spin Awareness

PERFORMANCE AND GROUND REFERENCE MANEUVERS

- ❑ Steep Turns
- ❑ Chandelles
- ❑ Lazy Eights
- ❑ Eights-On-Pylons
- ❑ Steep Spiral

NAVIGATION

- ❑ Pilotage and Dead Reckoning
- ❑ Navigation Systems and Radar Services
- ❑ Diversion
- ❑ Lost Procedures

HIGH ALTITUDE OPERATIONS

- ❑ Supplemental Oxygen Use
- ❑ Pressurization System Operation

AIRPORT OPERATIONS

- ❑ Radio Communications
- ❑ Lost Communication Procedures/ATC Light Signals
- ❑ Airport, Runway, and Taxiway Signs, Markings, and Lighting
- ❑ Traffic Patterns
- ❑ Runway Incursion Avoidance
- ❑ Wake Turbulence Avoidance

- ❑ Wind Shear Avoidance
- ❑ Land and Hold Short Operations (LAHSO)

EMERGENCY OPERATIONS
- ❑ Systems and Equipment Malfunctions
- ❑ Emergency Descent
- ❑ Emergency Approach and Landing (Simulated)
- ❑ Emergency Equipment and Survival Gear

TAKEOFFS, LANDINGS, AND GO-AROUNDS
(Includes operations in crosswinds)
- ❑ Rejected Takeoff
- ❑ Normal Takeoff and Climb
- ❑ Normal Approach and Landing
- ❑ Soft-Field Takeoff and Climb
- ❑ Soft-Field Approach and Landing
- ❑ Short-Field Takeoff and Maximum Performance Climb
- ❑ Short-Field Approach and Landing
- ❑ Power-Off 180° Accuracy Approach and Landing
- ❑ Go-Around/Rejected Landing

POSTFLIGHT PROCEDURES
- ❑ After Landing, Parking, and Securing

COMPLETION STANDARDS
- Demonstrate proficiency and competence required for commercial pilot certification by performing the outlined maneuvers with smoothness and coordination and using single-pilot resource management to manage risk and make effective decisions.
- Demonstrate the ability to meet or exceed the performance tolerances listed in the Commercial Pilot Airman Certification Standards.
- Demonstrate the ability to use single-pilot resource management to make effective decisions, maintain situational awareness, prevent CFIT, and manage risk, tasks, and automation.

POSTFLIGHT DEBRIEFING
- ❑ Critique maneuvers/procedures and SRM.
- ❑ Create a plan for skills that need improvement.
- ❑ Update the record folder and logbook.

STUDY ASSIGNMENT
Prepare for the Stage III Check in Flight Lesson 86 and the End-of-Course Flight Check in Flight Lesson 87.

FLIGHT LESSON 86

DUAL — LOCAL

STAGE III CHECK

OBJECTIVES

- Demonstrate proficiency in performing commercial maneuvers to the chief instructor, assistant chief, or a designated check instructor during the Stage III Check.
- Demonstrate proficiency in all IFR tasks listed to the chief instructor, assistant chief, or a designated check instructor during the Stage III Check.

NOTE: *The instrument competency portion of this stage check will be conducted on an "as required" basis. This part of the flight applies to students who are enrolled in the Instrument/Commercial Course concurrently and have not completed the FAA Instrument Rating Practical Test.*

PREFLIGHT DISCUSSION

❏ Student and Flight Check Instructor Roles and Expectations
❏ Questions to Test Student Knowledge

EVALUATE

PREFLIGHT PREPARATION

❏ Pilot Qualifications
❏ Airworthiness Requirements
❏ Weather Information
❏ Cross-Country Flight Planning
❏ National Airspace System
❏ Performance and Limitations
❏ Operation of Systems
❏ Human Factors

PREFLIGHT PROCEDURES

❏ Self-Assessment
❏ Preflight Inspection
❏ Flight Deck Management
❏ Engine Starting
❏ Taxiing
❏ Before Takeoff Check/Runup

SLOW FLIGHT AND STALLS

❏ Maneuvering During Slow Flight
❏ Power-Off Stalls
❏ Power-On Stalls
❏ Accelerated Stalls
❏ Spin Awareness

PERFORMANCE AND GROUND REFERENCE MANEUVERS

❏ Steep Turns
❏ Chandelles

- ❑ Lazy Eights
- ❑ Eights-On-Pylons
- ❑ Steep Spiral

NAVIGATION
- ❑ Pilotage and Dead Reckoning
- ❑ Navigation Systems and Radar Services
- ❑ Diversion
- ❑ Lost Procedures

HIGH ALTITUDE OPERATIONS
- ❑ Supplemental Oxygen Use
- ❑ Pressurization System Operation

AIRPORT OPERATIONS
- ❑ Radio Communications
- ❑ Lost Communication Procedures/ATC Light Signals
- ❑ Airport, Runway, and Taxiway Signs, Markings, and Lighting
- ❑ Traffic Patterns
- ❑ Runway Incursion Avoidance
- ❑ Wake Turbulence Avoidance
- ❑ Wind Shear Avoidance
- ❑ Land and Hold Short Operations (LAHSO)

EMERGENCY OPERATIONS
- ❑ Systems and Equipment Malfunctions
- ❑ Emergency Descent
- ❑ Emergency Approach and Landing (Simulated)
- ❑ Emergency Equipment and Survival Gear

TAKEOFFS, LANDINGS, AND GO-AROUNDS
(Includes operations in crosswinds)
- ❑ Normal Takeoff and Climb
- ❑ Normal Approach and Landing
- ❑ Soft-Field Takeoff and Climb
- ❑ Soft-Field Approach and Landing
- ❑ Short-Field Takeoff and Maximum Performance Climb
- ❑ Short-Field Approach and Landing
- ❑ Power-Off 180° Accuracy Approach and Landing
- ❑ Go-Around/Rejected Landing

PREFLIGHT PROCEDURES
- ❑ Airplane Systems Related to IFR Operations
- ❑ Airplane Flight Instruments and Navigation Equipment
- ❑ Instrument Flight Deck Check

AIR TRAFFIC CONTROL CLEARANCES AND PROCEDURES
- ❑ Compliance with ATC Clearances—Departure, Enroute, Arrival, Approach
- ❑ Holding Procedures

FLIGHT BY REFERENCE TO INSTRUMENTS
Instrument Flight (Full Panel and Partial Panel)
- ❑ Straight-and-Level Flight, Turns, Climbs, and Descents
- ❑ Recovery From Unusual Flight Attitudes
- ❑ GPS Course Interception and Tracking
- ❑ VOR Radial Interception and Tracking

Departure, Enroute, and Arrival Operations
- ❑ Standard Instrument Departure (SID)
- ❑ Obstacle Departure Procedure (ODP)
- ❑ Standard Terminal Arrival (STAR)

INSTRUMENT APPROACH PROCEDURES
Precision Approach
- ❑ ILS Approaches
- ❑ RNAV (GPS) Approaches (to LPV minimums with a DA less than 300 feet HAT)

Nonprecision Approach
- ❑ Localizer Approaches
- ❑ RNAV (GPS) Approaches
- ❑ VOR and VOR/DME Approaches

Landing from an Instrument Approach
- ❑ Straight-In Landing
- ❑ Circling Approach

EMERGENCY OPERATIONS
- ❑ Loss of Communications
- ❑ Approach with Loss of Primary Flight Instrument Indicators

POSTFLIGHT PROCEDURES
- ❑ Checking Instruments and Equipment
- ❑ After Landing, Parking, and Securing

COMPLETION STANDARDS
- Demonstrate proficiency in all commercial pilot tasks as required by the Commercial Pilot Airman Certification Standards.
- Demonstrate proficiency in all instrument rating tasks as required by the Instrument Rating Airman Certification Standards.
- Demonstrate the ability to use single-pilot resource management to make effective decisions, maintain situational awareness, prevent CFIT, and manage risk, tasks, and automation.

POSTFLIGHT DEBRIEFING
- ❑ Critique maneuvers/procedures and SRM.
- ❑ Create a plan for skills that need improvement.
- ❑ Update the record folder and logbook.

STUDY ASSIGNMENT
Prepare for the End-of-Course Flight Check in Flight Lesson 87.

FLIGHT LESSON 87

DUAL — LOCAL END-OF-COURSE FLIGHT CHECK FOR COURSE COMPLETION

OBJECTIVES

- Demonstrate proficiency in all listed IFR tasks to the chief instructor, assistant chief, or a designated check instructor during the End-of-Course Flight Check. The proficiency level must meet the requirements of the Instrument Rating Airman Certification Standards.
- Demonstrate proficiency in all listed commercial tasks to the chief instructor, assistant chief, or a designated check instructor during the End-of-Course Flight Check. The proficiency level must meet the requirements of the Commercial Pilot Airman Certification Standards.

NOTE: *The instrument competency portion of this stage check will be conducted on an "as required" basis. This part of the flight applies to students who are enrolled, in the Instrument/Commercial Course concurrently and have not completed the FAA practical test for the instrument rating.*

NOTE: *The types of navigation, holding procedures, and approach procedures evaluated will be based on the equipment in the training airplane.*

PREFLIGHT DISCUSSION

❑ Student and Flight Check Instructor Roles and Expectations
❑ Questions to Test Student Knowledge

EVALUATE

PREFLIGHT PREPARATION

❑ Pilot Qualifications
❑ Airworthiness Requirements
❑ Weather Information
❑ Cross-Country Flight Planning
❑ National Airspace System
❑ Performance and Limitations
❑ Operation of Systems
❑ Human Factors

PREFLIGHT PROCEDURES

❑ Self-Assessment
❑ Preflight Inspection
❑ Flight Deck Management
❑ Engine Starting
❑ Taxiing
❑ Before Takeoff Check/Runup

SLOW FLIGHT AND STALLS
- ❑ Maneuvering During Slow Flight
- ❑ Power-Off Stalls
- ❑ Power-On Stalls
- ❑ Accelerated Stalls
- ❑ Spin Awareness

PERFORMANCE AND GROUND REFERENCE MANEUVERS
- ❑ Steep Turns
- ❑ Chandelles
- ❑ Lazy Eights
- ❑ Eights-On-Pylons
- ❑ Steep Spiral

NAVIGATION
- ❑ Pilotage and Dead Reckoning
- ❑ Navigation Systems and Radar Services
- ❑ Diversion
- ❑ Lost Procedures

HIGH ALTITUDE OPERATIONS
- ❑ Supplemental Oxygen Use
- ❑ Pressurization System Operation

AIRPORT OPERATIONS
- ❑ Radio Communications
- ❑ Lost Communication Procedures/ATC Light Signals
- ❑ Airport, Runway, and Taxiway Signs, Markings, and Lighting
- ❑ Traffic Patterns
- ❑ Runway Incursion Avoidance
- ❑ Wake Turbulence Avoidance
- ❑ Wind Shear Avoidance
- ❑ Land and Hold Short Operations (LAHSO)

EMERGENCY OPERATIONS
- ❑ Systems and Equipment Malfunctions
- ❑ Emergency Descent
- ❑ Emergency Approach and Landing (Simulated)
- ❑ Emergency Equipment and Survival Gear

TAKEOFFS, LANDINGS, AND GO-AROUNDS
(Includes operations in crosswinds)
- ❑ Normal Takeoff and Climb
- ❑ Normal Approach and Landing
- ❑ Soft-Field Takeoff and Climb
- ❑ Soft-Field Approach and Landing
- ❑ Short-Field Takeoff and Maximum Performance Climb
- ❑ Short-Field Approach and Landing
- ❑ Power-Off 180° Accuracy Approach and Landing
- ❑ Go-Around/Rejected Landing

PREFLIGHT PROCEDURES
- ❑ Airplane Systems Related to IFR Operations
- ❑ Airplane Flight Instruments and Navigation Equipment
- ❑ Instrument Flight Deck Check

AIR TRAFFIC CONTROL CLEARANCES AND PROCEDURES

- ❑ Compliance with ATC Clearances—Departure, Enroute, Arrival, Approach
- ❑ Holding Procedures

FLIGHT BY REFERENCE TO INSTRUMENTS

Instrument Flight (Full and Partial Panel)

- ❑ Straight-and-Level Flight, Turns, Climbs, and Descents
- ❑ Recovery From Unusual Flight Attitudes
- ❑ GPS Course Interception and Tracking
- ❑ VOR Radial Interception and Tracking

Departure, Enroute, and Arrival Operations

- ❑ Standard Instrument Departure (SID)
- ❑ Obstacle Departure Procedure (ODP)
- ❑ Standard Terminal Arrival (STAR)

INSTRUMENT APPROACH PROCEDURES

Precision Approach

- ❑ ILS Approaches
- ❑ RNAV (GPS) Approaches (to LPV minimums with a DA less than 300 feet HAT)

Nonprecision Approach

- ❑ Localizer Approaches
- ❑ RNAV (GPS) Approaches
- ❑ VOR and VOR/DME Approaches

Landing from an Instrument Approach

- ❑ Straight-In Landing
- ❑ Circling Approach

EMERGENCY OPERATIONS

- ❑ Loss of Communications
- ❑ Approach with Loss of Primary Flight Instrument Indicators

POSTFLIGHT PROCEDURES

- ❑ Checking Instruments and Equipment
- ❑ After Landing, Parking, and Securing

COMPLETION STANDARDS

- Demonstrate proficiency in all commercial pilot tasks as required by the Commercial Pilot Airman Certification Standards.
- Demonstrate proficiency in all instrument rating tasks as required by the Instrument Rating Airman Certification Standards.
- Demonstrate the ability to use single-pilot resource management to make effective decisions, maintain situational awareness, prevent CFIT, and manage risk, tasks, and automation.

NOTE: *If the student has not taken the FAA Instrument Rating Practical Test, the Instrument Rating Practical Test Briefing also should be used during this Flight Lesson.*

POSTFLIGHT DEBRIEFING

- ❑ Evaluate maneuvers/procedures and SRM.
- ❑ Plan additional instruction for skills not meeting course completion standards.
- ❑ Update the record folder and logbook.

Commercial Pilot Flight Training Stage II TAA Option

If you selected the technically advanced airplane (TAA) option by checking the appropriate box in the Preface, you may conduct the lessons shown in this section for the TAA transition in place of the same numbered flight lessons shown in Stage II of the Commercial Course for the complex airplane transition. By doing so in this stage and in Stage III, the 10-hour TAA and total flight time requirements will be met. In addition, lessons in this stage that are not specifically identified as complex or TAA, such as dual and solo lessons focused on introducing and practicing commercial maneuvers, may be performed in a TAA or complex airplane.

TAA Transition	Complex Airplane Transition
Flight Lesson 46 **Dual — Local, TAA**	**Flight Lesson 46** **Dual — Local, Complex Airplane**
Flight Lessons 47 and 48 **Dual — Local, TAA**	**Flight Lessons 47 and 48** **Dual — Local, Complex Airplane**
Flight Lessons 49 and 50 **Dual — Local or Cross-Country, TAA**	**Flight Lessons 49 and 50** **Dual — Local, Complex Airplane**
Flight Lessons 51 – 65 *(TAA Optional)*	*Flight Lessons 51 – 65* *(Complex Airplane Optional)*
Flight Lessons 66 **Dual — Local or Cross-Country, TAA**	**Flight Lesson 66** **Dual — Local, Complex Airplane**
Flight Lesson 67 **Dual — Local, TAA** **Stage II Check**	**Flight Lesson 67** **Dual — Local, Complex Airplane** **Stage II Check**

STAGE OBJECTIVES

During this stage, the student gains proficiency in operating a technically advanced airplane (TAA). The student learns the procedures to operate the TAA's systems, manage information and automation, and handle equipment malfunctions and failures. In addition, the student gains skills to perform the flight maneuvers required for commercial pilot certification.

STAGE COMPLETION STANDARDS

This stage is complete when the student can demonstrate commercial pilot proficiency in the operation of the TAA and can correctly perform commercial maneuvers.

***NOTE:** A technically advanced airplane (TAA) is defined as an airplane equipped with an electronically advanced avionics system. At a minimum, this system must include the following:*
- *A primary flight display (PFD) with an airspeed indicator, turn coordinator, attitude indicator, heading indicator, altimeter, and vertical speed indicator;*
- *A multifunction display (MFD) with a moving map using GPS navigation to display the aircraft position;*
- *A two-axis autopilot integrated with the navigation and heading guidance system.*

FLIGHT LESSON 46

DUAL — LOCAL, TAA

OBJECTIVES

- Become familiar with operating technically advanced airplane (TAA) systems and equipment during ground and flight operations.
- Become familiar with high altitude operations, including the use of supplemental oxygen and pressurization equipment as applicable to the airplane.
- Properly configure the airplane and apply wind correction in the traffic pattern to perform takeoffs and landings.

PREFLIGHT DISCUSSION

❑ Pilot's Operating Handbook
❑ Airplane Performance and Limitations
❑ Avionics Operating Guide/Manual
❑ Digital Flight Instrument Systems
❑ GPS Equipment Operation
❑ Information Management

INTRODUCE

PREFLIGHT PREPARATION

❑ Pilot Qualifications
❑ Airworthiness Requirements
❑ Weather Information
❑ Performance and Limitations
❑ Operation of Systems
❑ Human Factors

PREFLIGHT PROCEDURES

❑ Self-Assessment
❑ Preflight Inspection
❑ Passenger Briefing
❑ Flight Deck Management
❑ Engine Starting
❑ Taxiing
❑ Before Takeoff Check/Runup
  ◊ GPS Programming
  ◊ PFD Setup
  ◊ MFD Setup

BASIC MANEUVERS

- ❑ Straight-and-Level Flight
- ❑ Climbs and Descents
- ❑ PFD Instrument Interpretation
- ❑ Use of MFD Features
- ❑ Power Settings and Mixture Control

AVIONICS OPERATION

- ❑ Checklists
- ❑ Engine Indication System
- ❑ Audio Panel
- ❑ Transponder
- ❑ Collision Avoidance—Traffic Information Operation and Interpretation
- ❑ Information Management

HIGH ALTITUDE OPERATIONS

- ❑ Supplemental Oxygen Use
- ❑ Pressurization System Operation

NOTE: *If high altitude systems are not applicable to the airplane to be used for the practical test, the student must still demonstrate knowledge of high altitude operations sufficient to meet the requirements specified in the FAA Commercial Pilot Airman Certification Standards.*

AIRPORT OPERATIONS

- ❑ Radio Communications
- ❑ Airport, Runway, and Taxiway Signs, Markings, and Lighting
- ❑ Traffic Patterns

TAKEOFFS, LANDINGS, AND GO-AROUNDS

(Includes operations in crosswinds)

- ❑ Rejected Takeoff
- ❑ Normal Takeoff and Climb
- ❑ Normal Approach and Landing
- ❑ Go-Around/Rejected Landing

POSTFLIGHT PROCEDURES

- ❑ After Landing, Parking, and Securing

COMPLETION STANDARDS

- Demonstrate understanding of the TAA systems and equipment.
- Demonstrate understanding of supplemental oxygen use and pressurization system operation.
- Perform takeoffs and landings using the proper configuration, airspeed and wind correction.

POSTFLIGHT DEBRIEFING

- ❑ Critique maneuvers/procedures and SRM.
- ❑ Create a plan for skills that need improvement.
- ❑ Update the record folder and logbook.

STUDY ASSIGNMENT

Ground Lessons 37, 38, and 39

Advanced Aerodynamics and Accelerated Stalls
Predicting Performance
Controlling Weight and Balance

FLIGHT LESSON 47

DUAL — LOCAL, TAA

NOTE: *To practice navigation, this lesson may be conducted as a flight to a nearby airport or to a waypoint.*

OBJECTIVES

- Become familiar with recognizing and recovering from power-off, power-on, and accelerated stalls.
- Become familiar with the navigation system, including programming and operating the GPS, using Direct-To navigation, and accessing airport/waypoint information.
- Become familiar with engaging the autopilot to perform basic maneuvers.
- Become familiar with attitude instrument flying in the TAA.
- Increase proficiency in performing basic flight maneuvers and takeoffs and landings in the TAA.

PREFLIGHT DISCUSSION

- ❑ Direct-To Navigation
- ❑ Airport/Waypoint Information
- ❑ Autopilot Functions
- ❑ Automation Management
- ❑ Stall Characteristics of Airplane
- ❑ Spin Awareness

INTRODUCE

SLOW FLIGHT AND STALLS

- ❑ Maneuvering During Slow Flight
- ❑ Power-Off Stalls
- ❑ Power-On Stalls
- ❑ Accelerated Stalls
- ❑ Spin Awareness

BASIC MANEUVERS (AUTOPILOT)

- ❑ Straight-and-Level Flight
- ❑ Climbs and Descents
- ❑ Turns to Headings
- ❑ Automation Management

FLIGHT BY REFERENCE TO INSTRUMENTS

Instrument Flight (Full and Partial Panel)

- ❑ Straight-and-Level Flight, Turns, Climbs, and Descents
- ❑ Recovery from Unusual Flight Attitudes

***NOTE:** The instrument portion of this lesson should be accomplished on an "as required" basis depending on an assessment of the student's capabilities. Students enrolled in the Commercial Pilot Certification Course only must complete 10 hours of instrument training to meet the requirements of Part 141, Appendix D.*

NAVIGATION SYSTEMS AND RADAR SERVICES
- ❑ VOR Radial Interception and Tracking
- ❑ GPS Course Interception and Tracking
- ❑ Autopilot Use
- ❑ Direct-To Navigation
- ❑ Airport/Waypoint Information
- ❑ Auxiliary Functions/Setup

REVIEW

PREFLIGHT PREPARATION
- ❑ Pilot Qualifications
- ❑ Airworthiness Requirements
- ❑ Weather Information
- ❑ Performance and Limitations
- ❑ Operation of Systems
- ❑ Human Factors

PREFLIGHT PROCEDURES
- ❑ Self-Assessment
- ❑ Preflight Inspection
- ❑ Passenger Briefing
- ❑ Flight Deck Management
- ❑ Engine Starting
- ❑ Taxiing
- ❑ Before Takeoff Check/Runup
  - ◊ GPS Programming
  - ◊ PFD Setup
  - ◊ MFD Setup

BASIC MANEUVERS
- ❑ Straight-and-Level Flight
- ❑ Climbs and Descents
- ❑ PFD Instrument Interpretation
- ❑ Use of MFD Features
- ❑ Power Settings and Mixture Control

AVIONICS OPERATION
- ❑ Checklists
- ❑ Engine Indication System
- ❑ Audio Panel
- ❑ Transponder
- ❑ Collision Avoidance—Traffic Information Operation and Interpretation
- ❑ Information Management

HIGH ALTITUDE OPERATIONS
- ❑ Supplemental Oxygen
- ❑ Pressurization System Operation

NOTE: *If high altitude systems are not applicable to the airplane to be used for the practical test, the student must still demonstrate knowledge of high altitude operations sufficient to meet the requirements specified in the FAA Commercial Pilot Airman Certification Standards.*

AIRPORT OPERATIONS

❑ Radio Communications
❑ Airport, Runway, and Taxiway Signs, Markings, and Lighting
❑ Traffic Patterns

TAKEOFFS, LANDINGS, AND GO-AROUNDS
(Includes operations in crosswinds)

❑ Rejected Takeoff
❑ Normal Takeoff and Climb
❑ Normal Approach and Landing
❑ Go-Around/Rejected Landing

POSTFLIGHT PROCEDURES

❑ After Landing, Parking, and Securing

COMPLETION STANDARDS

- Demonstrate understanding of power-off, power-on, and accelerated stall indications and recovery procedures.
- Properly engage the autopilot to perform basic maneuvers.
- Demonstrate how to use Direct-To navigation and access airport/waypoint information using the GPS equipment.
- Demonstrate proficiency in performing the traffic pattern, takeoffs, landings, and go-arounds.

POSTFLIGHT DEBRIEFING

❑ Critique maneuvers/procedures and SRM.
❑ Create a plan for skills that need improvement.
❑ Update the record folder and logbook.

STUDY ASSIGNMENT

Ground Lessons 40 and 41

Emergency Operations
Soft-Field and Short-Field Takeoffs and Landings

FLIGHT LESSON 48

DUAL — LOCAL, TAA

OBJECTIVES

- Become familiar with emergency procedures, including electrical system and electronic flight deck display malfunctions.
- Become familiar with performing soft-field and short-field takeoffs and landings in the complex airplane.
- Increase proficiency in performing basic flight maneuvers, navigation, and takeoffs and landings in the TAA.

PREFLIGHT DISCUSSION
- ❑ System and Equipment Malfunctions
- ❑ Emergency Procedures
- ❑ Task Management

INTRODUCE

EMERGENCY OPERATIONS
Systems and Equipment Malfunctions
- ❑ Partial Power Loss
- ❑ Electrical Malfunction
- ❑ Electronic Flight Display System Malfunction
- ❑ Landing Gear Malfunction, if applicable
- ❑ Flap Malfunction
- ❑ Inoperative Trim
- ❑ Smoke and Fire
- ❑ Airplane Specific Malfunctions
- ❑ Door Opening in Flight

Emergency Procedures
- ❑ Emergency Descent
- ❑ Emergency Approach and Landing (Simulated)
- ❑ Emergency Equipment and Survival Gear

FLIGHT BY REFERENCE TO INSTRUMENTS
Instrument Flight (Full Panel and Partial Panel)
- ❑ GPS Course Interception and Tracking
- ❑ VOR Radial Interception and Tracking

***NOTE:** The instrument portion of this lesson should be accomplished on an "as required" basis depending on an assessment of the student's capabilities. Students enrolled in the Commercial Pilot Certification Course only must complete 10 hours of instrument training to meet the requirements of Part 141, Appendix D.*

TAKEOFFS, LANDINGS, AND GO-AROUNDS
(Includes operations in crosswinds)
- ❑ Short-Field Takeoff and Maximum Performance Climb
- ❑ Short-Field Approach and Landing
- ❑ Soft-Field Takeoff and Climb
- ❑ Soft-Field Approach and Landing

REVIEW

PREFLIGHT PREPARATION
- ❑ Pilot Qualifications
- ❑ Airworthiness Requirements
- ❑ Weather Information
- ❑ Performance and Limitations
- ❑ Operation of Systems
- ❑ Human Factors

PREFLIGHT PROCEDURES
- ❑ Self-Assessment
- ❑ Preflight Inspection

- ❏ Flight Deck Management
- ❏ Engine Starting
- ❏ Taxiing
- ❏ Before Takeoff Check/Runup

HIGH ALTITUDE OPERATIONS
- ❏ Supplemental Oxygen Use
- ❏ Pressurization System Operation

NOTE: *If high altitude systems are not applicable to the airplane to be used for the practical test, the student must still demonstrate knowledge of high altitude operations sufficient to meet the requirements specified in the FAA Commercial Pilot Airman Certification Standards.*

SLOW FLIGHT AND STALLS
- ❏ Maneuvering During Slow Flight
- ❏ Power-Off Stalls
- ❏ Power-On Stalls
- ❏ Accelerated Stalls
- ❏ Spin Awareness

FLIGHT BY REFERENCE TO INSTRUMENTS

Instrument Flight (Full Panel and Partial Panel)
- ❏ Straight-and-Level Flight, Turns, Climbs, and Descents
- ❏ Recovery From Unusual Flight Attitudes

NAVIGATION SYSTEMS AND RADAR SERVICES
- ❏ VOR Radial Interception and Tracking
- ❏ GPS Course Interception and Tracking
- ❏ Autopilot Use
- ❏ Direct-To Navigation
- ❏ Airport/Waypoint Information
- ❏ Auxiliary Functions/Setup

TAKEOFFS, LANDINGS, AND GO-AROUNDS

(Includes operations in crosswinds)
- ❏ Rejected Takeoff
- ❏ Normal Takeoff and Climb
- ❏ Normal Approach and Landing
- ❏ Go-Around/Rejected Landing

POSTFLIGHT PROCEDURES
- ❏ After Landing, Parking, and Securing

COMPLETION STANDARDS

- Demonstrate understanding of how to manage systems and equipment malfunctions and perform the emergency procedures associated with the TAA.
- Demonstrate understanding of the proper airplane configurations to perform soft-field and short-field takeoffs and landings in the complex airplane.
- Demonstrate pilot-in-command proficiency while operating TAA systems and performing basic maneuvers.
- Demonstrate proficiency in recognizing and recovering from power-off, power-on, and accelerated stalls.

- Demonstrate proficiency in Direct-To navigation and accessing airport/waypoint information using the GPS equipment.
- Demonstrate proficiency in performing the traffic pattern, takeoffs, landings, and go-arounds.

POSTFLIGHT DEBRIEFING

❑ Critique maneuvers/procedures and SRM.
❑ Create a plan for skills that need improvement.
❑ Update the record folder and logbook.

FLIGHT LESSONS 49 AND 50

DUAL — LOCAL OR CROSS-COUNTRY, TAA

NOTE: *These lessons may be conducted as two separate flights to airports in the local area or the flight hours may be combined to accommodate a cross-country flight with at least one stop over 50 nautical miles from the original point of departure.*

OBJECTIVE

- Become familiar with programming a GPS flight plan and VNAV descents.
- Become familiar with interpreting data link weather and TAWS/terrain proximity data.
- Become familiar with using the GPS to navigate during a diversion, including using the Nearest feature.
- Gain proficiency in programming Direct-To navigation and accessing airport/waypoint information.
- Gain proficiency with operating the navigation system, including programming and operating the GPS, using Direct-To navigation, and accessing airport/waypoint information.
- Gain proficiency in soft-field and short-field takeoffs and landings in the complex airplane.

PREFLIGHT DISCUSSION

❑ Data Link Weather
❑ TAWS/Terrain Proximity Data
❑ Workload Management

INTRODUCE

PREFLIGHT PREPARATION

❑ Cross-Country Flight Planning
❑ National Airspace System

PREFLIGHT PROCEDURES

❑ GPS Flight Plan Programming

AVIONICS SYSTEM OPERATION

❑ Data Link Weather
❑ CFIT Avoidance—TAWS/Terrain Proximity Data

NAVIGATION SYSTEMS AND RADAR SERVICES
❑ Determining Groundspeed and ETA
❑ Diversion
❑ Nearest Function
❑ VNAV Descent Planning

REVIEW

NAVIGATION SYSTEMS AND RADAR SERVICES
❑ VOR Radial Interception and Tracking
❑ GPS Course Interception and Tracking
❑ Autopilot Use
❑ Direct-To Navigation
❑ Airport/Waypoint Information
❑ Auxiliary Functions/Setup

SLOW FLIGHT AND STALLS
❑ Maneuvering During Slow Flight
❑ Power-Off Stalls
❑ Power-On Stalls
❑ Accelerated Stalls
❑ Spin Awareness

EMERGENCY OPERATIONS
Systems and Equipment Malfunctions
❑ Partial Power Loss
❑ Electrical Malfunction
❑ Electronic Flight Display System Malfunction
❑ Landing Gear Malfunction
❑ Flap Malfunction
❑ Inoperative Trim
❑ Smoke and Fire
❑ Airplane Specific Malfunctions
❑ Door Opening in Flight
Emergency Procedures
❑ Emergency Descent
❑ Emergency Approach and Landing (Simulated)
❑ Emergency Equipment and Survival Gear

AVIONICS SYSTEM OPERATION
❑ Collision Avoidance—Traffic Information Operation and Interpretation
❑ Information Management
❑ Automation Management

FLIGHT BY REFERENCE TO INSTRUMENTS
Instrument Flight (Full Panel and Partial Panel)
❑ GPS Course Interception and Tracking
❑ VOR Radial Interception and Tracking

NOTE: *The instrument portion of this lesson should be accomplished on an "as required" basis depending on an assessment of the student's capabilities. Students enrolled in the Commercial Pilot Certification Course only must complete 10 hours of instrument training to meet the requirements of Part 141, Appendix D.*

TAKEOFFS, LANDINGS, AND GO-AROUNDS
(Includes operations in crosswinds)
- ❑ Short-Field Takeoff and Maximum Performance Climb
- ❑ Short-Field Approach and Landing
- ❑ Soft-Field Takeoff and Climb
- ❑ Soft-Field Approach and Landing

COMPLETION STANDARDS

- Demonstrate proficiency in displaying and interpreting data link weather and TAWS/terrain proximity data.
- Use the GPS to program a flight plan, perform a VNAV descent, and navigate during a diversion.
- Demonstrate proficiency in using the autopilot to navigate on a course and during abnormal and emergency situations.
- Demonstrate the ability to manage information and automation to make effective decisions as pilot in command of a TAA.

POSTFLIGHT DEBRIEFING

- ❑ Critique maneuvers/procedures and SRM.
- ❑ Create a plan for skills that need improvement.
- ❑ Update the record folder and logbook.

FLIGHT LESSON 66

DUAL — LOCAL, TAA

OBJECTIVES

To prepare for the Stage II Check:
- Review TAA operations and use of the navigation system.
- Review slow flight and stalls, commercial maneuvers, and takeoffs and landings.
- Review emergency operations.
- Correct any deficient knowledge and skill areas.

PREFLIGHT DISCUSSION

- ❑ TAA Equipment and Systems
- ❑ Single-Pilot Resource Management
- ❑ Commercial Pilot Airman Certification Standards

REVIEW

PREFLIGHT PREPARATION
- ❑ Pilot Qualifications
- ❑ Airworthiness Requirements
- ❑ Weather Information
- ❑ Cross-Country Flight Planning
- ❑ National Airspace System
- ❑ Performance and Limitations
- ❑ Operation of Systems
- ❑ Human Factors

PREFLIGHT PROCEDURES
- ❑ Self-Assessment
- ❑ Preflight Inspection
- ❑ Flight Deck Management
- ❑ Engine Starting
- ❑ Taxiing
- ❑ Before Takeoff Check/Runup
- ❑ GPS Flight Plan Programming

AVIONICS SYSTEM OPERATION
- ❑ Collision Avoidance—Traffic Information Operation and Interpretation
- ❑ Data Link Weather
- ❑ CFIT Avoidance—TAWS/Terrain Proximity Data
- ❑ Information Management
- ❑ Automation Management

HIGH ALTITUDE OPERATIONS
- ❑ Supplemental Oxygen Use
- ❑ Pressurization System Operation

NOTE: *If high altitude systems are not applicable to the airplane to be used for the practical test, the student must still demonstrate knowledge of high altitude operations sufficient to meet the requirements specified in the FAA Commercial Pilot Airman Certification Standards.*

EMERGENCY OPERATIONS

Systems and Equipment Malfunctions
- ❑ Partial Power Loss
- ❑ Electrical Malfunction
- ❑ Electronic Flight Display System Malfunction
- ❑ Landing Gear Malfunction
- ❑ Flap Malfunction
- ❑ Inoperative Trim
- ❑ Smoke and Fire
- ❑ Airplane Specific Malfunctions
- ❑ Door Opening in Flight

Emergency Procedures
- ❑ Emergency Descent
- ❑ Emergency Approach and Landing (Simulated)
- ❑ Emergency Equipment and Survival Gear

SLOW FLIGHT AND STALLS
- ❑ Maneuvering During Slow Flight
- ❑ Power-Off Stalls
- ❑ Power-On Stalls
- ❑ Accelerated Stalls
- ❑ Spin Awareness

PERFORMANCE AND GROUND REFERENCE MANEUVERS
- ❑ Steep Turns
- ❑ Chandelles
- ❑ Lazy Eights
- ❑ Eights-On-Pylons
- ❑ Steep Spiral

NAVIGATION SYSTEMS AND RADAR SERVICES
- ❏ VOR Radial Interception and Tracking
- ❏ GPS Course Interception and Tracking
- ❏ Autopilot Use
- ❏ Direct-To Navigation
- ❏ Airport/Waypoint Information
- ❏ Auxiliary Functions/Setup
- ❏ Determining Groundspeed and ETA
- ❏ Diversion
- ❏ Nearest Function
- ❏ VNAV Descent Planning

AIRPORT OPERATIONS
- ❏ Radio Communications
- ❏ Airport, Runway, and Taxiway Signs, Markings, and Lighting
- ❏ Traffic Patterns
- ❏ Runway Incursion Avoidance
- ❏ Wake Turbulence Avoidance
- ❏ Wind Shear Avoidance
- ❏ Land and Hold Short Operations (LAHSO)

TAKEOFFS, LANDINGS, AND GO-AROUNDS
(Includes operations in crosswinds)
- ❏ Rejected Takeoff
- ❏ Normal Takeoff and Climb
- ❏ Normal Approach and Landing
- ❏ Soft-Field Takeoff and Climb
- ❏ Soft-Field Approach and Landing
- ❏ Short-Field Takeoff and Maximum Performance Climb
- ❏ Short-Field Approach and Landing
- ❏ Power-Off 180° Accuracy Approach and Landing
- ❏ Go-Around/Rejected Landing

FLIGHT BY REFERENCE TO INSTRUMENTS
Instrument Flight (Full Panel and Partial Panel)
- ❏ Straight-and-Level Flight, Turns, Climbs, and Descents
- ❏ Recovery From Unusual Flight Attitudes
- ❏ GPS Course Interception and Tracking
- ❏ VOR Radial Interception and Tracking

NOTE: *The instrument portion of this lesson should be accomplished on an "as required" basis depending on an assessment of the student's capabilities. Students enrolled in the Commercial Pilot Certification Course only must complete 10 hours of instrument training to meet the requirements of Part 141, Appendix D.*

POSTFLIGHT PROCEDURES
- ❏ After Landing, Parking, and Securing

COMPLETION STANDARDS

- Demonstrates the ability to safely act as pilot in command of the TAA.
- Perform the listed maneuvers and procedures to the level required by the Commercial Pilot Airman Certification Standards in preparation for the Stage II Check.

POSTFLIGHT DEBRIEFING
- ❑ Critique maneuvers/procedures and SRM.
- ❑ Create a plan for skills that need improvement.
- ❑ Update the record folder and logbook.

STUDY ASSIGNMENT
Ground Lessons 45 and 46
Stage II Exam
Commercial Pilot End-Of-Course Exam

FLIGHT LESSON 67

DUAL — LOCAL, TAA

STAGE II CHECK

OBJECTIVE
Demonstrate proficiency as pilot in command of a TAA to the chief instructor, assistant chief, or a designated check instructor during the Stage II Check.

PREFLIGHT DISCUSSION
Conduct of the Stage II Check, including:
- ❑ Maneuvers and Procedures
- ❑ Acceptable Performance Criteria
- ❑ Applicable Rules

REVIEW

EVALUATE

PREFLIGHT PREPARATION
- ❑ Pilot Qualifications
- ❑ Airworthiness Requirements
- ❑ Weather Information
- ❑ Cross-Country Flight Planning
- ❑ National Airspace System
- ❑ Performance and Limitations
- ❑ Operation of Systems
- ❑ Human Factors

PREFLIGHT PROCEDURES
- ❑ Self-Assessment
- ❑ Preflight Inspection
- ❑ Flight Deck Management
- ❑ Engine Starting
- ❑ Taxiing
- ❑ Before Takeoff Check/Runup
- ❑ GPS Flight Plan Programming

AVIONICS SYSTEM OPERATION

- ❑ Collision Avoidance—Traffic Information Operation and Interpretation
- ❑ Data Link Weather
- ❑ CFIT Avoidance—TAWS/Terrain Proximity Data
- ❑ Information Management
- ❑ Automation Management

HIGH ALTITUDE OPERATIONS

- ❑ Supplemental Oxygen Use
- ❑ Pressurization System Operation

NOTE: *If high altitude systems are not applicable to the airplane to be used for the practical test, the student must still demonstrate knowledge of high altitude operations sufficient to meet the requirements specified in the FAA Commercial Pilot Airman Certification Standards.*

EMERGENCY OPERATIONS

Systems and Equipment Malfunctions

- ❑ Partial Power Loss
- ❑ Electrical Malfunction
- ❑ Electronic Flight Display System Malfunction
- ❑ Landing Gear Malfunction
- ❑ Flap Malfunction
- ❑ Inoperative Trim
- ❑ Smoke and Fire
- ❑ Airplane Specific Malfunctions
- ❑ Door Opening in Flight

Emergency Procedures

- ❑ Emergency Descent
- ❑ Emergency Approach and Landing (Simulated)
- ❑ Emergency Equipment and Survival Gear

SLOW FLIGHT AND STALLS

- ❑ Maneuvering During Slow Flight
- ❑ Power-Off Stalls
- ❑ Power-On Stalls
- ❑ Accelerated Stalls
- ❑ Spin Awareness

PERFORMANCE AND GROUND REFERENCE MANEUVERS

- ❑ Steep Turns
- ❑ Chandelles
- ❑ Lazy Eights
- ❑ Eights-On-Pylons
- ❑ Steep Spiral

NAVIGATION SYSTEMS AND RADAR SERVICES

- ❑ VOR Radial Interception and Tracking
- ❑ GPS Course Interception and Tracking
- ❑ Autopilot Use
- ❑ Direct-To Navigation
- ❑ Airport/Waypoint Information
- ❑ Auxiliary Functions/Setup
- ❑ Determining Groundspeed and ETA

- ❏ Diversion
- ❏ Nearest Function
- ❏ VNAV Descent Planning

AIRPORT OPERATIONS
- ❏ Radio Communications
- ❏ Airport, Runway, and Taxiway Signs, Markings, and Lighting
- ❏ Traffic Patterns
- ❏ Runway Incursion Avoidance
- ❏ Wake Turbulence Avoidance
- ❏ Wind Shear Avoidance
- ❏ Land and Hold Short Operations (LAHSO)

TAKEOFFS, LANDINGS, AND GO-AROUNDS
(Includes operations in crosswinds)
- ❏ Rejected Takeoff
- ❏ Normal Takeoff and Climb
- ❏ Normal Approach and Landing
- ❏ Soft-Field Takeoff and Climb
- ❏ Soft-Field Approach and Landing
- ❏ Short-Field Takeoff and Maximum Performance Climb
- ❏ Short-Field Approach and Landing
- ❏ Power-Off 180° Accuracy Approach and Landing
- ❏ Go-Around/Rejected Landing

FLIGHT BY REFERENCE TO INSTRUMENTS
Instrument Flight (Full Panel and Partial Panel)
- ❏ Straight-and-Level Flight, Turns, Climbs, and Descents
- ❏ Recovery From Unusual Flight Attitudes
- ❏ GPS Course Interception and Tracking
- ❏ VOR Radial Interception and Tracking

NOTE: *The instrument portion of this lesson should be accomplished on an "as required" basis depending on an assessment of the student's capabilities. Students enrolled in the Commercial Pilot Certification Course only must complete 10 hours of instrument training to meet the requirements of Part 141, Appendix D.*

POSTFLIGHT PROCEDURES
- ❏ After Landing, Parking, and Securing

COMPLETION STANDARDS

- Demonstrate commercial pilot proficiency as pilot in command of a TAA according to the criteria established by the Commercial Pilot Airman Certification Standards.
- Demonstrate the ability to use single-pilot resource management to make effective decisions, maintain situational awareness, prevent CFIT, and manage risk, tasks, and automation.

POSTFLIGHT DEBRIEFING

- ❏ Critique maneuvers/procedures and SRM.
- ❏ Create a plan for skills that need improvement.
- ❏ Update the record folder and logbook.

Commercial Pilot Flight Training Stage III TAA Option

If you selected the technically advanced airplane (TAA) option by checking the appropriate box in the Preface, you may conduct the lessons shown in this section for the TAA transition in place of the same numbered flight lessons shown in Stage III of the Commercial Course for the complex airplane transition. By doing so, the 10-hour TAA and total flight time requirements will be met. In addition, lessons in this stage that are not specifically identified as complex or TAA, such as dual and solo lessons focused on introducing and practicing commercial maneuvers, may be performed in a TAA or complex airplane.

TAA Transition	Complex Airplane Transition
Flight Lessons 68 – 77 *(TAA Optional)*	**Flight Lessons 68 – 77** *(Complex Airplane Optional)*
Flight Lesson 78 **Dual — Local, TAA**	**Flight Lesson 78** **Dual — Local, Complex Airplane**
Flight Lessons 79 – 81 *(TAA Optional)*	**Flight Lessons 79 – 81** *(Complex Airplane Optional)*
Flight Lesson 82 **Dual — Cross-Country, TAA**	**Flight Lesson 82** **Dual — Cross-Country, Complex Airplane**
Flight Lesson 83 **Dual — Local, TAA**	**Flight Lesson 83** **Dual — Local, Complex Airplane**
Flight Lessons 84 – 87 *(TAA Optional)*	**Flight Lessons 84 – 87** *(Complex Airplane Optional)*

STAGE OBJECTIVES

During this stage, the student performs maneuvers and procedures to attain the proficiency level required of a commercial pilot with an instrument rating.

STAGE COMPLETION STANDARDS

This stage is complete when the student can demonstrate all flight maneuvers and procedures at the level required by the Commercial Pilot Airman Certification Standards for a commercial pilot with an instrument rating. The student also successfully completes the Stage III and End-of-Course Flight Checks.

NOTE: *Completion of the instrument navigation, holding, and approach tasks listed in specific lessons must be based on the available aircraft equipment.* .

FLIGHT LESSON 78

DUAL — LOCAL, TAA

OBJECTIVES

- Increase proficiency in all commercial maneuvers and procedures in the TAA to the level required by the Commercial Pilot Airman Certification Standards.
- Operate airplane systems and equipment and perform normal and emergency procedures in the TAA to the level required by the Commercial Pilot Airman Certification Standards.

PREFLIGHT DISCUSSION

❑ TAA Systems and Equipment
❑ TAA Normal and Emergency Procedures
❑ Commercial Pilot Airman Certification Standards
❑ Single-Pilot Resource Management

REVIEW

PREFLIGHT PREPARATION

❑ Pilot Qualifications
❑ Airworthiness Requirements
❑ Weather Information
❑ Performance and Limitations
❑ Operation of Systems
❑ Human Factors

PREFLIGHT PROCEDURES

❑ Self-Assessment
❑ Preflight Inspection
❑ Flight Deck Management
❑ Engine Starting
❑ Taxiing
❑ Before Takeoff Check/Runup
❑ Flight Deck Management
❑ GPS Flight Plan Programming

AVIONICS OPERATION

❑ Collision Avoidance—Traffic Information Operation and Interpretation
❑ Data Link Weather
❑ CFIT Avoidance—TAWS/Terrain Proximity Data
❑ Information Management
❑ Automation Management

HIGH ALTITUDE OPERATIONS

❑ Supplemental Oxygen Use
❑ Pressurization System Operation

NOTE: *If high altitude systems are not applicable to the airplane to be used for the practical test, the student must still demonstrate knowledge of high altitude operations sufficient to meet the requirements specified in the FAA Commercial Pilot Airman Certification Standards.*

EMERGENCY OPERATIONS

Systems and Equipment Malfunctions

❑ Partial Power Loss
❑ Electrical Malfunction
❑ Electronic Flight Display Malfunction
❑ Landing Gear Malfunction, if Equipped
❑ Flap Malfunction
❑ Inoperative Trim
❑ Smoke and Fire
❑ Airplane Specific Malfunctions
❑ Door Opening in Flight

Emergency Procedures

❑ Emergency Descent
❑ Emergency Approach and Landing (Simulated)
❑ Emergency Equipment and Survival Gear

SLOW FLIGHT AND STALLS

❑ Maneuvering During Slow Flight
❑ Power-Off Stalls
❑ Power-On Stalls
❑ Accelerated Stalls
❑ Spin Awareness

PERFORMANCE AND GROUND REFERENCE MANEUVERS

❑ Steep Turns
❑ Chandelles
❑ Lazy Eights
❑ Eights-On-Pylons
❑ Steep Spirals

INSTRUMENT APPROACH PROCEDURES

Precision Approach (Full and Partial Panel)

❑ ILS Approaches
❑ RNAV (GPS) Approaches (to LPV minimums with a DA less than 300 feet HAT)

Nonprecision Approach (Full and Partial Panel)

❑ Localizer Approaches
❑ RNAV (GPS) Approaches
❑ VOR and VOR/DME Approaches

NOTE: *The instrument portion of this lesson should be accomplished on an "as required" basis depending on an assessment of the student's capabilities. Students enrolled in the Commercial Pilot Certification Course only must complete 10 hours of instrument training to meet the requirements of Part 141, Appendix D.*

TAKEOFFS, LANDINGS, AND GO-AROUNDS

(Includes operations in crosswinds)

❑ Rejected Takeoff
❑ Normal Takeoff and Climb
❑ Normal Approach and Landing
❑ Soft-Field Takeoff and Climb
❑ Soft-Field Approach and Landing
❑ Short-Field Takeoff and Maximum Performance Climb
❑ Short-Field Approach and Landing
❑ Power-Off 180° Accuracy Approach and Landing

- ❑ Rejected Takeoff
- ❑ Go-Around/Rejected Landing

COMPLETION STANDARDS

- Demonstrate proficiency in all commercial maneuvers and procedures in the TAA to the level required by the Commercial Pilot Airman Certification Standards.
- Demonstrate understanding of the TAA flight characteristics, systems, equipment, and emergency procedures by performing all operations to the level required by the Commercial Pilot Airman Certification Standards.

POSTFLIGHT DEBRIEFING

- ❑ Critique maneuvers/procedures and SRM.
- ❑ Create a plan for skills that need improvement.
- ❑ Update the record folder and logbook.

FLIGHT LESSON 82

DUAL — CROSS-COUNTRY, TAA

OBJECTIVES

- Increase proficiency in flight planning and cross-country operations in a TAA by performing a cross-country flight over 50 nautical miles from the original point of departure.
- Increase proficiency in using single-pilot resources management skills to make effective decisions during a cross-country flight in a TAA.

PREFLIGHT DISCUSSION

- ❑ Cross-Country Flight Planning
- ❑ Risk Management (5Ps, PAVE)

REVIEW

PREFLIGHT PREPARATION

- ❑ Pilot Qualifications
- ❑ Airworthiness Requirements
- ❑ Weather Information
- ❑ National Airspace System
- ❑ Operation of Systems
- ❑ Human Factors

Cross-Country Flight Planning

- ❑ Route Planning
- ❑ Altitude Selection
- ❑ Weight and Balance
- ❑ Performance and Limitations
- ❑ Determining ETA
- ❑ Fuel Requirements
- ❑ Sources of Flight Information
- ❑ Navigation Log
- ❑ VFR Flight Plan

PREFLIGHT PROCEDURES

- ❏ Self-Assessment
- ❏ Preflight Inspection
- ❏ Flight Deck Management
- ❏ Engine Starting
- ❏ Taxiing
- ❏ Before Takeoff Check/Runup
- ❏ GPS Flight Plan Programming

AVIONICS OPERATION

- ❏ Collision Avoidance—Traffic Information Operation and Interpretation
- ❏ Data Link Weather
- ❏ CFIT Avoidance—TAWS/Terrain Proximity Data
- ❏ Information Management
- ❏ Automation Management

NAVIGATION

- ❏ Pilotage and Dead Reckoning
- ❏ Diversion
- ❏ Lost Procedures

Navigation Systems and Radar Services

- ❏ VOR Radial Interception and Tracking
- ❏ GPS Course Interception and Tracking
- ❏ Use of ATC Services
- ❏ Autopilot Use
- ❏ Direct-To Navigation
- ❏ Airport/Waypoint Information
- ❏ Auxiliary Functions/Setup
- ❏ Course Interception
- ❏ Determining Groundspeed and ETA
- ❏ Diversion
- ❏ Nearest Function
- ❏ VNAV Descent Planning

CROSS-COUNTRY PROCEDURES

- ❏ Collision Avoidance
- ❏ Flight Deck Management
- ❏ Power Settings and Mixture Control
- ❏ CFIT Avoidance
- ❏ Estimating Visibility in Flight
- ❏ Flight on Federal Airways
- ❏ Opening and Closing Flight Plan

EMERGENCY OPERATIONS

Systems and Equipment Malfunctions

- ❏ Partial Power Loss
- ❏ Electrical Malfunction
- ❏ Electronic Flight Display Malfunction
- ❏ Landing Gear Malfunction, if Equipped
- ❏ Flap Malfunction
- ❏ Inoperative Trim
- ❏ Smoke and Fire
- ❏ Airplane Specific Malfunctions
- ❏ Door Opening in Flight

Emergency Procedures
- ❑ Emergency Descent
- ❑ Emergency Approach and Landing (Simulated)
- ❑ Emergency Equipment and Survival Gear

INSTRUMENT APPROACH PROCEDURES
Precision Approach (Full Panel and Partial Panel)
- ❑ ILS Approaches
- ❑ RNAV (GPS) Approaches (to LPV minimums with a DA less than 300 feet HAT)

Nonprecision Approach (Full Panel and Partial Panel)
- ❑ Localizer Approaches
- ❑ RNAV (GPS) Approaches
- ❑ VOR and VOR/DME Approaches

NOTE: *The instrument portion of this lesson should be accomplished on an "as required" basis depending on an assessment of the student's capabilities. Students enrolled in the Commercial Pilot Certification Course only must complete 10 hours of instrument training to meet the requirements of Part 141, Appendix D.*

AIRPORT OPERATIONS
- ❑ Radio Communications
- ❑ Lost Communication Procedures/ATC Light Signals
- ❑ Airport, Runway, and Taxiway Signs, Markings, and Lighting
- ❑ Traffic Patterns
- ❑ Runway Incursion Avoidance
- ❑ Wake Turbulence Avoidance
- ❑ Wind Shear Avoidance
- ❑ Land and Hold Short Operations (LAHSO)

TAKEOFFS, LANDINGS, AND GO-AROUNDS
(Includes operations in crosswinds)
- ❑ Normal Takeoff and Climb
- ❑ Normal Approach and Landing

COMPLETION STANDARDS
- Demonstrate the ability to safely act as pilot in command of the TAA during cross-country flights.
- Demonstrate proficiency in managing systems and equipment malfunctions and performing emergency procedures in a TAA during a cross-country flight.
- Demonstrate proficiency in using single-pilot resources management skills to make effective decisions during a cross-country flight in a TAA.

POSTFLIGHT DEBRIEFING
- ❑ Critique maneuvers/procedures and SRM.
- ❑ Create a plan for skills that need improvement.
- ❑ Update the record folder and logbook.

STUDY ASSIGNMENT
Prepare for the Stage III Check in Flight Lesson 86.

FLIGHT LESSON 83

DUAL — LOCAL, TAA

OBJECTIVE

Perform all maneuvers and procedures at the level required in the Commercial Pilot Airman Certification Standards in preparation for the Stage III Flight Check and the FAA Commercial Pilot Practical Test.

PREFLIGHT DISCUSSION

- ❑ TAA Systems and Equipment
- ❑ Commercial Pilot Airman Certification Standards
- ❑ Single-Pilot Resource Management

REVIEW

PREFLIGHT PREPARATION

- ❑ Pilot Qualifications
- ❑ Airworthiness Requirements
- ❑ Cross-Country Flight Planning
- ❑ Weather Information
- ❑ Performance and Limitations
- ❑ Operation of Systems
- ❑ Human Factors

PREFLIGHT PROCEDURES

- ❑ Self-Assessment
- ❑ Preflight Inspection
- ❑ Flight Deck Management
- ❑ Engine Starting
- ❑ Taxiing
- ❑ Before Takeoff Check/Runup
- ❑ GPS Flight Plan Programming

AVIONICS OPERATION

- ❑ Traffic Information Operation and Interpretation
- ❑ Data Link Weather
- ❑ Collision Avoidance—Traffic Information Operation and Interpretation
- ❑ CFIT Avoidance—TAWS/Terrain Proximity Data
- ❑ Information Management
- ❑ Automation Management

PERFORMANCE AND GROUND REFERENCE MANEUVERS

- ❑ Steep Turns
- ❑ Chandelles
- ❑ Lazy Eights
- ❑ Eights-On-Pylons
- ❑ Steep Spiral

TAKEOFFS, LANDINGS, AND GO-AROUNDS
(Includes operations in crosswinds)
- ❑ Rejected Takeoff
- ❑ Normal Takeoff and Climb
- ❑ Normal Approach and Landing
- ❑ Soft-Field Takeoff and Climb
- ❑ Soft-Field Approach and Landing
- ❑ Short-Field Takeoff and Maximum Performance Climb
- ❑ Short-Field Approach and Landing
- ❑ Power-Off 180° Accuracy Approach and Landing
- ❑ Go-Around/Rejected Landing

COMPLETION STANDARDS

Demonstrate proficiency in performing each of the listed maneuvers and procedures to the level required by the Commercial Pilot Airman Certification Standards.

POSTFLIGHT DEBRIEFING

- ❑ Critique maneuvers/procedures and SRM.
- ❑ Create a plan for skills that need improvement.
- ❑ Update the record folder and logbook.

STUDY ASSIGNMENT

Commercial Pilot Practical Test Briefing

Multi-Engine Rating Ground Training Stage I

STAGE OBJECTIVES

During this stage, the student learns multi-engine aerodynamics, operating procedures, systems, and performance considerations. The student learns to accurately use performance charts and compute weight and balance data for the multi-engine airplane. In addition, the student explores the principles, techniques, and procedures that apply to engine-out and instrument flight in the multi-engine airplane.

STAGE COMPLETION STANDARDS

The student must pass the Stage I Exam and the Multi-Engine End-of-Course Exam with a minimum score of 80 percent, and review each incorrect response with the instructor to ensure complete understanding.

GROUND LESSON 1

REFERENCES

Multi-Engine Textbook/e-Book
- Chapter 1 — Exploring the Multi-Engine Rating
- Chapter 4 — Performing Maneuvers and Procedures
  - Section A — Normal Operations

Commercial Pilot Multi-Engine Online
- Multi-Engine Maneuvers Lessons
  - ML — Normal Takeoff and Climb
  - ML — Normal Approach and Landing
  - ML — Short-Field Takeoff
  - ML — Short Field Landing

OBJECTIVES

Lesson Objective	Part 141/61 Aeronautical Knowledge	ACS Task
Become familiar with the human factors concepts that affect aeronautical decision making and judgment during multi-engine operations. Become familiar with the single-pilot resource management (SRM) techniques that increase flight safety during multi-engine operations. Describe normal operations in the multi-engine airplane, including the preflight, ground operations, and normal and short-field takeoff and landing procedures.	Aeronautical decision making and judgment	Human Factors
Describe normal operations in the multi-engine airplane, including the preflight inspection, ground operations, and normal and short-field takeoff and landing procedures.	Maneuvers, procedures, and emergency operations appropriate to the aircraft;	Airworthiness Requirements Operation of Systems Preflight Assessment Engine Starting Taxiing Normal Takeoff and Climb Normal Approach and Landing Short-Field Takeoff and Maximum Performance Climb Short-Field Approach and Landing Go-Around/Rejected Landing

CONTENT

CHAPTER 1A — SEEKING A NEW EXPERIENCE

- ❑ Why a Multi-Engine Rating?
- ❑ The Training Path

CHAPTER 1B — CONSIDERING SRM

- ❑ Multi-Engine Safety
- ❑ Aeronautical Decision Making
- ❑ Risk Management
- ❑ Task Management
- ❑ Situational Awareness
- ❑ Controlled Flight Into Terrain Awareness
- ❑ Automation Management

CHAPTER 4A — NORMAL OPERATIONS

MULTI-ENGINE MANEUVERS LESSONS

- ❑ Using Checklists
- ❑ Preflight Inspection (Including Airworthiness Requirements)
- ❑ Ground Operations
  - Engine Starting
  - Taxiing
  - Before-Takeoff Check
- ❑ Takeoff and Climb
- ❑ Propeller Synchronization
- ❑ Short-Field Takeoff and Maximum Performance Climb
- ❑ Cruise and Descent
- ❑ Approach and Landing
- ❑ Short-Field Approach and Landing
- ❑ Go-Around

COMPLETION STANDARDS

- Demonstrate understanding of the multi-engine training program and single-pilot resource management (SRM) concepts that apply to multi-engine airplane operations during oral quizzing by the instructor.
- Demonstrate understanding of normal operations in the multi-engine airplane during oral quizzing by the instructor.
- Complete with a minimum score of 80 percent: questions for Chapter 4A. With the instructor, review each incorrect response to ensure complete understanding before starting Ground Lesson 2.

STUDY ASSIGNMENT

Multi-Engine Textbook/e-Book

Chapter 2 — Understanding Your Airplane

Commercial Pilot Multi-Engine Online

GL — Light Twin System Differences
GL — Light Twin Performance

GROUND LESSON 2

REFERENCES

Multi-Engine Textbook/e-Book

Chapter 2 — Understanding Your Airplane

Commercial Pilot Multi-Engine Online

GL — Light Twin System Differences
GL — Light Twin Performance

OBJECTIVES

Lesson Objective	Part 141/61 Aeronautical Knowledge	ACS Task
Describe multi-engine systems and equipment including, powerplant, propeller, and retractable landing gear systems.	Principles and functions of aircraft systems	Operation of Systems
Explain weight and balance considerations for multi-engine airplanes and calculate weight and balance for multi-engine airplanes.	Weight and balance computations	Performance and Limitations
Determine performance for light twin airplanes operating on both engines and with an inoperative engine. Explain how the loss of an engine affects performance on a light twin.	Use of performance charts Significance and effects of exceeding aircraft performance limitations	Performance and Limitations

CONTENT

SECTION A — EXAMINING SYSTEMS

GL — LIGHT TWIN SYSTEM DIFFERENCES

RECIPROCATING-ENGINE-POWERED OPERATIONS

- ❑ Fuel Metering Systems
- ❑ Ignition and Starting Systems
- ❑ Lubrication Systems
- ❑ Induction Systems
- ❑ Cooling and Exhaust Systems
- ❑ Engine Indicating Systems
- ❑ Engine Accessory Systems
- ❑ Diesel Engines

CONSTANT-SPEED PROPELLER OPERATION

- ❑ Power Control
- ❑ Full Authority Digital Engine Control (FADEC)
- ❑ Propeller Synchronization
- ❑ Governor Checks
- ❑ Feathering
- ❑ Restarting

ELECTRICAL SYSTEMS

- ❑ Generation
- ❑ Storage and External Power
- ❑ Distribution Buses

FUEL SYSTEMS

- ❑ Fuel Pumps
- ❑ Fuel Selector Controls
- ❑ Cross Feeding
- ❑ Auxiliary Fuel Tanks

LANDING GEAR SYSTEMS
- ❑ Electrohydraulic Landing Gear
- ❑ Electric Landing Gear
- ❑ Gear Position Lights
- ❑ Gear Warning Horn
- ❑ Safety Switches
- ❑ Emergency Landing Gear Extension

ICE CONTROL SYSTEMS
- ❑ Propeller Anti-Ice System
- ❑ Wing and Tail Surface Deice Systems
- ❑ Windshield Anti-Ice Systems

CABIN ENVIRONMENTAL SYSTEMS
- ❑ Cabin Heating
- ❑ Oxygen Systems
- ❑ Cabin Pressurization Systems

SECTION B — CALCULATING WEIGHT AND BALANCE

GL — LIGHT TWIN PERFORMANCE

WEIGHT AND BALANCE TERMS
- ❑ Maximum Zero Fuel Weight
- ❑ Maneuvering Speed
- ❑ Center of Gravity

FINDING WEIGHT AND CG LOCATION
- ❑ Center of Gravity Limits
- ❑ Using the Weight Shift Formula

SECTION C — DETERMINING PERFORMANCE

GL — LIGHT TWIN PERFORMANCE

PERFORMANCE DEFINITIONS
- ❑ Power Required
- ❑ The Engine-Out Performance Penalty

USING PERFORMANCE DATA
- ❑ The Associated Conditions
- ❑ V-Speeds
- ❑ Takeoff and Climb
  - ◊ Accelerate-Stop Distance
  - ◊ Accelerate-Go Distance
  - ◊ Climb – Two Engine
  - ◊ Climb – One Engine Inoperative
- ❑ Cruise Flight
- ❑ Single-Engine Ceilings
- ❑ Descent Performance
- ❑ Landing Performance
- ❑ Engine-Out Go-Around

COMPLETION STANDARDS

- Demonstrate understanding of multi-engine airplane systems, including high-performance powerplants, constant-speed propellers, retractable landing gear, environmental systems, and ice control systems during oral quizzing by the instructor.
- Demonstrate understanding of weight and balance considerations for a multi-engine airplane during oral quizzing by the instructor. Correctly compute the weight and balance and performance for the training airplane based on at least two different loading conditions with the airport and environmental conditions as specified by the instructor.
- Demonstrate understanding of light twin performance with both engines operating and with an inoperative engine during oral quizzing by the instructor.
- Complete with a minimum score of 80 percent: questions for Chapter 2 or online exams for GL — Light Twin System Differences and GL — Light Twin Performance. With the instructor, review each incorrect response to ensure complete understanding before starting Ground Lesson 3.

STUDY ASSIGNMENT

Multi-Engine Textbook/e-Book

Chapter 3 — Discovering Aerodynamics
Chapter 4 — Performing Maneuvers and Procedures
  Section B — Maneuvers

Commercial Pilot Multi-Engine Online

GL — Light Twin Aerodynamics
Multi-Engine Maneuvers Lessons
  ML — Maneuvering During Slow Flight
  ML — Power-Off Stalls
  ML — Power-On Stalls

GROUND LESSON 3

REFERENCES

Multi-Engine Textbook/e-Book

Chapter 3 — Discovering Aerodynamics
Chapter 4 — Performing Maneuvers and Procedures
  Section B — Maneuvers

Commercial Pilot Mulit-Engine Online

GL — Light Twin Aerodynamics
Multi-Engine Maneuvers Lessons
  ML — Maneuvering During Slow Flight
  ML — Power-Off Stalls
  ML — Power-On Stalls

OBJECTIVES

Lesson Objective	Part 141/61 Aeronautical Knowledge	ACS Task
Explain multi-engine aerodynamics, including the characteristics of the boundary layer, induced flow, and high-speed flight. Describe the aerodynamic forces acting on a multi-engine airplane when an engine fails and how to counteract yaw and roll toward the inoperative engine and reduce drag when flying with an inoperative engine.	Basic aerodynamics and the principles of flight	Performance and Limitations
Identify the steps and techniques to perform steep turns, slow flight, stalls, and emergency descents in the multi-engine airplane. Develop stall/spin awareness and a clear understanding of the causes and recovery procedures that apply to stalls and spins in multi-engine airplanes.	Maneuvers, procedures, and emergency operations appropriate to the aircraft	Maneuvering During Slow Flight Power-Off Stalls Power-On Stalls Accelerated Stalls Spin Awareness Emergency Descent

CONTENT

CHAPTER 3A — INTRODUCING MULTI-ENGINE AERODYNAMICS

GL — LIGHT TWIN AERODYNAMICS

- ❑ Boundary Layer
- ❑ Induced Flow
- ❑ Turning Tendencies
- ❑ High-Speed Flight

CHAPTER 3B — MASTERING ENGINE-OUT AERODYNAMICS

GL — LIGHT TWIN AERODYNAMICS

- ❑ Engine Failure
- ❑ Yaw and Roll
- ❑ Critical Engine
- ❑ Cure for Yaw and Roll
- ❑ V_{MC}
- ❑ Windmilling Propeller
- ❑ Feathering
- ❑ Sideslip
- ❑ Zero Sideslip
- ❑ Controllability Versus Performance
  - ◊ Weight
  - ◊ Center of Gravity
  - ◊ Power

CHAPTER 4B — MANEUVERS

MULTI-ENGINE MANEUVERS LESSONS

- ❑ Steep Turns
- ❑ Slow Flight
- ❑ Stalls (Power-On and Power-Off)
- ❑ Spin Awareness
- ❑ Emergency Descent

COMPLETION STANDARDS

- Demonstrate understanding of aerodynamics, including the characteristics of the boundary layer, induced flow, and high-speed flight during oral quizzing by the instructor.
- Demonstrate understanding of engine-out aerodynamics and how to counteract the effects of a failed engine during oral quizzing by the instructor.
- Demonstrate understanding of the steps and techniques to perform steep turns, slow flight, stalls, and emergency descents in the multi-engine airplane during oral quizzing by the instructor.
- Demonstrate stall/spin awareness and a clear understanding of the causes and recovery procedures that apply to stalls and spins in multi-engine airplanes during oral quizzing by the instructor.
- Complete with a minimum score of 80 percent: questions for Chapter 3 and Chapter 4B or online exams for GL — Light Twin Aerodynamics. With the instructor, review each incorrect response to ensure complete understanding before starting Ground Lesson 4.

STUDY ASSIGNMENT

Multi-Engine Textbook/e-Book

Chapter 5 — Mastering Engine-Out Operations

Section A — When an Engine Fails

Section B — Engine-Out Maneuvers

Commercial Pilot Multi-Engine Online

Multi-Engine Maneuvers Lessons

ML — Engine Failure During Takeoff Before V_{MC}

ML — V_{MC} Demonstration

GROUND LESSON 4

REFERENCES

Multi-Engine Textbook/e-Book
Chapter 5 — Mastering Engine-Out Operations
Section A — When an Engine Fails
Section B — Engine-Out Maneuvers

Commercial Pilot Multi-Engine Online — Jeppesen Learning Center
Multi-Engine Maneuvers Lessons
ML — Engine Failure During Takeoff Before V_{MC}
ML — V_{MC} Demonstration

OBJECTIVES

Lesson Objective	Part 141/61 Aeronautical Knowledge	ACS Task
Explain the steps to take to manage an engine failure, including identifying the failed engine, maintaining control of the airplane, and securing the inoperative engine. Describe how to manage an engine failure during takeoff, climb, enroute, and landing. Identify the steps to perform the V_{MC} demonstration and drag demonstration.	Safe and efficient operation of aircraft Maneuvers, procedures, and emergency operations appropriate to the aircraft	Maneuvering with One Engine Inoperative V_{MC} Demonstration Engine Failure During Takeoff Before V_{MC} (Simulated) Engine Failure After Liftoff (Simulated) Approach and Landing with an Inoperative Engine (Simulated)

CONTENT

SECTION A — WHEN AN ENGINE FAILS

- ❑ Taking Action
  - ◊ Pitch
  - ◊ Power
  - ◊ Drag
  - ◊ Identify
  - ◊ Verify
  - ◊ Troubleshoot
- ❑ Feathering
  - ◊ After Actual Engine Failure
  - ◊ During Training
  - ◊ Restarting the Engine
- ❑ Establishing a Bank
- ❑ Securing the Inoperative Engine
- ❑ Monitoring the Operating Engine

SECTION B — ENGINE-OUT MANEUVERS

MULTI-ENGINE MANEUVERS LESSONS

- ❑ Engine Failure During Takeoff and Climb
  - ◊ Engine Failure During Takeoff Before V_{MC}
  - ◊ Engine Failure After Liftoff
  - ◊ Takeoff Briefing
- ❑ Enroute
- ❑ V_{MC} Demonstration
- ❑ Drag Demonstration
- ❑ Landing
- ❑ Engine-Out Go-Around

COMPLETION STANDARDS

- Demonstrate understanding of the steps to manage an engine failure in different phases of flight and making appropriate decisions about the continuation of flight during oral quizzing by the instructor.
- Demonstrate understanding of the steps to perform the V_{MC} demonstration and drag demonstration during oral quizzing by the instructor.
- Complete with a minimum score of 80 percent: questions for Chapter 5A and 5B. With the instructor, review each incorrect response to ensure complete understanding before starting Ground Lesson 5.

STUDY ASSIGNMENT

Multi-Engine Textbook/e-Book

Chapter 5 — Mastering Engine-Out Operations
    Section C — Operating on Instruments
Chapter 6 — Applying SRM

GROUND LESSON 5

REFERENCES

Multi-Engine Textbook/e-Book

Chapter 5 — Mastering Engine-Out Operations
    Section C — Operating on Instruments
Chapter 6 — Applying SRM

OBJECTIVES

Lesson Objective	Part 141/61 Aeronautical Knowledge	ACS Task
Recognize how to perform instrument procedures in the multi-engine airplane with both engines operating and with one engine inoperative.	Use of air navigation facilities Maneuvers, procedures, and emergency operations appropriate to the aircraft Procedures for operating within the National Airspace System	One Engine Inoperative (Simulated) (solely by Reference to Instruments) During Straight-and-Level Flight and Turns Instrument Approach and Landing with an Inoperative Engine (Simulated) (solely by Reference to Instruments)
Explain how to use single-pilot resource management (SRM) skills to make effective decisions as pilot in command of a multi-engine airplane.	Aeronautical decision making and judgment	Human Factors

CONTENT

CHAPTER 5C — OPERATING ON INSTRUMENTS

- ❑ Attitude Instrument Flying
- ❑ Departure
- ❑ Enroute
- ❑ Engine-Out Instrument Approach

CHAPTER 6 — APPLYING SRM

- ❑ Poor Judgment Chain
- ❑ Aeronautical Decision Making
- ❑ Risk Management
- ❑ Task Management
- ❑ Situational Awareness
- ❑ Controlled Flight Into Terrain Awareness
- ❑ Automation Management

COMPLETION STANDARDS

- Demonstrate understanding of performing instrument procedures in the multi-engine airplane with both engines operating and with one engine inoperative during oral quizzing by the instructor.
- Demonstrate understanding of how to use single-pilot resource management to make effective decisions, maintain situational awareness, prevent CFIT, and manage risk, tasks, and automation.
- Complete with a minimum score of 80 percent: questions for Chapters 5C and Chapter 6. With the instructor, review each incorrect response to ensure complete understanding before taking the Stage I Exam in Ground Lesson 7.

STUDY ASSIGNMENT

Review the content of Multi-Engine Ground Lessons 1 – 5 to prepare for the Stage I Exam.

GROUND LESSON 6

STAGE I EXAM

REFERENCES

Ground Lessons 1 – 5

OBJECTIVE

Demonstrate knowledge of the subjects covered in Multi-Engine Ground Lessons 1 – 5 by passing the Stage I Exam.

CONTENT

STAGE I EXAM

- ❏ Multi-Engine Operations
- ❏ Multi-Engine Systems
- ❏ Calculating Weight and Balance
- ❏ Determining Performance
- ❏ Multi-Engine Aerodynamics
- ❏ Engine-Out Aerodynamics
- ❏ Engine-Out Operations
- ❏ Multi-Engine Instrument Flight
- ❏ Applying SRM

COMPLETION STANDARDS

To complete the lesson and stage, pass the Stage I Exam with a minimum score of 80 percent. With the instructor, review each incorrect response to ensure complete understanding before taking the Multi-Engine End-of-Course Exam.

STUDY ASSIGNMENT

Review the content of Multi-Engine Ground Lessons 1 – 6 to prepare for the Multi-Engine End-of-Course Exam.

GROUND LESSON 7

END-OF-COURSE EXAM

REFERENCES

Ground Lessons 1-6

OBJECTIVE

Demonstrate comprehension of the material covered in Multi-Engine Ground Lessons 1 – 6 by passing the Multi-Engine End-of-Course Exam.

CONTENT

- ❏ Multi-Engine End-of-Course Exam

COMPLETION STANDARDS

To complete the lesson and the Multi-Engine Ground Training, pass the Multi-Engine End-of-Course Exam with a minimum score of 80 percent. Review each incorrect response with the instructor to ensure complete understanding.

Multi-Engine Rating Flight Training Stage I

STAGE OBJECTIVES

During Stage I, the student learns to fly the multi-engine airplane with both engines operating and in engine-out situations. The student learns to identify and manage an engine failure and perform engine-out maneuvers and procedures. Additionally, the student gains proficiency in IFR operations in the multi-engine airplane and learns to use single-pilot resource management (SRM) skills to make effective decisions in the multi-engine airplane.

STAGE COMPLETION STANDARDS

This stage is complete when the student demonstrates all multi-engine flight maneuvers and procedures at the proficiency level of a commercial pilot with an instrument rating as outlined in the multi-engine land sections of the Commercial Pilot Airman Certification Standards.

NOTE: *Completion of the navigation and instrument approach tasks listed in specific lessons must be based on the available aircraft equipment.*

FLIGHT LESSON 1

DUAL — LOCAL

NOTE: *Prior to this flight, complete Ground Lesson 1 and the Multi-Engine Operations and Systems Briefing.*

OBJECTIVES

- Become familiar with multi-engine operations: preflight preparation, preflight procedures, airport operations, basic maneuvers/procedures, takeoffs and landings, and postflight procedures.
- Become familiar with the attitudes, power settings, and configurations required for the performance of the listed maneuvers and procedures using outside visual reference and instrument reference.

PREFLIGHT DISCUSSION

❑ Multi-Engine Training Airplane Systems and Equipment
❑ Review of V-Speeds
❑ Positive Exchange of Flight Controls

INTRODUCE

PREFLIGHT PREPARATION
- ❏ Pilot Qualifications
- ❏ Airworthiness Requirements
- ❏ Weather Information
- ❏ Performance and Limitations
- ❏ Operation of Systems
- ❏ Human Factors

PREFLIGHT PROCEDURES
- ❏ Preflight Inspection
- ❏ Flight Deck Management
- ❏ Use of Checklists
- ❏ Engine Starting
- ❏ Taxiing
- ❏ Before Takeoff Check

BASIC MANEUVERS
- ❏ Straight-and-Level Flight
- ❏ Change of Airspeed
- ❏ Turns to Headings
- ❏ Climbs and Climbing Turns
- ❏ Descents and Descending Turns

FLIGHT BY REFERENCE TO INSTRUMENTS
Instrument Flight (Full Panel)
- ❏ Straight-and-Level Flight
- ❏ Change of Airspeed
- ❏ Standard-Rate Turns
- ❏ Constant Airspeed Climbs and Descents
- ❏ Constant Rate Climbs and Descents
- ❏ Climbing and Descending Turns

AIRPORT OPERATIONS
- ❏ Radio Communications
- ❏ Airport, Runway, and Taxiway Signs, Markings, and Lighting
- ❏ Traffic Patterns
- ❏ Runway Incursion Avoidance
- ❏ Wake Turbulence Avoidance
- ❏ Wind Shear Avoidance
- ❏ Land and Hold Short Operations (LAHSO)

TAKEOFFS, LANDINGS, AND GO-AROUNDS
(Includes operations in crosswinds)
- ❏ Normal Takeoff and Climb
- ❏ Normal Approach and Landing

POSTFLIGHT PROCEDURES
- ❏ After Landing, Parking, and Securing

COMPLETION STANDARDS
- Perform preflight preparation, preflight procedures, airport operations, basic maneuvers/procedures, takeoffs and landings, and postflight procedures with a minimum of instructor assistance.

- Demonstrate understanding of the attitudes and configurations necessary to perform the listed maneuvers and procedures.
- During flight solely by reference to instruments: maintain altitude ±200 feet, headings ±15°, airspeed ±15 knots, bank angles ±10°, and descent/climb rate ±150 feet per minute.

POSTFLIGHT DEBRIEFING

❏ Critique maneuvers/procedures and SRM.
❏ Create a plan for skills that need improvement.
❏ Update the record folder and logbook.

STUDY ASSIGNMENT

Ground Lesson 2

Multi-Engine Systems, Weight and Balance, and Performance

Multi-Engine Performance Considerations Briefing

FLIGHT LESSON 2

DUAL — LOCAL

OBJECTIVES

- Become familiar with the flight characteristics of the multi-engine airplane by performing slow flight, stalls, steep turns, and emergency operations.
- Become familiar with partial-panel attitude instrument flying and recovery from unusual attitudes.
- Gain proficiency in multi-engine operations: preflight preparation, preflight procedures, airport operations, basic maneuvers, takeoffs and landings, and postflight procedures.
- Gain proficiency in performing the listed maneuvers and procedures using outside visual reference and instrument reference.

PREFLIGHT DISCUSSION

❏ Multi-Engine Training Airplane Systems and Equipment
❏ Emergency Procedures
❏ Stall/Spin Awareness
❏ Single-Pilot Resource Management

INTRODUCE

PERFORMANCE MANEUVERS

❏ Steep Turns

SLOW FLIGHT AND STALLS

❏ Maneuvering During Slow Flight
❏ Power-Off Stalls
❏ Power-On Stalls
❏ Accelerated Stalls
❏ Spin Awareness

EMERGENCY OPERATIONS

Systems and Equipment Malfunctions

- ❑ Partial Power Loss
- ❑ Electrical Malfunction
- ❑ Instrument Malfunction
- ❑ Landing Gear Malfunction
- ❑ Flap Malfunction
- ❑ Inoperative Trim
- ❑ Smoke and Fire
- ❑ Airplane Specific Malfunctions
- ❑ Door Opening in Flight

Emergency Procedures

- ❑ Emergency Descent

FLIGHT BY REFERENCE TO INSTRUMENTS

Instrument Flight (Full Panel)

- ❑ Recovery From Unusual Flight Attitudes
- ❑ Autopilot Use, if Equipped

Instrument Flight (Partial Panel)

- ❑ Straight-and-Level Flight
- ❑ Change of Airspeed
- ❑ Compass Turns
- ❑ Timed Turns to Magnetic Compass Headings
- ❑ Constant Airspeed Climbs and Descents
- ❑ Constant Rate Climbs and Descents
- ❑ Climbing and Descending Turns

REVIEW

PREFLIGHT PREPARATION

- ❑ Pilot Qualifications
- ❑ Airworthiness Requirements
- ❑ Weather Information
- ❑ Performance and Limitations
- ❑ Operation of Systems
- ❑ Human Factors

PREFLIGHT PROCEDURES

- ❑ Preflight Inspection
- ❑ Flight Deck Management
- ❑ Use of Checklists
- ❑ Engine Starting
- ❑ Taxiing
- ❑ Before Takeoff Check

BASIC MANEUVERS

- ❑ Straight-and-Level Flight
- ❑ Change of Airspeed
- ❑ Turns to Headings
- ❑ Climbs and Climbing Turns
- ❑ Descents and Descending Turns

FLIGHT BY REFERENCE TO INSTRUMENTS

Instrument Flight (Full Panel)

❑ Straight-and-Level Flight
❑ Change of Airspeed
❑ Standard-Rate Turns
❑ Constant Airspeed Climbs and Descents
❑ Constant Rate Climbs and Descents
❑ Climbing and Descending Turns

AIRPORT OPERATIONS

❑ Radio Communications
❑ Airport, Runway, and Taxiway Signs, Markings, and Lighting
❑ Traffic Patterns
❑ Runway Incursion Avoidance
❑ Wake Turbulence Avoidance
❑ Wind Shear Avoidance
❑ Land and Hold Short Operations (LAHSO)

TAKEOFFS, LANDINGS, AND GO-AROUNDS

(Includes operations in crosswinds)

❑ Normal Takeoff and Climb
❑ Normal Approach and Landing

POSTFLIGHT PROCEDURES

❑ After Landing, Parking, and Securing

COMPLETION STANDARDS

- Perform the correct procedures for steep turns, maneuvering during slow flight, and stall entry and recovery.
- Perform the correct procedures for managing systems and equipment malfunctions and conducting an emergency descent.
- During flight solely by reference to instruments: maintain altitude ±100 feet, headings ±10°, airspeed ±10 knots, bank angles ±5°, and descent/climb rate ±50 feet per minute.
- Demonstrate the correct technique for partial-panel attitude instrument flying while performing basic flight maneuvers.
- Demonstrate the correct procedures for recognizing and recovering from unusual flight attitudes.
- Demonstrate proficiency in performing preflight preparation, preflight procedures, airport operations, basic maneuvers/procedures, takeoffs and landings, and postflight procedures.
- Demonstrate proficiency in properly configuring the airplane to perform the listed maneuvers and procedures.

POSTFLIGHT DEBRIEFING

❑ Critique maneuvers/procedures and SRM.
❑ Create a plan for skills that need improvement.
❑ Update the record folder and logbook.

FLIGHT LESSON 3

DUAL — LOCAL

OBJECTIVES

- Become familiar with short-field takeoffs and maximum performance climbs, short-field approaches and landings, and go-arounds.
- Become familiar with the high altitude operations, including the use of supplemental oxygen and pressurization.
- Gain proficiency in partial-panel attitude instrument flying and recovery from unusual attitudes.
- Increase proficiency in performing slow flight stalls, steep turns, and emergency operations.

PREFLIGHT DISCUSSION

❏ Short-Field Takeoff and Landing Configurations
❏ High Altitude Operations

INTRODUCE

TAKEOFFS, LANDINGS, AND GO-AROUNDS

(Includes operations in crosswinds)

❏ Rejected Takeoff
❏ Short-Field Takeoff and Maximum Performance Climb
❏ Short-Field Approach and Landing
❏ Go-Around/Rejected Landing

HIGH ALTITUDE OPERATIONS

❏ Supplemental Oxygen Use
❏ Pressurization System Operation

NOTE: *If high altitude systems are not applicable to the airplane to be used for the practical test, the student must still demonstrate knowledge of high altitude operations sufficient to meet the requirements specified in the FAA Commercial Pilot Airman Certification Standards.*

REVIEW

PERFORMANCE MANEUVERS

❏ Steep Turns

SLOW FLIGHT AND STALLS

❏ Maneuvering During Slow Flight
❏ Power-Off Stalls
❏ Power-On Stalls
❏ Accelerated Stalls
❏ Spin Awareness

EMERGENCY OPERATIONS

Systems and Equipment Malfunctions

- ❑ Partial Power Loss
- ❑ Electrical Malfunction
- ❑ Instrument Malfunction
- ❑ Landing Gear Malfunction
- ❑ Flap Malfunction
- ❑ Inoperative Trim
- ❑ Smoke and Fire
- ❑ Airplane Specific Malfunctions
- ❑ Door Opening in Flight

Emergency Procedures

- ❑ Emergency Descent

FLIGHT BY REFERENCE TO INSTRUMENTS

Instrument Flight (Full Panel)

- ❑ Recovery From Unusual Flight Attitudes
- ❑ Autopilot Use, if Equipped

Instrument Flight (Partial Panel)

- ❑ Straight-and-Level Flight
- ❑ Change of Airspeed
- ❑ Compass Turns
- ❑ Timed Turns to Magnetic Compass Headings
- ❑ Constant Airspeed Climbs and Descents
- ❑ Constant Rate Climbs and Descents
- ❑ Climbing and Descending Turns

TAKEOFFS, LANDINGS, AND GO-AROUNDS

(Includes operations in crosswinds)

- ❑ Normal Takeoff and Climb
- ❑ Normal Approach and Landing

POSTFLIGHT PROCEDURES

- ❑ After Landing, Parking, and Securing

COMPLETION STANDARDS

- Demonstrate understanding of short-field takeoffs and landings and high altitude operations using the correct procedures and maintaining positive control of the airplane.
- Demonstrate understanding of supplemental oxygen use and pressurization system operation.
- Demonstrate proficiency in partial-panel attitude instrument flying and recovery from unusual attitudes.
- Demonstrate proficiency in performing slow flight stalls, steep turns, and emergency operations.

POSTFLIGHT DEBRIEFING

- ❑ Critique maneuvers/procedures and SRM.
- ❑ Create a plan for skills that need improvement.
- ❑ Update the record folder and logbook.

STUDY ASSIGNMENT

Ground Lessons 3 and 4

Multi-Engine/Engine-Out Aerodynamics and Maneuvers
Engine-Out Operations

Engine-Out Operations Briefing

FLIGHT LESSON 4

DUAL — LOCAL

OBJECTIVES

- Become familiar with the procedures to identify, verify, feather, and secure the inoperative engine.
- Become familiar with applying the proper control inputs to counteract yaw and roll, reduce drag, and zero the sideslip after an engine failure.
- Become familiar with performing straight-and-level flight, climbs, descents, and turns with one engine inoperative.
- Become familiar with the V_{MC} characteristics and the significance of the relationship of V_{MC} to stall speed during the V_{MC} demonstration.
- Gain proficiency in high altitude operations.
- Gain proficiency in performing short-field takeoffs and landings, rejected takeoffs, and go-arounds.

PREFLIGHT DISCUSSION

❑ Engine-Out Procedures, Aerodynamics, and Performance
❑ Situational Awareness
❑ Task Management

INTRODUCE

MULTI-ENGINE OPERATIONS

Maneuvering with One Engine Inoperative

❑ Engine Failure During Cruise
❑ Identifying and Verifying Inoperative Engine
❑ Feathering and Securing Inoperative Engine
❑ Use of Controls to Counteract Yaw and Roll
❑ Drag Reduction
❑ Control Input for Zero Sideslip
❑ V_{MC} Demonstration

NOTE: *The V_{MC} demonstration must be completed no lower than 3,000 feet AGL or the manufacturer's recommended altitude, whichever is higher. In addition, it is imperative that instructors observe precautions applicable to the airplane being flown, particularly limitations associated with high density altitude conditions. In some high density altitude situations, the demonstration might not be practical and should not be attempted.*

BASIC MANEUVERS (ONE ENGINE INOPERATIVE)

- ❑ Straight-and-Level Flight
- ❑ Climbs and Descents
- ❑ Turns to Headings

REVIEW

TAKEOFFS, LANDINGS, AND GO-AROUNDS

(Includes operations in crosswinds)

- ❑ Rejected Takeoff
- ❑ Short-Field Takeoff and Maximum Performance Climb
- ❑ Short-Field Approach and Landing
- ❑ Go-Around/Rejected Landing

HIGH ALTITUDE OPERATIONS

- ❑ Supplemental Oxygen Use
- ❑ Pressurization System Operation

COMPLETION STANDARDS

- Perform the proper procedures to identify, verify, feather, and secure the inoperative engine.
- Apply the proper control inputs to counteract yaw and roll, reduce drag, and zero the sideslip after an engine failure.
- Demonstrate understanding of the effects of various airspeeds and configurations on engine-out performance.
- Maintain control of the airplane while performing straight-and-level flight, climbs, descents, and turns with one engine inoperative.
- Demonstrate knowledge of the cause, effect, and significance of engine-out minimum control speed (V_{MC}) and recognize the imminent loss of control.
- Demonstrate proficiency in short-field takeoffs and landings, rejected takeoffs, and go-arounds.

POSTFLIGHT DEBRIEFING

- ❑ Critique maneuvers/procedures and SRM.
- ❑ Create a plan for skills that need improvement.
- ❑ Update the record folder and logbook.

FLIGHT LESSON 5

DUAL — LOCAL

OBJECTIVES

- Become familiar with managing an engine failure during takeoff before V_{MC} and after liftoff.
- Become familiar with performing approaches and landings with an inoperative engine.
- Gain proficiency in the procedures to identify, verify, feather, and secure the inoperative engine and counteract yaw and roll, reduce drag, and zero the sideslip after an engine failure.

- Gain proficiency in performing straight-and-level flight, climbs, descents, and turns with one engine inoperative.
- Perform the V_{MC} demonstration and the proper recovery.

PREFLIGHT DISCUSSION

- ❑ Engine Failure on Takeoff and Initial Climb
- ❑ Factors Affecting V_{MC}

INTRODUCE

EMERGENCY OPERATIONS

- ❑ Engine Failure During Takeoff Before V_{MC} (Simulated)
- ❑ Engine Failure After Liftoff (Simulated)
- ❑ Approach and Landing with an Inoperative Engine (Simulated)

MULTI-ENGINE OPERATIONS

Maneuvering with One Engine Inoperative

- ❑ Full Feather and In-Flight Restart

REVIEW

MULTI-ENGINE OPERATIONS

Maneuvering with One Engine Inoperative

- ❑ Engine Failure During Cruise
- ❑ Identifying and Verifying Inoperative Engine
- ❑ Feathering and Securing Inoperative Engine
- ❑ Use of Controls to Counteract Yaw and Roll
- ❑ Drag Reduction
- ❑ Control Input for Zero Sideslip
- ❑ V_{MC} Demonstration

NOTE: *The V_{MC} demonstration must be completed no lower than 3,000 feet AGL or the manufacturer's recommended altitude, whichever is higher. In addition, it is imperative that instructors observe precautions applicable to the airplane being flown, particularly limitations associated with high density altitude conditions. In some high density altitude situations, the demonstration might not be practical and should not be attempted.*

BASIC MANEUVERS (ONE ENGINE INOPERATIVE)

- ❑ Straight-and-Level Flight
- ❑ Climbs and Descents
- ❑ Turns to Headings

COMPLETION STANDARDS

- Demonstrate understanding of the procedures to manage an engine failure during takeoff before V_{MC}, an engine failure after liftoff, and an approach and landing with an inoperative engine.
- Demonstrate understanding of the procedures to feather the propeller and restart an engine in flight.
- Promptly identify the inoperative engine and perform the correct procedures to verify, feather, and secure the inoperative engine.

- Properly counteract yaw and roll, reduce drag, and zero the sideslip after an engine failure.
- Gain proficiency in performing straight-and-level flight, climbs, descents, and turns with one engine inoperative.
- Perform the V_{MC} demonstration—correctly configure the airplane, reduce airspeed, recognize indications of loss of directional control or impending stall, and recover.

POSTFLIGHT DEBRIEFING

❏ Critique maneuvers/procedures and SRM.
❏ Create a plan for skills that need improvement.
❏ Update the record folder and logbook.

STUDY ASSIGNMENT

Ground Lesson 5

Multi-Engine Instrument Flight and Decision Making

Multi-Engine Instrument Flight Briefing

FLIGHT LESSON 6

DUAL — LOCAL

OBJECTIVE

- Become familiar with identifying an inoperative engine and performing engine-out procedures solely by reference to instruments.
- Gain proficiency in managing an engine failure during takeoff and after liftoff, performing a full feather and preflight restart, and performing an approach and landing with an inoperative engine.

PREFLIGHT DISCUSSION

❏ Engine-Out Instrument Procedures
❏ Situational Awareness
❏ Single-Pilot Resource Management

INTRODUCE

MULTI-ENGINE OPERATIONS

One Engine Inoperative (Simulated) (solely by Reference to Instruments) During Straight-and- Level Flight and Turns

❏ Identifying and Verifying Inoperative Engine
❏ Feathering and Securing Inoperative Engine
❏ Use of Controls to Counteract Yaw and Roll
❏ Drag Reduction
❏ Control Input for Zero Sideslip

REVIEW

EMERGENCY OPERATIONS
- ❑ Engine Failure During Takeoff Before V_{MC} (Simulated)
- ❑ Engine Failure After Liftoff (Simulated)
- ❑ Approach and Landing with an Inoperative Engine (Simulated)

MULTI-ENGINE OPERATIONS

Maneuvering with One Engine Inoperative
- ❑ Full Feather and In-Flight Restart
- ❑ V_{MC} Demonstration

NOTE: *The V_{MC} demonstration must be completed no lower than 3,000 feet AGL or the manufacturer's recommended altitude, whichever is higher. In addition, it is imperative that instructors observe precautions applicable to the airplane being flown, particularly limitations associated with high density altitude conditions. In some high density altitude situations, the demonstration might not be practical and should not be attempted.*

COMPLETION STANDARDS

- Demonstrate understanding of performing engine-out maneuvers and procedures solely by reference to instruments.
- Demonstrate proficiency in managing an engine failure during takeoff before V_{MC}, an engine failure after liftoff, and an approach and landing with an inoperative engine.
- Demonstrate proficiency in performing the procedures to feather the propeller and restart an engine in flight.
- Demonstrate proficiency in performing the correct procedures to identify, verify, feather, and secure the inoperative engine and to counteract yaw and roll, reduce drag, and zero the sideslip after an engine failure.
- Demonstrate proficiency in performing the V_{MC} demonstration.

POSTFLIGHT DEBRIEFING

- ❑ Critique maneuvers/procedures and SRM.
- ❑ Create a plan for skills that need improvement.
- ❑ Update the record folder and logbook.

FLIGHT LESSON 7

DUAL — LOCAL

OBJECTIVES

- Become familiar with performing instrument approaches, missed approach procedures, and holding with both engines operating.
- Increase proficiency in identifying an inoperative engine and performing engine-out procedures solely by reference to instruments.

PREFLIGHT DISCUSSION

- ❑ Instrument Approach Chart Review

INTRODUCE

NAVIGATION SYSTEMS

Intercepting and Tracking Navigational Systems and Arcs (Full Panel)

- ❏ GPS Course Interception and Tracking
- ❏ VOR Radial Interception and Tracking

AIR TRAFFIC CONTROL CLEARANCES AND PROCEDURES

Holding Procedures

- ❏ VOR Holding
- ❏ GPS Holding

INSTRUMENT APPROACH PROCEDURES

Precision Approach

- ❏ ILS Approaches
- ❏ RNAV (GPS) Approaches (to LPV minimums with a DA less than 300 feet HAT)

Nonprecision Approach

- ❏ Localizer Approaches
- ❏ RNAV (GPS) Approaches

APPROACH PROCEDURES

- ❏ Procedure Turn/Course Reversal
- ❏ Terminal Arrival Area (TAA)
- ❏ Vectors to the Approach Course
- ❏ Approach Procedure to Straight-In or Circling Landing Minimums
- ❏ Missed Approach

LANDING FROM AN INSTRUMENT APPROACH

- ❏ Straight-In Landing
- ❏ Circle-to-Land/Circling Approach
- ❏ Wake Turbulence Avoidance
- ❏ Wind Shear Avoidance
- ❏ Land and Hold Short Operations (LAHSO)

REVIEW

EMERGENCY OPERATIONS

- ❏ Engine Failure During Takeoff Before V_{MC} (Simulated)
- ❏ Engine Failure After Liftoff (Simulated)
- ❏ Approach and Landing with an Inoperative Engine (Simulated)

MULTI-ENGINE OPERATIONS

One Engine Inoperative (Simulated) (solely by Reference to Instruments) During Straight-and-Level Flight and Turns

- ❏ Identifying and Verifying Inoperative Engine
- ❏ Feathering and Securing Inoperative Engine
- ❏ Use of Controls to Counteract Yaw and Roll
- ❏ Drag Reduction
- ❏ Control Input for Zero Sideslip

COMPLETION STANDARDS

- Perform holding and instrument approaches using the correct procedures and positive aircraft control.

- Demonstrate proficiency in identifying an inoperative engine and performing engine-out procedures solely by reference to instruments.

POSTFLIGHT DEBRIEFING

- ❑ Critique maneuvers/procedures and SRM.
- ❑ Create a plan for skills that need improvement.
- ❑ Update the record folder and logbook.

FLIGHT LESSON 8

DUAL — CROSS-COUNTRY, DAY

OBJECTIVES

- Increase proficiency in basic instrument flight operations during a planned cross-country flight to at least one point more than 100 nautical miles straight-line distance from the departure point.
- Become familiar with engine-out approach procedures solely by reference to instruments.

PREFLIGHT DISCUSSION

- ❑ Cross-Country Flight Planning
- ❑ Instrument Approach Chart Review
- ❑ Engine Failure Considerations During Cross-Country Flight
- ❑ Risk Management (5Ps, PAVE)

INTRODUCE

IFR CROSS-COUNTRY FLIGHT

PREFLIGHT PREPARATION

Weather Information

- ❑ Departure, Enroute, Alternate, and Destination Meteorology
- ❑ Alternate Requirements

Cross-Country Flight Planning

- ❑ Route Planning and Alternate Selection
- ❑ Altitude Selection
- ❑ Weight and Balance
- ❑ Performance and Limitations
- ❑ Determining ETA
- ❑ Fuel Requirements
- ❑ Sources of Flight Information
- ❑ SIDs, ODPs, and STARs
- ❑ Navigation Log
- ❑ IFR Flight Plan
- ❑ Airframe Icing Considerations

PREFLIGHT PROCEDURES

Airplane Flight Instruments and Navigation Equipment

- ❑ GPS Programming
- ❑ VOR Equipment Operation

ATC CLEARANCES AND PROCEDURES
- ❏ Clearance Copying and Readback
- ❏ Compliance with ATC Clearances—Departure, Enroute, Arrival, Approach
- ❏ Holding Procedures

NAVIGATION SYSTEMS

Intercepting and Tracking Navigational Systems and Arcs (Full Panel and Partial Panel)
- ❏ GPS Course Interception and Tracking
- ❏ VOR Radial Interception and Tracking
- ❏ Localizer Course Interception and Tracking
- ❏ Intercepting and Tracking DME Arcs
- ❏ Autopilot Use for Navigation, if Equipped

Departure, Enroute, and Arrival Operations
- ❏ Standard Instrument Departure (SID)
- ❏ Obstacle Departure Procedure (ODP)
- ❏ Standard Terminal Arrival (STAR)
- ❏ Checklist Use
- ❏ Radio Communications
- ❏ ATC Services
- ❏ Use of Flight Deck Displays—Weather and Aeronautical Information

MULTI-ENGINE OPERATIONS

Instrument Approach and Landing with an Inoperative Engine (Simulated) (solely by Reference to Instruments)
- ❏ ILS Approaches
- ❏ Localizer Approaches
- ❏ RNAV (GPS) Approaches
- ❏ VOR and VOR/DME Approaches

Approach Procedures
- ❏ Procedure Turn/Course Reversal
- ❏ Terminal Arrival Area (TAA)
- ❏ Vectors to the Approach Course
- ❏ Approach Procedure to Straight-In or Circling Landing Minimums
- ❏ Missed Approach

Landing from an Instrument Approach
- ❏ Straight-In Landing
- ❏ Circle-to-Land/Circling Approach
- ❏ Wake Turbulence Avoidance
- ❏ Wind Shear Avoidance
- ❏ Land and Hold Short Operations (LAHSO)

NOTE: *Perform specific approach procedures as needed.*

REVIEW

EMERGENCY OPERATIONS
- ❏ Engine Failure During Takeoff Before V_{MC} (Simulated)
- ❏ Engine Failure After Liftoff (Simulated)
- ❏ Approach and Landing with an Inoperative Engine (Simulated)

TAKEOFFS, LANDINGS, AND GO-AROUNDS
(Includes operations in crosswinds)
- ❑ Rejected Takeoff
- ❑ Normal Takeoff and Climb
- ❑ Normal Approach and Landing
- ❑ Short-Field Takeoff and Maximum Performance Climb
- ❑ Short-Field Approach and Landing
- ❑ Go-Around/Rejected Landing

COMPLETION STANDARDS

- Demonstrate proficiency in IFR cross-country flight operations in the multi-engine airplane by performing an IFR cross-country over 100 nautical miles from the original point of departure.
- Demonstrate proficiency in IFR departure, enroute and arrival operations.
- Demonstrate understanding of the techniques to perform one-engine inoperative instrument approach procedures.
- Demonstrate the ability to use SRM to make effective decisions, maintain situational awareness, prevent CFIT, and manage risk, tasks, and automation.

POSTFLIGHT DEBRIEFING

- ❑ Critique maneuvers/procedures and SRM.
- ❑ Create a plan for skills that need improvement.
- ❑ Update the record folder and logbook.

FLIGHT LESSON 9

DUAL — CROSS-COUNTRY, NIGHT

OBJECTIVES

- Increase proficiency in flying instrument approaches, missed approach procedures, and holding with all engines operating and with one engine inoperative.
- Gain proficiency in basic cross-country and instrument flight operations at night by planning and performing a cross-country flight to a point more than 100 nautical miles straight-line distance from the departure point.

PREFLIGHT DISCUSSION

- ❑ Night Flying Considerations
- ❑ Cross-Country Flight Planning
- ❑ Instrument Approach Chart Review
- ❑ Engine Failure Considerations During Cross-Country Flight
- ❑ Risk Management (5Ps, PAVE)

INTRODUCE

IFR CROSS-COUNTRY FLIGHT

NIGHT FLIGHT
- ❑ Night Preparation—Visual Adaptation, Lighting, Equipment
- ❑ Night Operations—Orientation, Navigation, Chart Reading
- ❑ Collision Avoidance—Night

REVIEW

PREFLIGHT PREPARATION

Weather Information

- ❑ Departure, Enroute, Alternate, and Destination Meteorology
- ❑ Alternate Requirements

Cross-Country Flight Planning

- ❑ Route Planning and Alternate Selection
- ❑ Altitude Selection
- ❑ Weight and Balance
- ❑ Performance and Limitations
- ❑ Determining ETA
- ❑ Fuel Requirements
- ❑ Sources of Flight Information
- ❑ SIDs, ODPs, and STARs
- ❑ Navigation Log
- ❑ IFR Flight Plan
- ❑ Airframe Icing Considerations

PREFLIGHT PROCEDURES

Airplane Flight Instruments and Navigation Equipment

- ❑ GPS Programming
- ❑ VOR Equipment Operation

ATC CLEARANCES AND PROCEDURES

- ❑ Clearance Copying and Readback
- ❑ Compliance with ATC Clearances—Departure, Enroute, Arrival, Approach
- ❑ Holding Procedures

NAVIGATION SYSTEMS

Intercepting and Tracking Navigational Systems and Arcs (Full Panel and Partial Panel)

- ❑ GPS Course Interception and Tracking
- ❑ VOR Radial Interception and Tracking
- ❑ Localizer Course Interception and Tracking
- ❑ Intercepting and Tracking DME Arcs
- ❑ Autopilot Use for Navigation, if Equipped

Departure, Enroute, and Arrival Operations

- ❑ Standard Instrument Departure (SID)
- ❑ Obstacle Departure Procedure (ODP)
- ❑ Standard Terminal Arrival (STAR)
- ❑ Checklist Use
- ❑ Radio Communications
- ❑ ATC Services
- ❑ Use of Flight Deck Displays—Weather and Aeronautical Information

MULTI-ENGINE OPERATIONS

Instrument Approach and Landing with an Inoperative Engine (Simulated) (solely by Reference to Instruments)

- ❑ ILS Approaches
- ❑ Localizer Approaches
- ❑ RNAV (GPS) Approaches
- ❑ VOR and VOR/DME Approaches

Approach Procedures
- ❑ Procedure Turn/Course Reversal
- ❑ Terminal Arrival Area (TAA)
- ❑ Vectors to the Approach Course
- ❑ Approach Procedure to Straight-In or Circling Landing Minimums
- ❑ Missed Approach

Landing from an Instrument Approach
- ❑ Straight-In Landing
- ❑ Circle-to-Land/Circling Approach
- ❑ Wake Turbulence Avoidance
- ❑ Wind Shear Avoidance
- ❑ Land and Hold Short Operations (LAHSO)

NOTE: *Perform specific approach procedures as needed.*

EMERGENCY OPERATIONS
- ❑ Engine Failure During Takeoff Before V_{MC} (Simulated)
- ❑ Engine Failure After Liftoff (Simulated)
- ❑ Approach and Landing with an Inoperative Engine (Simulated)

TAKEOFFS, LANDINGS, AND GO-AROUNDS
(Includes operations in crosswinds)
- ❑ Rejected Takeoff
- ❑ Normal Takeoff and Climb
- ❑ Normal Approach and Landing
- ❑ Short-Field Takeoff and Maximum Performance Climb
- ❑ Short-Field Approach and Landing
- ❑ Go-Around/Rejected Landing

COMPLETION STANDARDS

- Demonstrate proficiency in night IFR cross-country flight operations in the multi-engine airplane by performing a night IFR cross-country over 100 nautical miles from the original point of departure.
- Demonstrate proficiency in IFR departure, enroute, and arrival operations.
- Demonstrate proficiency in performing one-engine inoperative instrument approach procedures—maintain altitude ±100 feet or minimum sink rate if applicable, airspeed ±10 knots, selected heading ±10°, and on the final approach segment, vertical (as applicable) and lateral guidance within ¾-scale deflection.
- Demonstrate the ability to use SRM to make effective decisions, maintain situational awareness, prevent CFIT, and manage risk, tasks, and automation.

POSTFLIGHT DEBRIEFING

- ❑ Critique maneuvers/procedures and SRM.
- ❑ Create a plan for skills that need improvement.
- ❑ Update the record folder and logbook.

STUDY ASSIGNMENT

Ground Lesson 6
Stage I Exam

Multi-Engine Rating Practical Test Briefing

Stage I Check

Prepare for the Stage I Check in Flight Lesson 10.

FLIGHT LESSON 10

DUAL — LOCAL
STAGE I CHECK

OBJECTIVE

Demonstrate to the chief instructor, the assistant chief instructor, or the designated check instructor, proficiency in performing:

- Slow flight, stalls, steep turns, normal and short-field takeoffs and landings, and emergency operations.
- The procedures to manage an engine failure during takeoff before V_{MC}, an engine failure after liftoff, and an approach and landing with an inoperative engine.
- The procedures to verify, feather, and secure the inoperative engine, counteract yaw and roll, reduce drag, and zero the sideslip after an engine failure.
- The V_{MC} demonstration.
- One engine inoperative (simulated) solely by reference to instruments during straight-and-level flight and turns.
- An instrument approach and landing with an inoperative engine (simulated) solely by reference to instruments.

PREFLIGHT DISCUSSION

❑ Student and Flight Check Instructor Roles and Expectations
❑ Questions to Test Student Knowledge

EVALUATE

PREFLIGHT PREPARATION

❑ Pilot Qualifications
❑ Airworthiness Requirements
❑ Weather Information
❑ Performance and Limitations
❑ Operation of Systems
❑ Human Factors

PREFLIGHT PROCEDURES

❑ Preflight Inspection
❑ Flight Deck Management
❑ Use of Checklists
❑ Engine Starting
❑ Taxiing
❑ Before Takeoff Check

PERFORMANCE MANEUVERS

❑ Steep Turns

SLOW FLIGHT AND STALLS
- ❑ Maneuvering During Slow Flight
- ❑ Power-Off Stalls
- ❑ Power-On Stalls
- ❑ Accelerated Stalls
- ❑ Spin Awareness

HIGH ALTITUDE OPERATIONS
- ❑ Supplemental Oxygen Use
- ❑ Pressurization System Operation

NOTE: *If high altitude systems are not applicable to the airplane to be used for the practical test, the student must still demonstrate knowledge of high altitude operations sufficient to meet the requirements specified in the FAA Commercial Pilot Airman Certification Standards.*

EMERGENCY OPERATIONS
- ❑ Systems and Equipment Malfunctions
- ❑ Emergency Descent
- ❑ Engine Failure During Takeoff Before V_{MC} (Simulated)
- ❑ Engine Failure After Liftoff (Simulated)
- ❑ Approach and Landing with an Inoperative Engine (Simulated)

MULTI-ENGINE OPERATIONS
- ❑ Maneuvering with One Engine Inoperative
- ❑ V_{MC} Demonstration

NOTE: *The V_{MC} demonstration must be completed no lower than 3,000 feet AGL or the manufacturer's recommended altitude, whichever is higher. In addition, it is imperative that instructors observe precautions applicable to the airplane being flown, particularly limitations associated with high density altitude conditions. In some high density altitude situations, the demonstration might not be practical and should not be attempted.*

MULTI-ENGINE OPERATIONS

One Engine Inoperative (Simulated) (solely by Reference to Instruments) During Straight-and-Level Flight and Turns
- ❑ Identifying and Verifying Inoperative Engine
- ❑ Feathering and Securing Inoperative Engine
- ❑ Use of Controls to Counteract Yaw and Roll
- ❑ Drag Reduction
- ❑ Control Input for Zero Sideslip

Instrument Approach and Landing with an Inoperative Engine (Simulated) (solely by Reference to Instruments)
- ❑ ILS Approaches
- ❑ Localizer Approaches
- ❑ RNAV (GPS) Approaches
- ❑ VOR and VOR/DME Approaches

AIRPORT OPERATIONS
- ❑ Radio Communications
- ❑ Airport, Runway, and Taxiway Signs, Markings, and Lighting
- ❑ Traffic Patterns
- ❑ Runway Incursion Avoidance

- ❑ Wake Turbulence Avoidance
- ❑ Wind Shear Avoidance
- ❑ Land and Hold Short Operations (LAHSO

TAKEOFFS, LANDINGS, AND GO-AROUNDS
(Includes operations in crosswinds)

- ❑ Rejected Takeoff
- ❑ Normal Takeoff and Climb
- ❑ Normal Approach and Landing
- ❑ Short-Field Takeoff and Maximum Performance Climb
- ❑ Short-Field Approach and Landing
- ❑ Go-Around/Rejected Landing

POSTFLIGHT PROCEDURES

- ❑ After Landing, Parking, and Securing

COMPLETION STANDARDS

- Demonstrate proficiency in all the maneuvers and procedures listed for review at the level required by multi-engine land sections of the Commercial Pilot Airman Certification Standards.
- Demonstrate the ability to use single-pilot resource management to make effective decisions, maintain situational awareness, prevent CFIT, and manage risk, tasks, and automation.

POSTFLIGHT DEBRIEFING

- ❑ Evaluate maneuvers/procedures and SRM.
- ❑ Plan additional instruction for skills not meeting course completion standards.
- ❑ Update the record folder and logbook.

STUDY ASSIGNMENT

Ground Lesson 7

Multi-Engine Rating End-of-Course Exam

Flight Lesson 11

Prepare for the End-of-Course Flight Check.

FLIGHT LESSON 11

DUAL — LOCAL

END-OF-COURSE FLIGHT CHECK FOR COURSE COMPLETION

OBJECTIVE

Demonstrate proficiency in all listed tasks to the chief instructor, assistant chief, or a designated check instructor during the End-of-Course Flight Check. The proficiency level must meet the requirements of the multi-engine land sections of the Commercial Pilot Airman Certification Standards.

PREFLIGHT DISCUSSION

- ❏ Student and Flight Check Instructor Roles and Expectations
- ❏ Questions to Test Student Knowledge

EVALUATE

PREFLIGHT PREPARATION

- ❏ Pilot Qualifications
- ❏ Airworthiness Requirements
- ❏ Weather Information
- ❏ Performance and Limitations
- ❏ Operation of Systems
- ❏ Human Factors

PREFLIGHT PROCEDURES

- ❏ Preflight Inspection
- ❏ Flight Deck Management
- ❏ Use of Checklists
- ❏ Engine Starting
- ❏ Taxiing
- ❏ Before Takeoff Check

PERFORMANCE MANEUVERS

- ❏ Steep Turns

SLOW FLIGHT AND STALLS

- ❏ Maneuvering During Slow Flight
- ❏ Power-Off Stalls
- ❏ Power-On Stalls
- ❏ Accelerated Stalls
- ❏ Spin Awareness

HIGH ALTITUDE OPERATIONS

- ❏ Supplemental Oxygen Use
- ❏ Pressurization System Operation

NOTE: *If high altitude systems are not applicable to the airplane to be used for the practical test, the student must still demonstrate knowledge of high altitude operations sufficient to meet the requirements specified in the FAA Commercial Pilot Airman Certification Standards.*

EMERGENCY OPERATIONS

- ❏ Systems and Equipment Malfunctions
- ❏ Emergency Descent
- ❏ Engine Failure During Takeoff Before V_{MC} (Simulated)
- ❏ Engine Failure After Liftoff (Simulated)
- ❏ Approach and Landing with an Inoperative Engine (Simulated)

MULTI-ENGINE OPERATIONS

- ❏ Maneuvering with One Engine Inoperative
- ❏ V_{MC} Demonstration

NOTE: *The V_{MC} demonstration must be completed no lower than 3,000 feet AGL or the manufacturer's recommended altitude, whichever is higher. In addition, it is imperative that instructors observe precautions applicable to the airplane being* *flown, particularly limitations associated with high density altitude conditions. In some high density altitude situations, the demonstration might not be practical and should not be attempted.*

MULTI-ENGINE OPERATIONS

One Engine Inoperative (Simulated) (solely by Reference to Instruments) During Straight-and-Level Flight and Turns

- ❏ Identifying and Verifying Inoperative Engine
- ❏ Feathering and Securing Inoperative Engine
- ❏ Use of Controls to Counteract Yaw and Roll
- ❏ Drag Reduction
- ❏ Control Input for Zero Sideslip

Instrument Approach and Landing with an Inoperative Engine (Simulated) (solely by Reference to Instruments)

- ❏ ILS Approaches
- ❏ Localizer Approaches
- ❏ RNAV (GPS) Approaches
- ❏ VOR and VOR/DME Approaches

AIRPORT OPERATIONS

- ❏ Radio Communications
- ❏ Airport, Runway, and Taxiway Signs, Markings, and Lighting
- ❏ Traffic Patterns
- ❏ Runway Incursion Avoidance
- ❏ Wake Turbulence Avoidance
- ❏ Wind Shear Avoidance
- ❏ Land and Hold Short Operations (LAHSO)

TAKEOFFS, LANDINGS, AND GO-AROUNDS

(Includes operations in crosswinds)

- ❏ Rejected Takeoff
- ❏ Normal Takeoff and Climb
- ❏ Normal Approach and Landing
- ❏ Short-Field Takeoff and Maximum Performance Climb
- ❏ Short-Field Approach and Landing
- ❏ Go-Around/Rejected Landing

POSTFLIGHT PROCEDURES

- ❏ After Landing, Parking, and Securing

COMPLETION STANDARDS

- Demonstrate proficiency in all the maneuvers and procedures listed for review at the level required by multi-engine land sections of the Commercial Pilot Airman Certification Standards.
- Demonstrate the ability to use single-pilot resource management to make effective decisions, maintain situational awareness, prevent CFIT, and manage risk, tasks, and automation.

POSTFLIGHT DEBRIEFING

- ❏ Evaluate maneuvers/procedures and SRM.
- ❏ Plan additional instruction for skills not meeting course completion standards.
- ❏ Update the record folder and logbook.

Appendix A — Pilot Briefing Questions

Instrument Rating

Course Briefings

INSTRUMENT APPROACHES BRIEFING

These questions help prepare the student for flying instrument approach procedures. The student should demonstrate understanding of these questions and any additional questions that develop during the briefing before practicing instrument approach procedures.

1. Describe the segments of a typical instrument approach and the purpose of each segment.
2. What does the notation "NoPT" on an approach chart mean?
3. If a standard procedure turn symbol is shown, what type of course reversals are authorized? If a teardrop or holding pattern is shown? If no procedure turn symbol is shown?
4. What does the phrase "...cleared for straight-in approach" mean?
5. What determines the aircraft approach category?
6. If you fly a Category A airplane at an approach speed appropriate to Category B, which minimums should you use and why?
7. At what point during a circling approach may you begin descent from the MDA?
8. How should you initiate a missed approach if you lose visual contact during a circling approach?
9. What does the term "...cleared approach" mean?
10. What requirements must you meet to descend below the DA/MDA?
11. Is it permissible to land a civil aircraft when the visibility is below minimums if you have the runway environment in sight?
12. If one or more approach components are inoperative, unusable, or not utilized, how do you determine the adjustments required in approach minimums?
13. What is RVR? If both RVR and prevailing visibility are reported, which takes precedence?
14. Where is the MAP on a precision approach? On an APV? On a nonprecision approach?
15. What is the lowest possible DA and visibility for a Category I ILS approach?
16. What is the CDI sensitivity of a localizer signal compared to a VOR signal?
17. Do you ever use an ILS glide slope with a back course approach?
18. How do you determine the allowable uses for the specific GPS installation in your airplane?
19. Describe the characteristics of a terminal arrival area (TAA).

20. What airplane equipment do you need to fly an RNAV (GPS) approach to LNAV minimums? LNAV/VNAV minimums? LPV minimums?
21. What are the characteristics of an RNAV (GPS) approach to LP minimums?
22. If RAIM is not available when you set up an RNAV (GPS) approach, what should you do?
23. What is the minimum navigation equipment required for a VOR/DME approach?
24. Given an approach chart, brief the approach.
25. Compare and contrast visual and contact approaches.

IFR CROSS-COUNTRY BRIEFING

These questions help prepare the student for IFR cross-country flight operations. The student should demonstrate understanding of these questions and any additional questions that develop during the briefing before performing IFR cross-country flight operations.

1. If you plan to fly a SID or a STAR, how do you indicate this on your flight plan? How do you indicate that you do not wish to use SIDs or STARs?
2. What aircraft equipment code do you indicate on your IFR flight plans?
3. What standard takeoff minimums apply to flights conducted under Part 91 as compared to commercial operators?
4. When are you required to have an alternate airport for a flight under IFR?
5. What are the IFR fuel requirements?
6. List the items of an IFR clearance in the normal sequence.
7. After receiving a takeoff clearance from the tower, when do you contact departure control?
8. What reports should you make to ATC without request when operating in a radar environment?
9. What additional reports should you make to ATC in a nonradar environment? Where must you make position reports?
10. On a direct route segment, what points are considered to be compulsory reporting points?
11. Give an example of a position report.
12. Explain a VFR-on-top clearance.
13. Explain a clearance to climb to VFR-on-top.
14. What does flight at or above an MEA guarantee? At or above the MOCA?
15. What is the significance of an MRA? Of an MCA?
16. What altimeter setting should you use during IFR flight below 18,000 feet? For flight at or above 18,000 feet?
17. What are the appropriate IFR cruising altitudes below and above 18,000 feet?
18. What procedures should you follow if you lose two-way radio communications under IFR?
19. How can you obtain weather information enroute on an IFR flight?
20. What temperature range normally is conducive to structural icing when you are operating in visible moisture?
21. If you encounter icing conditions in flight, what actions should you take?
22. You are being radar vectored with your last assigned altitude as 9,000 feet. ATC then issues your approach clearance. At what point during the approach can you descend to a lower altitude?

INSTRUMENT RATING PRACTICAL TEST BRIEFING

These questions help prepare the student for the FAA Instrument Rating Practical Test. The student should demonstrate understanding of these questions and any additional questions that develop during the briefing before taking the End-of Course Flight Check and FAA Instrument Rating Practical Test.

These sample questions are examples of the types of questions that the examiner might ask during the oral and flight portions of the practical test. The examiner may ask questions at any time to determine if the student's knowledge of a subject area is adequate. Preparation for the practical test should include a review of FAR Parts 61, 91, and NTSB 830, with emphasis on the rules that apply to instrument pilots. In addition, thoroughly discuss each FAA question incorrectly answered on the knowledge test because the examiner might emphasize these areas.

AIRPLANE REQUIREMENTS

1. What equipment, in addition to that required for a VFR flight, must the airplane have for a flight under IFR?
2. What airplane and equipment inspections are required for flight under IFR? How often are these inspections required? Locate each entry for the training airplane in the aircraft logbooks.
3. How often must the VOR equipment be operationally checked when you use VORs for a flight conducted under IFR?
4. What are the acceptable methods of checking the airplane's VOR equipment, and what are the allowable errors for each method?
5. Under what conditions must you have a transponder for flight under VFR or IFR?
6. What are the differences in aircraft equipment requirements for flight under IFR in controlled and uncontrolled airspace?
7. How do you determine that the required instruments are working properly prior to flight?

PILOT REQUIREMENTS

1. What currency requirements must you meet to act as pilot in command of a flight under IFR? How much time and how many approaches may you conduct in an approved FTD or simulator?
2. Assume your instrument currency expires on June 1. What is the latest date that you can regain your currency without having to pass an instrument proficiency check?
3. What are the differences in pilot requirements to act as pilot in command of an airplane flying IFR in controlled and uncontrolled airspace?

APPROACH CHARTS AND PROCEDURES

To answer questions 1 through 15, use an ILS approach chart from the local area.

1. What is the approach category of your airplane?

2. What is the DA and visibility requirements for the ILS approach with all components operating? If the approach lighting systems are inoperative?
3. What is the localizer frequency and identifier?
4. Can you use DME for this approach? Is DME required?
5. What is the minimum procedure turn altitude?
6. What is the minimum glide slope intercept altitude?
7. Where does the final approach segment begin?
8. What is the final approach course?
9. How is the missed approach point determined for this approach?
10. What is the height of the electronic glide slope at the runway threshold?
11. Are there any limitations noted for the straight-in or circle-to-land procedures?
12. What is the elevation of the touchdown zone?
13. What are the landing minimum requirements if the glide slope is inoperative?
14. During a localizer approach (if applicable to the procedure), where does the final approach segment begin and how do you determine the missed approach point?
15. If applicable, what is the MSA to the east? What does flight at or above an MSA guarantee and when can you use an MSA?

To answer questions 16 through 24, use an RNAV (GPS) approach chart from the local area.

16. How will you obtain the latest weather observation at this airport before you begin the approach?
17. If applicable, at which IAFs must you perform a course reversal? Name any IAFs at which a course reversal is not authorized.
18. Where does the final approach segment begin?
19. At what point may you begin a descent from the procedure turn altitude, if applicable?
20. What is the final approach course?
21. If applicable for the approach procedure, answer the following questions. What requirements must your airplane's GPS equipment meet for you to fly the approach to LNAV minimums? To LNAV/VNAV minimums? To LPV minimums?
22. If applicable for the approach procedure, answer the following questions. What are the ceiling and visibility requirements when flying the approach to LNAV minimums? To LNAV/VNAV minimums? To LPV minimums?
23. Where is the missed approach point?
24. What is the missed approach procedure?

To answer questions 25 through 33, use a VOR approach chart from the local area.

25. What is the frequency and identification of the primary facility?
26. What is the minimum procedure turn altitude for the approach?
27. What types of course reversal(s) may you use for the procedure turn?
28. Where does the final approach segment begin?
29. At what point may you begin a descent from the procedure turn altitude?
30. What is the final approach course?

31. What are the landing minimum requirements for a Category C aircraft?
32. Where is the missed approach point?
33. Assume you are flying a Category A aircraft at an approach speed of 100 knots during a circle-to-land maneuver. Which minimums should you use and why?

AIR TRAFFIC CONTROL

1. When may you deviate from a clearance?
2. When may you cancel IFR?
3. Assume you have been issued a clearance to climb from 5,000 feet to 8,000 feet. What rate(s) of climb does ATC expect you to maintain?
4. If you reach a clearance limit before you receive a further clearance, what action should you take?
5. What does the phrase *"...radar service terminated"* mean?
6. What does the phrase *"...resume own navigation"* mean?
7. What is the maximum indicated airspeed you can use in any civil aircraft in a holding pattern below 6,000 feet MSL?
8. What are the requirements for a visual approach, and who may initiate the procedure?
9. What are the requirements for a contact approach, and who may initiate the procedure?
10. How is your IFR flight plan closed at an airport served by an operating control tower? At an airport not served by a control tower?
11. How is your flight plan closed at an airport not served by a control tower or flight service station?
12. What procedures should you follow if you are unable to contact ATC on an assigned frequency?

Commercial Pilot Certification Course Briefings

CROSS-COUNTRY PROCEDURES BRIEFING

These questions help review VFR cross-country flight planning and flight operations. The student should demonstrate understanding of these questions and any additional questions that develop during the briefing before performing VFR cross-country flight operations.

1. Explain what weather product you would use to obtain the most current weather condition at your destination.
2. What is the meaning of code "9900" found on a winds aloft forecast?

To answer questions 3 through 8, use the appropriate pilot's operating handbook.

3. Based on the following conditions, determine the distance required to take off and clear a 50-foot obstacle, assuming maximum takeoff weight and a 10-knot headwind.
   - Field elevation..4,000 ft
   - Temperature..24°C
   - Altimeter setting..30.00
4. Determine the time, fuel, and distance needed to climb from a field elevation of 2,000 feet to a cruising altitude of 7,500 feet. Assume standard conditions and calm wind.
5. Based on a cruise altitude of 7,500 feet and standard conditions, determine the true airspeed and fuel flow at approximately 65% power. What is the airplane's maximum range with full fuel?
6. Based on the following conditions, determine the distance required to land over a 50-foot obstacle with a calm wind.
   - Field elevation..................................3,000 ft
   - Temperature..24°C
   - Altimeter Setting..................................29.92
7. What are the standard service volumes of the three classes of VORs? What basic restriction affects VOR signal reception? How can you verify that a VOR is usable?
8. What are the different methods for conducting a VOR check?
9. Using a sectional chart, identify how each class of airspace is depicted. What are the basic VFR weather minimums and pilot and equipment requirements to operate in each class?
10. What is a special VFR clearance? Can you request it at night? What visibility and cloud clearances apply?
11. Name the various types of special use airspace and explain the restrictions they impose.
12. How can you tell when a part-time control tower is operating?
13. If your route takes you through Class C airspace and you have established two-way radio contact with the approach controller but have not received a clearance to enter Class C airspace yet, what should you do? What if the airspace is Class B?

14. What if ATC issues a clearance that would cause you to enter a cloud in Class C or Class B airspace. Should you comply with the clearance? Explain.
15. If ATIS indicates the ceiling is 800 feet overcast and the visibility is two miles, can you land under VFR at an airport with Class C airspace?
16. Assume the same weather as in the previous question and clear skies above the ceiling. Can you legally operate above the cloud ceiling in Class C airspace without obtaining a special VFR clearance?
17. What minimum weather conditions must exist for you to enter Class D, C or B airspace without requesting special VFR?

COMPLEX AIRPLANE/TAA TRANSITION BRIEFING

These questions help prepare the student for flying a complex airplane, a technically advanced airplane (TAA), or both. Because a wide variety of complex airplanes and TAAs exist, determine the questions appropriate to the specific training airplane. The student should demonstrate understanding of these questions and any additional questions that develop during the briefing before operating the complex airplane and/or TAA.

ELECTRICAL SYSTEM

1. What equipment provides the electrical power?
2. How are the electrical system components protected?
3. What is the voltage of the electrical system when the alternator is operating and when it is off?
4. What is the difference between an ammeter and a loadmeter? How is an alternator failure indicated on an ammeter or on a loadmeter? Which is installed in your airplane?
5. What should you expect if the alternator fails?
6. What is the correct procedure for resetting a popped circuit breaker?
7. What should you do in the case of an electrical fire?

FUEL SYSTEM

1. Is your airplane equipped with a carburetor or a fuel injection system?
2. How many fuel tanks does your airplane have? What is the total amount of usable fuel?
3. What is the minimum allowable grade of fuel that you can use with your airplane? What color is it?
4. Describe the recommended fuel management procedures in the POH.
5. When should you switch fuel tanks during a flight? What is the procedure for switching fuel tanks?
6. What is the purpose of the fuel pump, if appropriate, on your airplane? When should you use it?
7. Where are the fuel tank vents located and what is their purpose?
8. Where are the fuel drains located on your airplane? When should you use them?
9. Some fuel tanks have a tab located within them that is visible with the fuel cap removed. What is its purpose?

LANDING GEAR SYSTEM

1. Explain how the landing gear system operates.
2. At what point during the takeoff should you retract the landing gear?
3. When approaching to land, where do you normally extend the landing gear?
4. Explain the procedure for manually extending the landing gear if the primary power source fails.
5. After extending the landing gear manually as a training procedure, is it advisable or possible to retract it normally? Is it possible to retract the landing gear manually?
6. What airspeed limitations exist during landing gear extension and retraction? Is there an additional limitation when the gear is down and locked?
7. Explain the purpose of each annunciator light of the landing gear system.
8. What procedure should you follow if a gear-down annunciator light fails to illuminate?
9. Explain the operation of the landing gear warning system.

COWL FLAPS

1. What is the purpose of the cowl flaps and how are they controlled?
2. What gauge/instrument helps you determine how to position the cowl flaps?
3. Generally, how should you position the cowl flaps for takeoff, during climb, in cruise flight, during descent, approach, and after landing?

CONSTANT-SPEED PROPELLERS

1. Explain the advantages and disadvantages of constant-speed and fixed-pitch propellers.
2. Explain how a constant-speed propeller operates.
3. Explain how you should set the propeller control or takeoff, climb, cruise, and landing. What gauge/instrument do you use to set the propeller?
4. When you apply power by using the throttle, what gauge/instrument indicates the increase in power?
5. What does the manifold pressure gauge indicate when the airplane is sitting on the ramp after the engine is shut down? Why?
6. What gauge/instrument do you use to set the propeller?
7. As a general rule, when decreasing power, do you move the throttle or the propeller control first? Which do you move first to increase power?
8. If the oil pressure to the propeller governor is cut off, what pitch setting does the propeller go to in most single-engine airplanes?
9. Why do you check the oil pressure when cycling the propeller during engine runup?
10. What should you do if you are ready for takeoff before the oil temperature is in the normal operating range?

WEIGHT AND BALANCE

1. What is the basic empty weight for your airplane?
2. Compute the weight and balance of your airplane as you typically operate it during training with full fuel. What is the airplane's maximum payload? How must you distribute the weight to keep the airplane in balance?

3. Compute a weight and balance problem, assuming yourself and three 170-pound passengers, each with 20 pounds of baggage. How much fuel can the airplane carry? With that fuel load, how must you load the baggage to keep the airplane in balance?

GENERAL CONSIDERATIONS

1. List the following airspeeds for your airplane and, where applicable, the corresponding airspeed indicator color codes.
   - Stalling speed in the landing configuration
   - Stalling speed in a specified configuration
   - Best angle-of-climb speed
   - Best rate-of-climb speed
   - Normal approach speed
   - Approach speed with the flaps retracted
   - Short-field landing approach speed
   - Maximum flap extension speed(s)
   - Maximum landing gear extended speed
   - Maximum landing gear operating speed
   - Design maneuvering speed
   - Maximum structural cruising speed
   - Never-exceed speed
2. Where is the ELT located?
3. Explain the proper procedures for leaning the mixture for your airplane.
4. Where is the alternate static source and how do you use it?
5. Explain the procedures for dealing with an engine fire during flight.
6. What configuration and airspeed provides the greatest glide distance?

PRIMARY FLIGHT DISPLAY (PFD)

1. What is the function of the altitude and heading reference system (AHRS)?
2. What is a magnetometer?
3. Where is the slip/skid indicator on the PFD?
4. What does the trend vector indicate on the HSI? On the airspeed indicator? On the altimeter?
5. What is the function of the air data computer (ADC)?
6. How are instrument failures indicated on the PFD?
7. How does an integrated display system compensate for a PFD failure?
8. How do you manage a complete electrical failure?
9. Describe the backup instruments in your airplane.

AUTOPILOT

1. How do you program the autopilot to:
   - Hold your current heading and altitude?
   - Climb or descend to a specific altitude?
   - Navigate on a course?
   - Perform an instrument approach?
2. How do you disengage the autopilot?
3. What is an automation surprise?

MFD/GPS FUNCTIONS

1. How do you set up the MFD map page?
2. How can you access information about an airport on the MFD?
3. How do you create a GPS flight plan?
4. What feature can you use to fly directly to a waypoint from your current position?
5. Explain how to use MFD functions in the event you need to divert.
6. How do you enter and activate an instrument departure, approach, or arrival procedure?
7. Describe features of your avionics system, including
   - Checklists
   - Engine Indication System
   - Audio Panel
   - Transponder
   - Traffic Information
   - Data Link Weather
   - TAWS/Terrain Proximity Data

COMMERCIAL FLIGHT MANEUVERS BRIEFING

These questions help prepare the student for flying commercial flight maneuvers and expand the student's understanding of the aerodynamics of these maneuvers. Consult the current FAA Commercial Pilot Airman Certification Standards for the required maneuvers.

SHORT-FIELD AND SOFT-FIELD TAKEOFFS AND LANDINGS

1. What flap setting should you use for a short-field takeoff? For a soft-field takeoff?
2. During a short-field approach and landing over a 50-foot obstacle, why is it necessary to establish a constant angle of descent over the obstacle?
3. Explain the effects of torque and P-factor on airplane control during short-field takeoffs.
4. What climb speed should you use during the initial portion of the short-field takeoff?
5. During a short-field approach and landing, how accurately must you land the airplane relative to a selected touchdown point?
6. How can you increase braking effectiveness during the landing roll after a short-field approach and landing?
7. At approximately what airspeed will the airplane become airborne during a soft-field takeoff?
8. At what point during the soft-field takeoff do you begin a climb? At what point during the soft-field takeoff do you retract the flaps?
9. Explain how you use power during the landing flare and touchdown during a soft-field landing.
10. Explain how to position the controls during crosswind takeoffs and landings.

11. What is the maximum demonstrated crosswind component for your airplane? Is this a limitation? Explain.
12. What effect does flap extension have on approach speed and descent angle?
13. If the airplane is low and slow on final approach, what corrective action should you take?
14. What is the significance of the key position during a landing?
15. Explain the procedures for performing a go-around.

STALL/SPIN AWARENESS

1. When practicing stall recognition and recovery, at what point should you initiate the recovery maneuver?
2. What is an accelerated stall? Explain how to perform and recover from an accelerated stall.
3. Are the manufacturer's spin recovery techniques included in the POH proven for the airplane and, if not, why not?
4. Describe the conditions required for a spin, the indications of an incipient spin and a full spin, and the spin recovery techniques for your airplane.

STEEP TURNS, CHANDELLES, AND STEEP SPIRALS

1. At what altitude and airspeed should you enter steep turns and chandelles?
2. How do you perform a steep turn? What bank angle should you use?
3. If an airplane weighs 2,500 pounds, how much weight must the wings support during a level turn with a 60° bank?
4. Explain the changes in elevator (or stabilator) pressure necessary to maintain level flight during the roll from a steep turn in one direction to a turn in the opposite direction.
5. What is the maximum recommended angle of bank for the chandelle?
6. Explain how you adjust the power during a chandelle.
7. What should your airspeed be at the completion of the chandelle?
8. Describe the differences in control pressures between the rollout from a chandelle to the right and one to the left. Where is the rudder pressure greatest?
9. Explain how you should recover from a chandelle. Why is altitude gain not the basis for judging the quality of a chandelle?
10. Describe the steps to perform a steep spiral.

LAZY EIGHTS AND EIGHTS-ON-PYLONS

1. What altitude and airspeed should you use to enter lazy eights?
2. What reference points do you use during lazy eights?
3. Where do the highest and lowest altitudes occur during lazy eights?
4. Do you use pitch or power to control the altitude and symmetry of the loops during lazy eights? Explain.
5. At what point during lazy eights do you use the greatest control pressures?
6. Compare and contrast turns around a point and eights-on-pylons.
7. How does wind direction affect the entry for eights-on-pylons?
8. At what altitude should you enter eights-on-pylons? How do you determine the pivotal altitude?
9. What is the maximum angle of bank that you should use during eights-on-pylons? Where does this bank angle occur?

10. Describe how you make changes in altitude during eights-on-pylons to hold the pylon position relative to the wing. Where do the highest and lowest altitudes occur?

POWER-OFF 180° ACCURACY APPROACHES AND LANDINGS

1. What is the objective of power-off accuracy landings?
2. What is the key position and why is it important?
3. What are some techniques to conserve or dissipate altitude?
4. Name the advantages and disadvantages of flaps and slips.
5. In which direction should you perform a slip when a crosswind exists?

COMMERCIAL PILOT PRACTICAL TEST BRIEFING

These questions help prepare the student for the FAA Commercial Pilot Practical Test. The student should demonstrate understanding of these questions and any additional questions that develop during the briefing before taking the End-of Course Flight Check and the FAA Commercial Pilot Practical Test.

These sample questions are examples of the types of questions that the examiner might ask during the oral and flight portions of the practical test. The examiner may ask questions at any time to determine if the student's knowledge of a subject area is adequate. Preparation for the practical test should include a review of FAR Parts 61, 91, and NTSB 830, with emphasis on the rules that apply to commercial pilots. Ensure the student knows what regulations apply to agricultural operations (Part 137), external load operations (Part 133), and air transportation of hazardous materials (HMR 175). In addition, thoroughly discuss each FAA question incorrectly answered on the knowledge test because the examiner might emphasize these areas.

AIRPLANE REQUIREMENTS

1. What certificates and documents must you have on board the airplane?
2. Locate the following inspections, as appropriate, in the airframe and engine logbooks: annual, 100-hour, pitot-static, altimeter, and transponder.
3. What equipment, in addition to that required for flight during the day, must you have for night operations?
4. When is an electric landing light required?
5. Must all airplanes be equipped with an ELT? If your airplane requires an ELT to be installed, when may you fly without one?

PILOT REQUIREMENTS

1. What recency of experience requirements must you meet to act as a pilot in command of an aircraft carrying passengers during the day? At night?
2. Can the holder of a commercial pilot certificate rent an airplane (with a recent 100-hour inspection) from a fixed-base operator and use it to carry passengers for hire?

3. What minimum class of medical certificate must you hold when exercising commercial privileges? How long is the appropriate medical certificate valid for operations that require a commercial pilot certificate?
4. Define the term "commercial operator."

THE FLIGHT ENVIRONMENT

1. What is the significance of 14,500 feet MSL in relation to Class E airspace?
2. What are the prerequisites for flight within Class A airspace?
3. Explain the vertical limit for Class D airspace.
4. Explain the pilot and equipment requirements within Class B and C airspace.
5. What is the maximum authorized airspeed below 10,000 feet MSL within a Class D airspace area below the floor of associated Class B airspace?
6. What are the minimum visibility and cloud clearance requirements for VFR flight in both controlled and uncontrolled airspace?
7. Explain when you may operate within the following areas: prohibited, restricted, warning, alert, and MOA.
8. Under what conditions must you file a VFR flight plan?
9. What are the pilot and passenger oxygen requirements?
10. Explain the meaning of ATC light gun signals to aircraft on the ground and in flight.

AVIATION PHYSIOLOGY

1. Explain the four types of hypoxia.
2. Discuss the similarities and differences between the conditions of hypoxia and hyperventilation. What are the symptoms and effects for each condition, and what corrective actions should you take in each case?
3. If a passenger exhibits symptoms that could be attributed to more than one condition, what should you do?
4. What are the rules concerning alcohol use and the operation of an airplane?
5. Name several common medications that you should not take before or during a flight.
6. What is spatial disorientation, when is it most likely to occur, and what corrective action should you take if you become spatially disoriented?
7. What are the effects of fatigue on a pilot?
8. What are the effects of nitrogen on a SCUBA diver, and what precautions need to be observed prior to flight?

AIRPLANE EQUIPMENT AND SYSTEMS

To answer the following questions, refer to the pilot's operating handbook for the airplane used for the practical test.

1. What is your airplane's total fuel capacity? Total usable fuel quantity?
2. What is the fuel grade and corresponding color of the fuel used in your airplane? If the recommended fuel grade is not available, what grade(s) of fuel can you use?
3. Explain fuel management for your airplane.
4. Where is the battery located in your airplane and what is its voltage?
5. Explain the information displayed by your airplane's ammeter or load meter.
6. What are the procedures for dealing with an electrical fire in flight?

7. What are the maximum and minimum allowable flap settings for takeoff?
8. Explain the cold and hot starting procedures for your airplane.
9. Explain the manual landing gear extension procedures for your airplane.
10. List the best rate-of-climb (V_Y) and best angle of climb (V_X) speeds for your airplane when loaded to its maximum allowable weight at sea level.
11. What is your airplane's stalling speed at maximum weight in level flight? In a 45° bank?
12. List the following speeds for your airplane: V_{FE}, V_{LO}, and V_{LE}.
13. What is the maximum demonstrated crosswind component for your airplane? Is this an airplane limitation?
14. What is the minimum required ground roll for takeoff at maximum takeoff weight if the field elevation is 5,000 feet and the temperature is 26°C?
15. Assuming the same conditions given in the previous question, what is your rate of climb with gear and flaps retracted at the best rate-of-climb airspeed?
16. What does the term "service ceiling" mean?
17. What are the service and absolute ceilings for your airplane?
18. Assume you are flying at a pressure altitude of 4,000 feet under ISA+10°C conditions. What are the predicted true airspeed and fuel flow values for 65% power?
19. What are the maximum allowable baggage compartment weights?
20. If you do not know an adult passenger's weight, what should you use for weight and balance computations? When should you not use standard weights?
21. Calculate the weight and balance for your airplane as it will be loaded for the practical flight test and assume the examiner weighs 180 pounds.
22. Explain how a constant-speed propeller operates on a multi-engine airplane.
23. What is the maximum continuous operating power setting for your airplane? Why is it important to comply with these limitations?
24. Explain the procedures to apply and reduce power.
25. Explain the propeller synchronizing system.

Multi-Engine Rating Course Briefings

These questions help prepare the student for flying a multi-engine airplane. Because a wide variety of multi-engine training airplanes exist, determine the questions appropriate to the specific training airplane. The student should demonstrate understanding of these questions and any additional questions that develop during the briefing before operating the multi-engine airplane.

MULTI-ENGINE OPERATIONS AND SYSTEMS BRIEFING

PILOT REQUIREMENTS AND SRM

1. Is a multi-engine rating a category or class rating?
2. What tests are required to obtain a multi-engine rating?
3. What is required if you are an instrument-rated pilot and desire to operate a multi-engine airplane in instrument conditions?
4. Explain SRM considerations that apply to flying a multi-engine airplane.
5. Describe the risk factors that apply if you operate more than one type of multi-engine airplane on a regular basis.

PROCEDURES AND MANEUVERS

1. Explain the elements contributing to the left-turning tendency in a conventional twin (non-counterrotating propellers) with both engines operating.
2. Why does torque cause a rolling moment in conventional twin-engine airplanes? Why are the effects of torque eliminated in airplanes with counter-rotating propellers?
3. Explain the uses of differential power during taxi and takeoff.
4. Define the V-speeds for your airplane, and include the airspeed indicator color codes, where applicable.
5. Describe the preflight planning considerations necessary for a typical multi-engine cross-country flight.
6. Describe the correct procedures and sequence of events for a normal takeoff and a short-field takeoff with a maximum performance climb.
7. What guidelines determine the point of gear retraction following liftoff?
8. When is the first power reduction normally made during departure?
9. What determines the configuration of the cowl flaps during climb?
10. What are the advantages of performing a cruise climb to altitude?
11. Explain the procedure for maneuvering during slow flight.
12. Explain the procedure for setting up and performing stalls in the gear down and full flaps, as well as the gear up, flaps up configurations.
13. Explain the factors involved in planning the descent.
14. Explain the correct procedures and sequence of events for a normal landing and a short-field approach and landing over an obstacle.
15. Describe the correct procedures for performing a go-around.

SYSTEMS AND EQUIPMENT

1. Explain how a constant-speed propeller operates on a multi-engine airplane.
2. What is the maximum continuous operating power setting for your airplane?
3. Why is it important to comply with these limitations?
4. Explain the procedures to apply and reduce power.
5. Explain the propeller synchronizing system.
6. Is an autofeather system installed on your airplane? If so, explain how the system works.
7. How does a reversible propeller system work? Can it be used in flight?
8. Diagram and explain the fuel system used in your airplane.
9. Explain the crossfeed system on the airplane. When is it used?
10. What is the normal fuel pressure and what are some of the things that cause low pressure?
11. Explain the fuel injection system.
12. Explain turbocharging operation.
13. Explain the electrical system including the primary sources of electrical power and how the electrical power is distributed.
14. What is the function of a voltage regulator?
15. Explain the purpose of an over-voltage relay.
16. Explain what adjustments have to be made with one alternator inoperative.
17. Explain the landing gear system. How do accomplish emergency landing gear extension?
18. Explain the following ice control systems, if installed on your airplane: propeller, wing and tail surfaces, and windshield.
19. Explain how the cabin heating system operates. How do you regulate the cabin temperature?

MULTI-ENGINE PERFORMANCE CONSIDERATIONS BRIEFING

These questions help ensure that the student understands the performance considerations that apply to a multi-engine airplane and can determine performance prior to flight operations in a light twin. The student should demonstrate understanding of these questions and any additional questions that develop during the briefing before performing maneuvers in the multi-engine airplane.

WEIGHT AND BALANCE

1. What are the maximum ramp, maximum takeoff, maximum landing, and basic empty weights for your airplane?
2. Which weights are required for weight computations?
3. Where is the basic empty weight found?
4. Which items are included in the payload?
5. What guidelines are used for making weight and balance computations if the weights of the passengers are unknown?
6. What is the purpose of a maximum zero fuel weight and does your airplane have this limitation?

7. If the airplane is loaded to maximum capacity, will the greatest movement in the center of gravity occur when weight is shifted from the fuel, baggage, or passenger loading station?
8. Assuming the listed conditions, determine whether your airplane is loaded within the center of gravity range.
   - Pilot and front passenger ....340 lbs
   - Rear passengers ....370 lbs
   - Fuel tanks..Full
   - Baggage..95 lbs
9. Assuming that your airplane is loaded with the CG at the extreme aft limit, explain the handling characteristics of the airplane during normal operations, such as takeoffs and landings.

PERFORMANCE CHARTS

1. Explain the relationship between power available versus power required as it relates to engine-out performance.
2. Define accelerate-stop distance, and explain why it is an important performance consideration.
3. Given the following conditions, determine the accelerate-stop distance, the normal takeoff ground run, and the takeoff distance necessary to clear a 50-foot obstacle.
   - Field elevation ....2,000 ft
   - Temperature ....30°C
   - Altimeter setting.....................................29.72
   - Runway......................................Hard surfaced
   - Weight....................................Maximum gross
   - Headwind component ....10 knots
4. Assuming the airplane is loaded to maximum gross weight, compute the average rate of climb at 5,000 feet and 20°C with both engines operating and with an inoperative engine.
5. Given the following conditions, determine the normal landing roll and the landing distance over a 50-foot obstacle.
   - Field elevation ....3,500 ft
   - Temperature ....30°C
   - Altimeter setting......................................30.32
   - Weight.....................................Maximum gross
6. Explain why the climb performance of a twin-engine airplane is decreased more than 50 percent with one engine inoperative.
7. Explain the operational significance of the single-engine service ceiling an the single-engine absolute ceiling. How are V_{YSE} and V_{XSE} related to single-engine ceilings?

MANEUVERS

1. When practicing stall recognition and recovery, at what point should you initiate the recovery maneuver?
2. What is an accelerated stall? Explain how to perform and recover from an accelerated stall.
3. Are the manufacturer's spin recovery techniques included in the POH proven for the airplane and, if not, why not?
4. What are the conditions required for a spin to occur, the indications of an incipient spin and a full spin, and the spin recovery techniques for your training airplane?
5. What are the most likely emergencies that might require an emergency descent in a multi-engine airplane? What are the steps to perform an emergency descent?

ENGINE-OUT OPERATIONS BRIEFING

These questions prepare the student to manage engine failures and perform engine-out operations. The student should demonstrate understanding of these questions and any additional questions that develop during the briefing before performing engine-out maneuvers and procedures in the multi-engine airplane.

AERODYNAMICS

1. What effect does induced flow have on the total lift generated by a multi-engine airplane, and what might result from a sudden power reduction during a slow final approach?
2. Define critical engine. Explain why airplanes with counterrotating propellers do not have a critical engine.
3. Define V_{MC}. Explain the factors that affect V_{MC}.
4. Why is the airplane directionally uncontrollable during flight below V_{MC}?
5. Is it possible for the airplane to enter a engine-out stall before V_{MC} is reached? Explain.
6. Why should you feather the propeller of the inoperative engine if you cannot restart the engine?
7. Identify and explain all the factors that contribute to the yawing and rolling tendency in the direction of the inoperative engine.
8. Explain why some airplanes might not be able to maintain altitude after an engine failure.
9. What guidelines should you follow when making turns with one engine inoperative?

PROCEDURES AND MANEUVERS

1. Describe the steps you take immediately after an engine failure. How do you identify the inoperative engine? Why is the throttle of the suspected inoperative engine retarded prior to beginning the feathering process?
2. Explain why you should bank the airplane toward the operative engine during engine-out flight.
3. Explain why the takeoff and climb are considered to be the most critical phases of flight for an engine failure.

4. What indications do you have that the airplane is approaching V_{MC}?
5. What procedure do you use to regain airplane control if an engine failure occurs during flight below V_{MC}?
6. Is a successful engine-out go-around probable from a low altitude when the airspeed is below V_{YSE}? Explain your answer.
7. Describe the use of the landing gear and wing flaps during an engine-out approach and landing.
8. When considering an engine failure, which is more valuable, airspeed in excess of V_{YSE} or additional altitude? Why?
9. Does the shutdown of either engine affect the operation of the landing gear, flaps, hydraulic system, or electrical system?
10. If a positive engine-out rate of climb is not possible, how do you obtain the minimum rate of descent?
11. Explain the steps to secure the engine after complete shutdown.

MULTI-ENGINE INSTRUMENT FLIGHT BRIEFING

These questions help prepare the student for flying instrument procedures with both engines operating and with an inoperative engine. The student should demonstrate understanding of these questions and any additional questions that develop during the briefing before performing instrument operations in the multi-engine airplane.

NORMAL PROCEDURES

1. Why is important to know the proper power settings to maintain the desired attitudes and airspeeds?
2. Describe the recommended trim technique during airspeed and/or attitude changes.
3. What are the primary considerations for a departure under IFR?
4. What is the recommended holding pattern airspeed?
5. Why is preflight planning important for instrument approaches?
6. What are the main tasks you must perform during an instrument approach with all engines operating?

INSTRUMENT PROCEDURES WITH ONE ENGINE INOPERATIVE

1. Describe the main tasks you must perform when one engine fails during instrument conditions.
2. What indications should the turn coordinator show during straight-and-level flight with one engine inoperative?
3. During engine-out flight, what approximate bank angle provides the best turning performance?
4. What type of approach should you request with one engine inoperative?
5. What deviations from normal procedures, if any, are recommended for an engine-out instrument approach?
6. What is recommended concerning an engine-out missed approach in instrument conditions?

MULTI-ENGINE RATING PRACTICAL TEST BRIEFING

These questions help prepare the student for the FAA Multi-Engine Rating Practical Test. The student should demonstrate understanding of these questions and any additional questions that develop during the briefing before taking the End-of Course Flight Check and the FAA Multi-Engine Rating Practical Test.

These sample questions are examples of the types of questions that the examiner might ask during the oral and flight portions of the practical test. The examiner may ask questions at any time to determine if the student's knowledge of a subject area is adequate.

AIRPLANE REQUIREMENTS

1. What documents are required to be onboard the airplane during flight? Explain the significance of each.
2. Explain FAR 91.213 with regard to how it applies to flight with inoperative instruments or equipment.
3. Review the V-speeds for your airplane, and include the airspeed indicator color codes, where applicable.
4. Calculate the weight and balance for your airplane as it will be loaded for the practical flight test and assume the examiner weighs 180 pounds.
5. Based upon the following data, determine the CG location.
   - Pilot and front passenger......................350 lbs
   - Rear passengers....................................335 lbs
   - Fuel tanks..Full
   - Baggage..75 lbs
6. What does the term "zero fuel weight" mean? Does your airplane have a zero fuel weight limitation? If so, what is it?
7. Use the weight and balance data from the previous question and assume that when an intermediate stop is made, the airplane has consumed 28 gallons of fuel and a 150-pound center-seat passenger deplanes. How many inches will the center of gravity move, and in which direction?
8. What grade and type of fuel and oil are specified for your airplane?
9. Determine the amount of oxygen required for a flight at 15,000 feet MSL for two hours with a total of three people onboard. How is the oxygen system checked and serviced?

PERFORMANCE

1. Define accelerate-stop distance and its significance.
2. Determine the accelerate-stop distance under the following conditions:
   - Field pressure altitude..........................2,500 ft
   - Temperature...52°F
   - Weight.................................Maximum takeoff
   - Headwind component..........................10 knots

3. Compute the takeoff distance over a 50-foot obstacle based on the following conditions.
   - Field elevation......................................3,000 ft
   - Temperature..68°F
   - Altimeter setting.....................................30.20
   - Runway....................................Hard surfaced
   - Weight.................................Maximum takeoff
   - Headwind component........................15 knots
4. Using the data from the previous question, determine the takeoff distance with no obstacles.
5. What power setting will produce 65 percent rated power at 7,000 feet if the temperature is 2°C.?
6. Determine the true airspeed and maximum range if the airplane is loaded to maximum gross weight.
7. Given the following conditions, determine the average single-engine rate of climb at 2,000 feet MSL.
   - Altimeter...29.92
   - Temperature at 2,000 ft. ....25°C
   - Weight.................................Maximum takeoff
8. What is the single-engine service ceiling for your airplane and what is its significance in relation to takeoffs and go-arounds?
9. Explain the relationship between density altitude and the single-engine service ceiling.
10. Given the following data, determine the landing distance required over a 50-foot obstacle.
    - Field pressure altitude........................1,500 ft.
    - Temperature..27°C
    - Weight................................Maximum landing
    - Headwind component........................ 15 knots

SYSTEMS AND EQUIPMENT

To answer the following questions, refer to the pilot's operating handbook for the airplane used for the practical test.

1. Explain the electrical system installed in your airplane.
2. During single-engine operations, are there any restrictions and/or recommendations placed on the electrical system?
3. Discuss the hot starting procedure for your airplane and explain how you determine when this procedure is necessary.
4. Describe the procedure for correcting an engine overheating problem.
5. Explain the correct and most accurate engine leaning procedure.
6. Explain and diagram your airplane's fuel system.
7. Discuss the proper procedure for fuel management for both twin-engine and engine-out operations.
8. Describe your airplane's landing gear system.
9. What is the purpose of the landing gear safety switch, and where is it located?

10. How many seconds are required for the landing gear to retract fully? In what situation could this become critical?
11. Explain the manual landing gear extension procedure.
12. Explain the landing procedure and configuration if the nosewheel will not extend and the two main wheels extend normally.
13. What action should you take in the event the propeller de-icing equipment fails on one propeller?
14. If the airplane is autopilot equipped, is there any limitation placed on autopilot operation during engine-out flight?
15. What type of system provides heated air to the cabin? Is there any limitation on restrictions on this equipment's operation?

ENGINE-OUT OPERATIONS

1. Does your airplane have a critical engine? Explain.
2. What procedure do you follow if an engine failure occurs below VMC on the takeoff ground run?
3. How do you determine the inoperative engine?
4. Explain the propeller feathering procedures.
5. Is there any engine RPM limitation on propeller feathering?
6. Explain the in-flight engine restart procedure if a propeller is feathered.
7. Explain why it is advisable to bank the airplane up to five degrees toward the operating engine during single-engine operations. What bank angle is appropriate for your airplane?
8. What airspeed should you maintain immediately after an engine failure? Why?
9. What gear/flap configurations and conditions were used to determine the published V_{MC}?
10. What is the proper recovery method if you inadvertently allow the speed to dissipate to V_{MC} after an engine failure?
11. Is the greatest amount of drag created by the extension of the landing gear, extension of full flaps, or a windmilling propeller?

Appendix B FAR Requirements

The tables in this appendix depict how the objectives and tasks listed in the ground training and flight training lessons of each course correspond to the aeronautical knowledge training and flight training areas of operation required by FAR Part 141, FAR Part 61, and the FAA Airman Certification Standards (ACS).

FAA inspectors and school administrators should refer to these tables to verify that the courses include the required knowledge and flight training areas. Instructors should consult these tables and the pertinent sections of the regulations when teaching the courses to ensure that no aeronautical knowledge areas, flight training areas of operation or tasks are omitted during pilot training and that requirements are documented in appropriate records and endorsements. I

TABLES

The following tables are included in this appendix:

- Instrument Rating Course
    - Instrument Ground Training — Aeronautical Knowledge Areas
    - Instrument Flight Training — Areas of Operation
- Commercial Pilot Certification Course
    - Commercial Ground Training — Aeronautical Knowledge Areas
    - Commercial Flight Training — Areas of Operation
- Multi-Engine Rating Course
    - Multi-Engine Ground Training — Aeronautical Knowledge Areas
    - Multi-Engine Flight Training — Areas of Operation

INTERPRETING THE TABLES

Instructors can use the check boxes to in each table row to record that the required tasks have been completed before endorsing the student for the applicable airman knowledge test or practical test. Review the following examples to understand how to interpret the information in the ground training and flight training tables.

Ground Training Tables

	Aeronautical Knowledge	Ground Lesson
1. ☐	Applicable Federal Aviation Regulations for IFR flight operations	GL 1, 2, 5, 8, 22, 24; **E 9, 25, 26**
2. ☐	Appropriate information in the *Aeronautical Information Manual*	GL 6, 10, 11, 12, 13, 14, 15; **E 9, 19, 26**
3. ☐	Air traffic control system and procedures for instrument flight operations	GL 7, 10, 11, 12, 13, 14, 15, 16, 17, 18; **E 9, 19, 26**
4. ☐	IFR navigation and approaches by use of navigation systems	GL 4, 22; **E 9, 25, 26**
5. ☐	Use of IFR enroute and instrument approach procedure charts	GL 10, 13, 14, 15, 16, 17, 18, 22; **E 19, 25, 26**
6.	Procurement and use of aviation weather reports and forecasts, and the elements of forecasting	GL 21, 22; E 25, 26

The ground training tables list the aeronautical knowledge areas required by Part 141 and Part 61. The ground lessons (GL) and exams (E) that apply to each knowledge area are listed. For example, GL 4 and 22 include subjects that apply to "IFR navigation and approaches by use of navigation systems." This knowledge area is evaluated in GL 9, 25, and 26.

In the ground lesson, the knowledge area appears next to the lesson objective(s).

GROUND LESSON 4

OBJECTIVES

Lesson Objective	Part 141/61 Aeronautical Knowledge	ACS Task
Explain the operation and limitations of VOR, DME, and GPS equipment. Identify how to navigate using VOR, DME, and GPS equipment	IFR navigation and approaches by use of navigation systems	Airplane Flight Instruments and Navigation Equipment Intercepting and Tracking Navigational Systems and Arcs

Ground lessons also contain knowledge areas that apply to the flight training areas of operation and tasks specified in the Airman Certification Standards (ACS). For example, the area of operation, "Navigation Systems" and task, "Intercepting and Tracking Navigational Systems and Arcs" *in the Instrument Rating ACS applies* to GL 4.

Flight Training Tables

FAR/ACS	Area of Operation, Tasks	Stage	Introduce	Review	Evaluate
Part 141 Appendix C (5) FAR 61.65 (5) ACS V.	Navigation Systems				
ACS V. A. ☐	Intercepting and Tracking Navigational Systems and Arcs	I	GL 4 FL 8, 9, 11	FL 9, 10, 11, 12	FL 13
		II	GL 16, 17, 18	FL 14, 15	
		III	FL 24	FL 25, 26, 27	FL 28, 29

Flight Training Tables

You can find the area of operation, Preflight Procedures, in the flight training requirements under Part 141 Appendix C (2) and FAR 61.65 (2). Preflight Procedures is also listed as Area of Operation II in the *Instrument Rating Airman Certification Standards (ACS).*

FAR/ACS	Area of Operation, Tasks	Stage	Introduce	Review	Evaluate
ACS I. C. ☐	Cross-Country Flight Planning	I	GL 5		
		II			
		III	GL 21, 22 FL 24	FL 25, 26, 27	FL 28, 29
Part 141 Appendix C (2) FAR 61.65 (2) ACS II	Preflight Procedures				
ACS II. A. ☐	Airplane Systems Related to IFR Operations	I	FL 2	FL 3, 4, 5, 12	FL 13
		II			
		III	GL 20		FL 29
ACS II. B. ☐	Airplane Flight Instruments and Navigation Equipment	I	GL 2, 4 FL 2	FL 3, 4, 5, 12	FL 13
		II			
		III	FL 24		FL 29
ACS II. B. ☐	Airplane Flight Instruments and Navigation Equipment	I	GL 2, 4 FL 8, 9	FL 9, 10, 11, 12	FL 13
		II			
		III	FL 24	FL 25, 26, 27	FL 28, 29
ACS II. C. ☐	Instrument Flight Deck Check	I	GL 2 FL 2, 8, 9	FL 3, 4, 5, 9, 10, 12	FL 13
		II			
		III			FL 29

The ACS specifies tasks that apply to each area of operation. For example, "Airplane Systems Related to IFR Operations," "Airplane Flight Instruments and Navigation Equipment" (which is divided into two tasks in the syllabus) and "Instrument Flight Deck Check" are tasks under the area of operation, "Preflight Procedures."

This table indicates the training stage and ground and/or flight lesson in which each task is introduced, reviewed, and evaluated. For example, Flight Lesson 2 introduces three of the tasks under "Preflight Procedures."

FLIGHT LESSON 2

INTRODUCE

PREFLIGHT PROCEDURES
- ❑ Airplane Systems Related to IFR Operations (Anti-icing and Deicing)
- ❑ Airplane Flight Instruments Operation
- ❑ Instrument Flight Deck Check

INSTRUMENT GROUND TRAINING AERONAUTICAL KNOWLEDGE AREAS

This table specifies the ground lessons in which each aeronautical knowledge area required by FAR Part 141 and FAR Part 61 is presented in the Instrument Rating Ground Training Syllabus. Use the check boxes to ensure that each required aeronautical knowledge area is completed before the student receives an instructor endorsement to take the Instrument Rating Airman Knowledge Test and the Instrument Rating Practical Test.

GL — Ground Lesson; E — Stage Exam/End of Course Exam

Appendix C to Part 141 — Instrument Rating Course

3. Aeronautical Knowledge Training

(b) Ground training / aeronautical knowledge areas

Part 61 Subpart B — Aircraft Ratings and Pilot Authorizations

61.65 Instrument Rating Requirements

(b) Aeronautical knowledge

	Aeronautical Knowledge	Ground Lesson
1. ☐	Applicable Federal Aviation Regulations for IFR flight operations	GL 1, 2, 5, 8, 22, 24; **E 9, 25, 26**
2. ☐	Appropriate information in the *Aeronautical Information Manual*	GL 6, 10, 11, 12, 13, 14, 15; **E 9, 19, 26**
3. ☐	Air traffic control system and procedures for instrument flight operations	GL 7, 10, 11, 12, 13, 14, 15, 16, 17, 18; **E 9, 19, 26**
4. ☐	IFR navigation and approaches by use of navigation systems	GL 4, 22; **E 9, 25, 26**
5. ☐	Use of IFR enroute and instrument approach procedure charts	GL 10, 13, 14, 15, 16, 17, 18, 22; **E 19, 25, 26**
6. ☐	Procurement and use of aviation weather reports and forecasts, and the elements of forecasting weather trends on the basis of that information and personal observation of weather conditions	GL 21, 22; **E 25, 26**
7. ☐	Safe and efficient operation of aircraft under instrument flight rules and conditions	GL 2, 3, 10, 11, 12, 13, 14, 15, 16, 17, 18, 24; **E 9, 19, 25, 26**
8. ☐	Recognition of critical weather situations and wind shear avoidance	GL 20; **E 25, 26**
9. ☐	Aeronautical decision making and judgment	GL 1, 23, 24; **E 25, 26**
10. ☐	Crew resource management, to include crew communication and coordination	GL 23, 24; **E 25, 26**

INSTRUMENT FLIGHT TRAINING
AREAS OF OPERATION

This table specifies the flight lessons in which each area of operation and task required by FAR Part 141, FAR Part 61, and the Instrument Rating Airman Certification Standards (ACS) is introduced, reviewed, and evaluated in the Instrument Rating Flight Training Syllabus. This table also lists ground lessons containing knowledge areas that apply to the flight training areas of operation and tasks specified in the ACS. The name of the task as it appears in the syllabus lessons is shown in bold if it differs from the task name in the FAR/ACS. Use the check boxes to ensure each required task is completed before the student receives an instructor endorsement to take the Instrument Rating Practical Test.

FL — Flight Lesson; N — Night; C — Cross-Country

Appendix C to Part 141 — Instrument Rating Course

4. Flight Training

(d) Areas of operation appropriate to the instrument aircraft category and class rating (if class rating is appropriate)

Part 61 Subpart B — Aircraft Ratings and Pilot Authorizations

61.65 Instrument Rating Requirements

(c) Flight proficiency

Instrument Rating — Airplane Airman Certification Standards

FAR/ACS	Area of Operation, Task	Stage	Introduce	Review	Evaluate
Part 141 Appendix C 4. (d) (1) FAR 61.65 (c) (1) ACS I.	Preflight Preparation				
ACS I. A. ☐	Pilot Qualifications	I	GL 1 FL 1	FL 2, 12	FL 13
		II			
		III			FL 29
ACS I. B. ☐	Weather Information	I	FL 1	FL 2, 12	FL 13
		II			
		III	GL 20, 21 FL 24	FL 25, 26, 27	GL 25 FL 28, 29
ACS I. C. ☐	Cross-Country Flight Planning	I	GL 5		
		II			
		III	GL 21, 22 FL 24	FL 25, 26, 27	FL 28, 29
Part 141 Appendix C 4. (d) (2) FAR 61.65 (c) (2) ACS II.	Preflight Procedures				

Table continued on next page.

FAR/ACS	Area of Operation, Task	Stage	Introduce	Review	Evaluate
ACS II. A. ☐	Airplane Systems Related to IFR Operations	I	FL 2	FL 3, 4, 5, 12	FL 13
		II			
		III	GL 20		FL 29
ACS II. B. ☐	Airplane Flight Instruments and Navigation Equipment	I	GL 2, 4 FL 2	FL 3, 4, 5, 12	FL 13
		II			
		III	FL 24		FL 29
ACS II. B. ☐	Airplane Flight Instruments and Navigation Equipment	I	GL 2, 4 FL 8, 9	FL 9, 10, 11, 12	FL 13
		II			
		III	FL 24	FL 25, 26, 27	FL 28, 29
ACS II. C. ☐	Instrument Flight Deck Check	I	GL 2 FL 2, 8, 9	FL 3, 4, 5, 9, 10, 12	FL 13
		II			
		III			FL 29
Part 141 Appendix C 4. (d) (3) FAR 61.65 (c) (3) ACS III.	Air Traffic Control Clearances and Procedures				
ACS III. A. ☐	Compliance with Air Traffic Control Clearances	I		GL 5, 6, 7, 8	
		II	FL 14, 16	GL 12 FL 15, 16, 17, 18, 19, 22	FL 23
		III	FL 24	FL 25, 26, 27	FL 28, 29
ACS III. B. ☐	Holding Procedures	I			
		II	GL 12 FL 14, 15	FL 15, 16, 22	FL 23
		III	FL 24	FL 25, 26, 27	FL 28, 29
Part 141 Appendix C 4. (d) (4) FAR 61.65 (c) (4) ACS IV.	Flight by Reference to Instruments				
ACS IV. A. ☐	Instrument Flight ***NOTE:*** *Instrument Flight includes a variety of maneuvers performed using a full and partial panel.*	I	GL 3 FL 1, 3, 4, 5, 6	FL 2, 3, 4, 5, 6, 7, 8, 12	FL 13
		II			
		III			FL 29
ACS IV. B. ☐	Recovery from Unusual Flight Attitudes	I	GL 3 FL 4, 6	FL 5, 7, 12	FL 13
		II			
		III			FL 29

Table continued on next page.

FAR/ACS	Area of Operation, Task	Stage	Introduce	Review	Evaluate
Part 141 Appendix C 4. (d) (5) FAR 61.65 (c) (5) ACS V.	Navigation Systems				
ACS V. A. ☐	Intercepting and Tracking Navigational Systems and Arcs	I	GL 4 FL 8, 9, 11	FL 9, 10, 11, 12	FL 13
		II	GL 16, 17, 18	FL 14, 15	
		III	FL 24	FL 25, 26, 27	FL 28, 29
ACS V. B. ☐	Departure, Enroute, and Arrival Operations	I			
		II	GL 10, 11, 12		
		III	FL 24	FL 25, 26, 27	FL 28, 29
Part 141 Appendix C 4. (d) (6) FAR 61.65 (c) (6) ACS VI.	Instrument Approach Procedures				
ACS VI. A. ☐	Nonprecision Approach	I			
		II	GL 14, 15, 16, 17, 18 FL 16, 18, 19, 20	FL 17, 18, 19, 21, 22	FL 23
		III	FL 24	FL 25, 26, 27	FL 28, 29
ACS VI. B. ☐	Precision Approach	I			
		II	GL 14, 15, 16, 17 FL 17, 18, 20	FL 17, 18, 19, 22	FL 23
		III	FL 24	FL 25, 26, 27	FL 28, 29
ACS VI. C. ☐	Missed Approach	I			
		II	GL 14, 15, 16, 17, 18 FL 16, 20	FL 17, 18, 19, 21, 22	FL 23
		III	FL 24	FL 25, 26, 27	FL 28, 29
ACS VI. D. ☐	Circling Approach	I			
		II	GL 14, 15 FL 16	FL 17, 18, 19, 22	FL 23
		III	FL 24	FL 25, 26, 27	Fl 28, 29
ACS VI. E. ☐	Landing from an Instrument Approach	I			
		II	GL 14, 15, 16, 17, 18 FL 16	FL 17, 18, 19, 22	FL 23
		III	FL 24	FL 25, 26, 27	FL 28, 29
Part 141 Appendix C 4. (d) (7) FAR 61.65 (c) (7) ACS VII.	Emergency Operations				

Table continued on next page.

FAR/ACS	Area of Operation, Task	Stage	Introduce	Review	Evaluate
ACS VII. A. ☐	Loss of Communications	I	GL 24		
		II			
		III	FL 25	FL 26, 27	FL 28, 29
ACS VII. B. MEL	One Engine Inoperative (Simulated) during Straight-and-Level Flight and Turns	***NOTE:*** *The initial Instrument Rating Course outlined in this syllabus is for single-engine airplanes. These tasks are covered in the Multi-Engine Rating Course when adding a multi-engine rating to the Commercial Pilot Certification Course.*			
ACS VII. C. MEL	Instrument Approach and Landing with an Inoperative Engine (Simulated)				
ACS VII. D. ☐	Approach with Loss of Primary Flight Instrument Indicators *Includes:* Loss of Primary Flight Instrument Indicators	I	GL 3 FL 5	FL 6, 12	FL 13
		II	FL 20	FL 21, 22	FL 23
		III	GL 24, 25 FL 25	FL 26, 27	FL 28, 29
Part 141 Appendix C 4. (d) (8) FAR 61.65 (c) (8) ACS VIII.	Postflight Procedures				
ACS VIII.A. ☐	Checking Instruments and Equipment	I	GL 2 FL 2	FL 3, 4, 5, 12	FL 13
		II			
		III			FL 29

APPENDIX B ■ **FAR Requirements**

COMMERCIAL GROUND TRAINING AERONAUTICAL KNOWLEDGE AREAS

This table specifies the ground lessons in which each aeronautical knowledge area required by FAR Part 141 and FAR Part 61 is presented in the Commercial Pilot Ground Training Syllabus of the Commercial Pilot Certification Course. Use the check boxes to ensure that each required aeronautical knowledge area is completed before the student receives an instructor endorsement to take the Commercial Pilot Airman Knowledge Test and the Commercial Pilot Practical Test.

GL — Ground Lesson; E — Stage Exam/End of Course Exam

Appendix D to Part 141 — Commercial Pilot Certification Course

3. Aeronautical Knowledge Training

(b) Ground training / aeronautical knowledge areas

Part 61 Subpart F — Commercial Pilots

61.125 Aeronautical Knowledge

(b) Aeronautical knowledge areas

	Aeronautical Knowledge	Ground Lesson
1. ☐	Federal Aviation Regulations that apply to commercial pilot privileges, limitations, and flight operations	GL 27, 32; **E 33, 46**
2. ☐	Accident reporting requirements of the National Transportation Safety Board	GL 32; **E 33, 46**
3. ☐	Basic aerodynamics and the principles of flight	GL 37; **E 45, 46**
4. ☐	Meteorology, to include recognition of critical weather situations, wind shear recognition and avoidance, and the use of aeronautical weather reports and forecasts	GL 29; **E 33, 46**
5. ☐	Safe and efficient operation of aircraft	GL 34, 35, 36; **E 45, 46**
6. ☐	Weight and balance computations	GL 39; **E 45, 46**
7. ☐	Use of performance charts	GL 38; **E 45, 46**
8. ☐	Significance and effects of exceeding aircraft performance limitations	GL 37, 38; **E 45, 46**
9. ☐	Use of aeronautical charts and a magnetic compass for pilotage and dead reckoning	GL 30; **E 33, 46**
10. ☐	Use of air navigation facilities	GL 30; **E 33, 46**
11. ☐	Aeronautical decision making and judgment	GL 31, 44; **E 33, 45, 46**
12. ☐	Principles and functions of aircraft systems	GL 34, 35, 36; **E 45, 46**
13. ☐	Maneuvers, procedures, and emergency operations appropriate to the aircraft	GL 40, 41, 42, 43; **E 45, 46**
14. ☐	Night and high-altitude operations	GL 31, 35; **E 33, 45, 46**
15. ☐	Descriptions of and procedures for operating within the National Airspace System	GL 28, 30; **E 33, 46**

COMMERCIAL PILOT FLIGHT TRAINING AREAS OF OPERATION

This table specifies the flight lessons in which each task required by FAR Part 141, FAR Part 61, and the Commercial Pilot Airman Certification Standards (ACS) is introduced, reviewed, and evaluated in the Commercial Pilot Flight Training Syllabus. This table also lists ground lessons containing knowledge areas that apply to the flight training areas of operation and tasks specified in the ACS. The name of the task as it appears in the syllabus lessons is shown in bold if it differs from the task name in the FAR/ACS. Use the check boxes to ensure each required task is completed before the student receives an instructor endorsement to take the Commercial Pilot Practical Test.

FL — Flight Lesson; S — Solo; N — Night; C — Cross-Country

Appendix D to Part 141 — Commercial Pilot Certification Course

4. Flight Training

(d) Areas of operation that are appropriate to the aircraft category and class rating
(1) For an airplane single-engine airplane course

Part 61 Subpart F — Commercial Pilots

61.127 Flight Proficiency

(b) Areas of operation
(1) For an airplane category rating with a single-engine class rating

Commercial Pilot — Airplane Airman Certification Standards

FAR/ACS	Area of Operation, Task	Stage	Introduce	Review	Evaluate
Part 141 Appendix D 4. (d) (1) (i) FAR 61.127 (b) (1) (i) ACS I.	Preflight Preparation				
ACS I. A. ☐	Pilot Qualifications	I	GL 27, 32 FL 30C, 32N, 33NC	FL 31SC, 34SN, 35SN, 36SNC, 37SC, 38SC, 39SC, 40SC, 41SC, 42C, 43SC	GL 33, 46 FL 44C
		II	FL 46	FL 47, 48, 66	FL 67
		III		FL 78, 82C, 83, 84, 85	FL 86, 87
ACS I. B. ☐	Airworthiness Requirements	IV	GL 32 FL 30C, 31SC, 32N, 33NC	FL 34SN, 35SN, 36SNC, 37SC, 38SC, 39SC, 40SC, 41SC, 42C, 43SC	GL 33, 46 FL 44C
		V	FL 46	FL 47, 48, 66	FL 67
		VI		FL 78, 82C, 83, 84, 85	FL 86, 87
ACS I. C. ☐	Weather Information	IV	GL 29 FL 30C, 32N, 33NC	FL 31SC, 34SN, 35SN, 36SNC, 37SC, 38SC, 39SC, 40SC, 41SC, 42C, 43SCC	GL 33, 46 FL 44
		V	FL 46	FL 47, 48, 66	GL 46 FL 67
		VI		FL 73S, 74S, 75S 76, 77, 78, 79S, 80S, 81S, 82C, 83, 84, 85	FL 86, 87

Table continued on next page.

FAR/ACS	Area of Operation, Task	Stage	Introduce	Review	Evaluate
ACS I. D. ☐	Cross-Country Flight Planning	I	GL 30 FL 30C, 33NC	FL 31SC, 36SNC, 37SC, 38SC, 39SC, 40SC, 41SC, 42C, 43SC	GL 33 FL 44C
		II	FL 49, 50	FL 66	GL 46 FL 67
		III		FL 73S, 74S, 75S, 76, 77, 79S, 80S, 81S, 82C, 83	FL 86, 87
ACS I. E. ☐	National Airspace System	I	GL 28, 30 FL 30C, 33NC	FL 31SC, 36SNC, 37SC, 38SC, 39SC, 40SC, 41SC, 42C, 43SC	GL 33 FL 44C
		II	FL 49, 50	FL 66	GL 46 FL 67
		III		FL 82C, 83, 84, 85	FL 86, 87
ACS I. F. ☐	Performance and Limitations	I	FL 30C, 33NC	FL 31SC, 36SNC, 37SC, 38SC, 39SC, 40SC, 41SC, 42C, 43SC	FL 44
		II	GL 39 FL 46	FL 47, 48, 66	GL 45, 46 FL 67
		III		FL 78, 82C, 83, 84, 85	FL 86, 87
ACS I. G. ☐	Operation of Systems	I	FL 30C, 32N, 33NC	FL 31SC, 34SN, 35SN, 36SNC, 37SC, 38SC, 39SC, 40SC, 41SC, 42C, 43SC	FL 44C
		II	GL 34, 35, 36 FL 46	FL 47, 48, 66	GL 45, 46 FL 67
		III		FL 78, 82C, 83, 84, 85	FL 86, 87
ACS I. H. ☐	Human Factors	I	GL 31 FL 30C, 32N, 33NC	FL 31SC, 34SN, 35SN, 36SNC, 37SC, 38SC, 39SC, 40SC, 41SC, 42C, 43SC	GL 33 FL 44C
		II	GL 44 FL 46	FL 47, 48, 66	GL 45, 46 FL 67
		III		FL 78, 82C, 83, 84, 85	FL 86, 87
Part 141 Appendix D 4. (d) (1) (ii) FAR 61.127 (b) (1) (ii) ACS II..	Preflight Procedures				
ACS II. A. ☐	Preflight Assessment **Self-Assessment** **Preflight Inspection**	I	FL 30C, 32N, 33NC	FL 31SC, 34SN, 35SN, 36SNC	FL 44C
		II	FL 46	FL 47, 48, 66	FL 67
		III		FL 78, 82C, 83, 84, 85	FL 86, 87
ACS II. B. ☐	Flight Deck Management	I	FL 30C, 32N, 33NC	FL 31SC, 34SN, 35SN, 36SNC, 37-41SC, 42C, 43SC	FL 44C
		II	FL 46	FL 47, 48, 66	FL 67
		III		FL 78, 82C, 83, 84, 85	FL 86, 87

Table continued on next page.

FAR/ACS	Area of Operation, Task	Stage	Introduce	Review	Evaluate
ACS II. C. ☐	Engine Starting	I	FL 30C, 32N, 33NC	FL 31SC, 34SN, 35SN, 36SNC	FL 44C
		II	FL 46	FL 47, 48, 66	FL 67
		III		FL 78, 82C, 83, 84, 85	FL 86, 87
ACS II. D. ☐	Taxiing	I	FL 30C, 32N, 33NC	FL 31SC, 34SN, 35SN, 36SNC	FL 44C
		II	FL 46	FL 47, 48, 66	FL 67
		III		FL 78, 82C, 83, 84, 85	FL 86, 87
ACS II. F. ☐	Before Takeoff Check **Before Takeoff Check/ Runup**	I	FL 30C, 32N, 33NC	FL 31SC, 34SN, 35SN, 36SNC	FL 44C
		II	FL 46	FL 47, 48, 66	FL 67
		III		FL 78, 82C, 83, 84, 85	FL 86, 87
Part 141 Appendix D 4. (d) (1) (iii) FAR 61.127 (b) (1) (iii) ACS III.	Airport and Seaplane Base Operations				
ACS III. A. ☐	**Communications,** Light Signals, and Runway Lighting Systems **Radio Communications**	I	GL 32 FL 30C, 32N, 33NC	FL 31SC, 34SN, 35SN, 36SNC, 37SC, 38SC, 39SC, 40SC, 41SC, 42C, 43SC	GL 33 FL 44
		II	FL 46	FL 47, 66	FL 67
		III		FL 82C, 84, 85	FL 86, 87
ACS III. A ☐	Communications, **Light Signals,** and Runway Lighting Systems **Lost Communication Procedures/ATC Light Signals**	I	FL 30C, 32N, 33NC	FL 42C	FL 44
		II			GL 46
		III		FL 82C, 84, 85	FL 86, 87
ACS III. A. ☐	Communications, Light Signals, and **Runway Lighting Systems** **Airport, Runway, and Taxiway Signs, Markings, and Lighting**	I	GL 28 FL 30C, 32N, 33NC	FL 31SC, 34SN, 35SN, 36SNC, 37SC, 38SC, 39SC, 40SC, 41SC, 42C, 43SC	GL 33 FL 44
		II	FL 46	FL 47, 66	GL 46 FL 67
		III		FL 82C, 84, 85	FL 86, 87
ACS III. B. ☐	Traffic Patterns	I	FL 30C, 32N, 33NC	FL 31SC, 34SN, 35SN, 36SNC, 37SC, 38SC, 39SC, 40SC, 41SC, 42C, 43SC	FL 44
		II	FL 46	FL 47, 66	FL 67
		III		FL 82C, 84, 85	FL 86, 87
Part 141 Appendix D 4. (d) (1) (iv) FAR 61.127 (b) (1) (iv) ACS IV.	Takeoffs, Landings, and Go-Arounds				

Table continued on next page.

FAR/ACS	Area of Operation, Task	Stage	Introduce	Review	Evaluate
ACS IV. A. ☐	Normal Takeoff and Climb	I	FL 30C, 32N, 33NC	FL 31C, 34SN, 35SN, 36SNC, 37SC, 38SC, 39SC, 40SC, 41SC, 42C	FL 44C
		II	FL 46	FL 45S, 47, 48, 66	FL 67
		III		FL 73S, 74S, 75S, 78, 79S, 80S, 81S, 82C, 83, 84, 85	FL 86, 87
ACS IV. B. ☐	Normal Approach and Landing	I	FL 30C, 32N, 33NC	FL 31C, 34SN, 35SN, 36SNC, 37SC, 38SC, 39SC, 40SC, 41SC, 42C	FL 44C
		II	FL 46	FL 45S, 47, 48, 66	FL 67
		III		FL 73S, 74S, 75S, 78, 79S, 80S, 81S, 82C, 83, 84, 85	FL 86, 87
ACS IV. C. ☐	Soft-Field Takeoff and Climb	I			
		II	GL 41 FL 48	FL 49, 50, 51, 52, 55S, 56S, 57S, 62S, 63S, 64, 65, 66	GL 45, 46 FL 67
		III		FL 73S, 74S, 75S, 76, 77, 78, 79S, 80S, 81S, 83, 84, 85	FL 86, 87
ACS IV. D. ☐	Soft-Field Approach and Landing	I			
		II	GL 41 FL 48	FL 49, 50, 51, 52, 55S, 56S, 57S, 62S, 63S, 64, 65, 66	GL 45, 46 FL 67
		III		FL 73S, 74S, 75S, 76, 77, 78, 79S, 80S, 81S, 83, 84, 85	FL 86, 87
ACS IV. E. ☐	Short-Field Takeoff and Maximum Performance Climb	I			
		II	GL 41 FL 48	FL 49, 50, 51, 52, 55S, 56S, 57S, 62S, 63S, 64, 65, 66	GL 45, 46 FL 67
		III		FL 73S, 74S, 75S, 76, 77, 78, 79S, 80S, 81S, 83, 84, 85	FL 86, 87
ACS IV. F. ☐	Short-Field Approach and Landing	I			
		II	GL 41 FL 48	FL 49, 50, 51, 52, 55S, 56S, 57S, 62S, 63S, 64, 65, 66	GL 45, 46 FL 67
		III		FL 73S, 74S, 75S, 76, 77, 78, 79S, 80S, 81S, 83, 84, 85	FL 86, 87
ACS IV. M. ☐	Power-Off 180° Accuracy Approach and Landing	I			
		II	GL 43 FL 53	FL 54, 55S, 56S, 57S, 62S, 63S, 64, 65, 66	GL 45, 46 FL 67
		III		FL 73S, 74S, 75S, 76, 77, 78, 79S, 80S, 81S, 83, 84, 85	FL 86, 87
ACS IV. N. ☐	Go-Around/Rejected Landing	I	30C, 32N, 33NC	FL 42C	FL 44C
		II	FL 46	FL 47, 48, 64, 65, 66	FL 67
		III		FL 76, 77, 78, 83, 84, 85	FL 86, 87

 Table continued on next page.

FAR/ACS	Area of Operation, Task	Stage	Introduce	Review	Evaluate
Part 141 Appendix D 4. (d) (1) (v) FAR 61.127 (b) (1) (v) ACS V.	Performance and Ground Reference Maneuvers				
ACS V. A. ☐	Steep Turns	I	FL 32N		
		II	GL 37, 42 FL 52	FL 45, 53, 54, 55S, 56S, 57S, 59S, 60S, 61S, 64, 65, 66	GL 45, 46 FL 67
		III		FL 68, 69, 70S, 71S, 72, 73S, 74S, 75S, 76, 77, 78, 79S, 80S, 81S, 83, 84, 85	FL 86, 87
ACS V. B. ☐	Steep Spirals	I			
		II	GL 43 FL 53	FL 54, 55S, 56S, 57S, 59S, 60S, 61S, 64, 65, 66	GL 45, 46 FL 67
		III		FL 68, 69, 70S, 71S, 72, 73S, 74S, 75S, 76, 77, 78, 79S, 80S, 81S, 83, 84, 85	FL 86, 87
ACS V. C. ☐	Chandelles	I			
		II	GL 37, 42 FL 52	FL 53, 54, 55S, 56S, 57S, 59S, 60S, 61S, 64, 65, 66	GL 45, 46 FL 67
		III		FL 68, 69, 70S, 71S, 72, 73S, 74S, 75S, 76, 77, 78, 79S, 80S, 81S, 83, 84, 85	FL 86, 87
ACS V. D. ☐	Lazy Eights	I			
		II	GL 37, 42 FL 52	FL 53, 54, 55S, 56S, 57S, 59S, 60S, 61S, 64, 65, 66	GL 45, 46 FL 67
		III		FL 68, 69, 70S, 71S, 72, 73S, 74S, 75S, 76, 77, 78, 79S, 80S, 81S, 83, 84, 85	FL 86, 87
ACS V. E. ☐	Eights on Pylons	I			
		II	GL 37, 43 FL 53	FL 54, 55S, 56S, 57, 59S, 60S, 61S, 64, 65, 66	GL 45, 46 FL 67
		III		FL 68, 69, 70S, 71S, 72, 73S, 74S, 75S, 76, 77, 78, 79S, 80S, 81S, 83, 84, 85	FL 86, 87
Part 141 Appendix D 4. (d) (1) (vi) FAR 61.127 (b) (1) (vi) ACS VI..	Navigation				
ACS VI. A. ☐	Pilotage and Dead Reckoning	I	GL 30 FL 30C, 33NC	FL 31SC, 36SNC, 37SC, 38SC, 39SC, 40SC, 41SC, 42C, 43SC	GL 33, 46 FL 44C
		II			
		III		FL 73S, 74S, 75S, 76, 77, 79S, 80S, 81S, 82C, 84, 85	FL 86, 87

Table continued on next page.

FAR/ACS	Area of Operation, Task	Stage	Introduce	Review	Evaluate
ACS VI. B. ☐	Navigation Systems and Radar Services	I	GL 30 FL 30C, 33NC	FL 31SC, 36SNC, 37SC, 38SC, 39SC, 40SC, 41SC, 42C, 43SC	GL 33, 46 FL 44C
		II	FL 47	FL 48, 49, 50, 66	FL 67
		III		FL 73S, 74S, 75S, 76, 77, 79S, 80S, 81S, 82C, 84, 85	FL 86, 87
ACS VI. C. ☐	Diversion	I	GL 30 FL 30C, 33NC	FL 42C	FL 44C
		II			
		III		FL 76, 77, 82C, 84, 85	FL 86, 87
ACS VI. D. ☐	Lost Procedures	I	FL 30C, 33NC	FL 42C	FL 44C
		II			
		III		FL 76, 77, 82C, 84, 85	FL 86, 87
Part 141 Appendix D 4. (d) (1) (vii) FAR 61.127 (b) (1) (vii) ACS VII.	Slow Flight and Stalls				
ACS VII. A. ☐	Maneuvering During Slow Flight	I	FL 32N		
		II	GL 37 FL 47	FL 45S, 48, 49, 50, 51, 55S, 56S, 57S, 59S, 60S, 61S, 64, 65, 66	GL 45, 46 FL 67
		III		FL 76, 77, 78, 79S, 80S, 81S, 84, 85	FL 86, 87
ACS VII. B. ☐	Power-Off Stalls	I	FL 32N		
		II	GL 37 FL 47	FL 45S, 48, 49, 50, 51, 55S, 56S, 57S, 59S, 60S, 61S, 64, 65, 66	GL 45, 46 FL 67
		III		FL 76, 77, 78, 79S, 80S, 81S, 84, 85	FL 86, 87
ACS VII. C. ☐	Power-On Stalls	I	FL 32N		
		II	GL 37 FL 47	FL 45S, 48, 49, 50, 51, 55S, 56S, 57S, 59S, 60S, 61S, 64, 65, 66	GL 45, 46 FL 67
		III		FL 76, 77, 78, 79S, 80S, 81S, 84, 85	FL 86, 87
ACS VII. D. ☐	Accelerated Stalls	I			
		II	GL 37 FL 47	FL 48, 49, 50, 51, 55S, 56S, 57S, 58, 59S, 60S, 61S, 64, 65, 66	GL 45, 46 FL 67
		III		FL 76, 77, 78, 79S, 80S, 81S, 84, 85	FL 86, 87
ACS VII. E. ☐	Spin Awareness	I	FL 32N		
		II	GL 37 FL 47	FL 48, 49, 50, 51, 55S, 56S, 57S, 59S, 60S, 61S, 64, 65, 66	GL 45, 46 FL 67
		III		FL 76, 77, 78, 79S, 80S, 81S, 84, 85	FL 86, 87

Table continued on next page.

FAR/ACS	Area of Operation, Task	Stage	Introduce	Review	Evaluate
Part 141 Appendix D 4. (d) (1) (viii) FAR 61.127 (b) (1) (viii) ACS VIII.	High Altitude Operations				
ACS VIII. A. ☐	Supplemental Oxygen **Supplemental Oxygen Use**	I			
		II	GL 35 FL 46	FL 47, 48, 66	GL 45 FL 67
		III		FL 78, 84, 85	FL 86, 87
ACS VIII. B. ☐	Pressurization **Pressurization System Operation**	I			
		II	GL 35 FL 46	FL 47, 48, 66	FL 45 FL 67
		III		FL 78, 84, 85	FL 86, 87
Part 141 Appendix D 4. (d) (1) (ix) FAR 61.127 (b) (1) (ix) ACS IX.	Emergency Operations				
ACS IX. A. ☐	Emergency Descent	I	GL 40 FL 30C, 33N	FL 42	FL 44
		II	GL 40 FL 48	FL 49, 50, 51, 58, 66	GL 45, 46 FL 67
		III		FL 68, 69, 78, 82C, 84, 85	FL 86, 87
ACS IX. B. ☐	Emergency Approach and Landing (Simulated)	I	GL 40 FL 30C, 33N	FL 42	FL 44
		II	GL 40 FL 48	FL 49, 50, 51, 58, 66	GL 45, 46 FL 67
		III		FL 68, 69, 78, 82C, 84, 85	FL 86, 87
ACS IX. C. ☐	Systems and Equipment Malfunctions	I	GL 40 FL 30C, 33N	FL 42	FL 44
		II	GL 43 FL 48	FL 49, 50, 51, 58, 66	GL 45, 46 FL 67
		III		FL 68, 69, 78, 82C, 84, 85	FL 86, 87
ACS IX.D. ☐	Emergency Equipment and Survival Gear	I	GL 40 FL 30C, 33N	FL 42	FL 44
		II	GL 40 FL 48	FL 49, 50, 51, 58, 66	GL 45, 46 FL 67
		III		FL 68, 69, 78, 82C, 84, 85	FL 86, 87
Part 141 Appendix D (1) (xi) **FAR 61.107 (xi)** **ACS XI.**	Postflight Procedures				
ACS XI.A. ☐	After Landing, Parking and Securing	I	FL 30C, 32N, 33NC	FL 31SC, 34SN, 35SN. 36SNC	FL 44C
		II	FL 46	FL 47, 48, 64, 65, 66	FL 67
		III		FL 78, 84, 85	FL 86, 87

MULTI-ENGINE GROUND TRAINING AERONAUTICAL KNOWLEDGE AREAS

This table specifies the ground lessons in which each aeronautical knowledge area required by FAR Part 141 and FAR Part 61 is presented in the Multi-Engine Rating Ground Training Syllabus. Use the check boxes to ensure that each required aeronautical knowledge area is completed before the student receives an instructor endorsement to take the Multi-Engine Rating Practical Test.

GL — Ground Lesson; E — Stage Exam/End of Course Exam

Appendix I to Part 141 — Additional Aircraft Category and/or Class Rating Course

3. Aeronautical Knowledge Training

(c) Commercial pilot ground training / aeronautical knowledge areas

Part 61 Subpart B — Aircraft Ratings and Pilot Authorizations

61.63 Additional Aircraft Ratings

(c) Additional class rating

(1) Aeronautical knowledge areas appropriate to FAR 61.125 (b)

NOTE: The following table lists the knowledge areas required by Part 141. The additional knowledge areas that apply to FAR 61.125 (b) are included in the Commercial Pilot Certification Course.

	Aeronautical Knowledge	Ground Lesson
1. ☐	Applicable regulations issued by the Federal Aviation Administration for commercial pilot privileges, limitations, and flight operations *NOTE: This knowledge area is covered in the initial Commercial Pilot Certification Course.*	GL 27, 32; **E 33, 46**
2. ☐	Basic aerodynamics and the principles of flight	ME GL 3; **E 6, 7**
3. ☐	Safe and efficient operation of aircraft	ME GL 4; **E 6, 7**
4. ☐	Weight and balance computations	ME GL 4; **E 6,7**
5. ☐	Use of performance charts	ME GL 4; **E 6,7**
6. ☐	Significance and effects of exceeding aircraft performance limitations	ME GL 2; **E 6, 7**
7. ☐	Principles and functions of aircraft systems	ME GL 2; **E 6, 7**
8. ☐	Maneuvers, procedures, and emergency operations appropriate to the aircraft	ME GL 1, 3, 4, 5; **E 6, 7**
9. ☐	Night and high-altitude operations *NOTE: The knowledge area of night operations is covered in the initial Commercial Pilot Certification Course.*	GL 31, 35; **E 33, 45, 46** ME GL 5; **E 6, 7**

MULTI-ENGINE FLIGHT TRAINING
AREAS OF OPERATION

This table specifies the flight lessons in which each task required by FAR Part 141, FAR Part 61, and the Commercial Pilot Airman Certification Standards (ACS) is introduced, reviewed, and evaluated. This table also lists ground lessons containing knowledge areas that apply to the flight training areas of operation and tasks specified in the ACS. The name of the task as it appears in the syllabus lessons is shown in bold if it differs from the task name in the FAR/ACS. Use the check boxes to ensure each required task is completed before the student receives an instructor endorsement to take the Multi-Engine Rating Practical Test.

FL — Flight Lesson; N — Night; C — Cross-Country

Appendix I To Part 141 — Additional Aircraft Category and/or Class Rating Course

4. Flight Training

(2) Areas of operation appropriate to Part 141 Appendix D, 4. Flight Training (d) (2) for an airplane multi-engine course

Part 61 Subpart B — Aircraft Ratings and Pilot Authorizations

61.63 Additional Aircraft Ratings

(c) Additional class rating
(1) Areas of operation appropriate to FAR 61.127 (b)(2)

Commercial Pilot — Airplane Airman Certification Standards

Additional Rating Task Table — Addition of an Airplane Multi-Engine Land Rating to an Existing Commercial Pilot Certificate

*NOTE: ACS areas of operation that are required for the addition of an airplane multi-engine land rating to an existing commercial pilot airplane single-engine land rating are indicated by an asterisk.

FAR/ACS	Area of Operation, Task	Stage	Introduce	Review	Evaluate
Part 141 Appendix D 4. (d) (2) (i) FAR 61.127 (b) (2) (i) ACS I.	Preflight Preparation				
ACS I. A. ☐	Pilot Qualifications	I	FL 1	FL 2	FL 10, 11
ACS I. B. ☐	Airworthiness Requirements	I	FL 1	FL 2	FL 10, 11
ACS I. C. ☐	Weather Information	I	ME FL 1, 8C, 9NC	ME FL 2, 9NC	ME FL 10, 11
ACS I. D. ☐	Cross-Country Flight Planning	I	ME FL 8C	ME FL 9NC	FL 10, 11
*ACS I. F. ☐	Performance and Limitations	I	ME GL 2, 3 ME FL 1, 8C	ME FL 2, 9NC	ME FL 10, 11

Table continued on next page.

FAR/ACS	Area of Operation, Task	Stage	Introduce	Review	Evaluate
*ACS I. G. ☐	Operation of Systems	I	ME GL 1, 2 ME FL 1	ME FL 2	ME FL 10, 11
ACS I. H. ☐	Human Factors	I	ME FL 1	ME FL 2	ME FL 10, 11
Part 141 Appendix D 4. (d) (2) (ii) FAR 61.127 (b) (2) (ii) ACS II.	Preflight Procedures				
*ACS II. A. ☐	Preflight Assessment **Self-Assessment Preflight Inspection**	I			
*ACS II. B. ☐	Flight Deck Management	I	ME FL 1	ME FL 2	ME FL 10, 11
*ACS I. C. ☐	Engine Starting	I	ME GL 1 ME FL 1	ME FL 2	ME FL 10, 11
*ACS I. D. ☐	Taxiing	I	ME FL 1	ME FL 2	ME FL 10, 11
*ACS I. F. ☐	Before Takeoff Check **Before Takeoff Check/ Runup**	I	ME FL 1	ME FL 2	ME FL 10, 11
Part 141 Appendix D 4. (d) (2) (iii) FAR 61.127 (b) (2) (iii) ACS II.	Airport and Seaplane Base Operations				
ACS III. A. ☐	Communications, Light Signals, and Runway Lighting Systems **Radio Communications**	I	ME FL 1	ME FL 2	ME FL 10, 11
ACS III. A. ☐	**Communications, Light Signals, and Runway Lighting Systems** **Airport, Runway, and Taxiway Signs, Markings, and Lighting**	I	ME FL 1	ME FL 2	ME FL 10, 11
ACS III. B. ☐	Traffic Patterns	I	ME FL 1	ME FL 2	ME FL 10, 11
Part 141 Appendix D 4. (d) (2) (iv) FAR 61.127 (b) (2) (iv) ACS II.	Takeoffs, Landings, and Go-Arounds				
*ACS IV. A. ☐	Normal Takeoff and Climb	I	ME GL 1 ME FL 1	ME FL 2, 3, 8C, 9NC	ME FL 10, 11

Table continued on next page.

	Area of Operation, Task	Stage	Introduce	Review	Evaluate
*ACS IV. B. ☐	Normal Approach and Landing	I	ME GL 1 ME FL 1	ME FL 2, 3, 8C, 9NC	FL 10, 11
*ACS IV. E. ☐	Short-Field Takeoff and Maximum Performance Climb	I	ME GL 1 ME FL 3	ME FL 4, 8C, 9NC	ME FL 10, 11
*ACS IV. F. ☐	Short-Field Approach and Landing	I	ME GL 1 ME FL 3	ME FL 4, 8C, 9NC	ME FL 10, 11
ACS IV. N. ☐	Go-Around/Rejected Landing	I	ME GL 1 ME FL 3	ME FL 4	ME FL 10, 11
Part 141 Appendix D 4. (d) (2) (v) FAR 61.127 (b) (2) (v) ACS V.	Performance and Ground Reference Maneuvers				
*ACS V. A. ☐	Steep Turns	I	ME GL 1 ME FL 2	ME FL 3	ME FL 10, 11
Part 141 Appendix D 4. (d) (2) (vii) FAR 61.127 (b) (2) (vii) ACS VII.	Slow Flight and Stalls				
*ACS VII. A. ☐	Maneuvering During Slow Flight	I	ME FL 2	ME FL 3	ME FL 10, 11
*ACS VII. B. ☐	Power-Off Stalls	I	ME GL 3 ME FL 2	ME FL 3	ME FL 10, 11
*ACS VII. C. ☐	Power-On Stalls	I	ME GL 3 ME FL 2	ME FL 3	ME FL 10, 11
*ACS VII. D. ☐	Accelerated Stalls	I	ME GL 3 ME FL 2	ME FL 3	ME FL 10, 11
*ACS VII. E. ☐	Spin Awareness	I	ME GL 3 ME FL 2	ME FL 3	ME FL 10, 11
Part 141 Appendix D 4. (d) (2) (viii) FAR 61.127 (b) (2) (viii) ACS VIII.	High Altitude Operations				
ACS VIII. A. ☐	Supplemental Oxygen **Supplemental Oxygen Use**	I	ME FL 3	ME FL 4	ME FL 10, 11
ACS VIII. B. ☐	Pressurization **Pressurization System Operation**	I	ME FL 3	ME FL 4	ME FL 10, 11

Table continued on next page.

FAR/ACS	Area of Operation, Task	Stage	Introduce	Review	Evaluate
Part 141 Appendix D 4. (d) (2) (ix) FAR 61.127 (b) (2) (ix) ACS IX.	Emergency Operations				
ACS IX. A. ☐	Emergency Descent	I	ME FL 2	ME FL 3	ME FL 10, 11
ACS IX. C. ☐	Systems and Equipment Malfunctions	I	FL 2	FL 3	FL 10, 11
*ACS IX. E. ☐	Engine Failure During Takeoff Before VMC (Simulated)	I	ME GL 4 ME FL 5	ME FL 6, 7, 8C, 9NC	ME FL 10, 11
*ACS IX. F. ☐	Engine Failure After Liftoff (Simulated)	I	ME GL 4 ME FL 5	ME FL 6, 7, 8C, 9NC	ME FL 10, 11
*ACS IX. G. ☐	Approach and Landing with an Inoperative Engine (Simulated	I	ME GL 4 ME FL 5	FL 6, 7, 8C, 9NC	ME FL 10, 11
Part 141 Appendix D 4. (d) (2) (x) FAR 61.127 (b) (2) (x) ACS X.	Emergency Operations				
*ACS X. A. ☐	Maneuvering with One Engine Inoperative	I	ME GL 4 ME FL 4	ME FL 5, 6	ME FL 10, 11
*ACS X. B. ☐	V_{MC} Demonstration	I	ME GL 4 ME FL 4	ME FL 5, 6	ME FL 10, 11
*ACS X. C. ☐	One Engine Inoperative (Simulated) (solely by Reference to Instruments) During Straight-and- Level Flight and Turns	I	ME GL 5 ME FL 6	ME FL 7, 8, 9	ME FL 10, 11
*ACS X. D. ☐	Instrument Approach and Landing with an Inoperative Engine (Simulated) (solely by Reference to Instruments)	I	ME GL 5 ME FL 8	ME FL 9	ME FL 10, 11
Part 141 Appendix D 4. (d) (2) (xi) FAR 61.127 (b) (2) (xi) ACS XI..	Postflight Procedures				
ACS XI. A. ☐	After Landing, Parking and Securing	I	ME FL 1	ME FL 2, 3	ME FL 10, 11

This is to certify that

____

is enrolled in the
Federal Aviation Administration

approved ____________________________ course

conducted by ________________________ .

____________________ ____________________

Date of Enrollment Chief Instructor

This is to certify that

____

is enrolled in the
Federal Aviation Administration

approved ______________________________ course

conducted by ________________________ .

____________________ ____________________

Date of Enrollment Chief Instructor

This is to certify that

____

is enrolled in the
Federal Aviation Administration

approved ______________________ course

conducted by ______________________ .

______________________ ______________________

Date of Enrollment Chief Instructor

This is to certify that

____

has successfully completed all stages, tests, and course requirements and has graduated from the FEDERAL AVIATION ADMINISTRATION approved ____________________ course conducted by ____________________.

The graduate has completed the cross-country training specified in FAR Part 141.

- o Instrument Rating Course — Appendix C, Paragraph 4(c)(1)(ii)
- o Commercial Pilot Certification Course — Appendix D, Paragraphs 4 and 5
- o Multi-Engine Course — Appendix I, Paragraph 4

I certify the above statements are true.

____

Chief Instructor

____

School Certificate Number

____

Date of Graduation

This is to certify that

____

has successfully completed all stages, tests, and course requirements and has graduated from the FEDERAL AVIATION ADMINISTRATION approved __________________________ course conducted by ____________________________.

The graduate has completed the cross-country training specified in FAR Part 141.

o Instrument Rating Course — Appendix C, Paragraph 4(c)(1)(ii)
o Commercial Pilot Certification Course — Appendix D, Paragraphs 4 and 5
o Multi-Engine Course — Appendix I, Paragraph 4

I certify the above statements are true.

____

Chief Instructor

____

School Certificate Number

____

Date of Graduation

This is to certify that

____

has successfully completed all stages, tests, and course requirements and has graduated from the FEDERAL AVIATION ADMINISTRATION approved ________________________ course conducted by ________________________.

The graduate has completed the cross-country training specified in FAR Part 141.

o Instrument Rating Course — Appendix C, Paragraph 4(c)(1)(ii)
o Commercial Pilot Certification Course — Appendix D, Paragraphs 4 and 5
o Multi-Engine Course — Appendix I, Paragraph 4

I certify the above statements are true.

____

Chief Instructor

____

School Certificate Number

____

Date of Graduation